COLD WAR III

HOW THE U.S. NAVY CAN DEFEAT PUTIN
AND HALT CLIMATE CHANGE

COLD WAR III

HOW THE U.S. NAVY CAN DEFEAT PUTIN
AND HALT CLIMATE CHANGE

W. CRAIG REED

FIRST EDITION

Library of Congress Cataloging-in-Publication Data has been applied for.

ISBN 978-0-9908930-1-1

Cover photographs of ICEX 2011 courtesy of U.S. Navy

For Sarah, my family, the Us4Warriors Foundation,
and everyone who has ever served their country.

TABLE OF CONTENTS

INTRODUCTION

More than five decades ago, the world was brought to the brink of destruction when Soviet President Nikita Khrushchev sent four *Foxtrot* submarines toward Cuba. Each one carried a nuclear torpedo. Officers aboard all four vessels, when backed against the wall by President John F. Kennedy's naval forces, came within a breath of firing their torpedoes and starting World War III. I was the first author to bring the entire chilling story to light in my book, *Red November: Inside the Secret U.S.–Soviet Submarine War*. For the first time in print, I revealed why Khrushchev really backed down and removed his missiles from Cuba. Kennedy trumped the Soviet president by playing an ace that averted a nuclear war and changed the course of history. The ace was a new technology invented by scientists at the Naval Research Labs (NRL) in Washington, D.C., and deployed worldwide by my father, U.S. Navy Lieutenant William Reed.

Today, human population is skyrocketing, natural resources are dwindling, Russian and Chinese aggressions are escalating, and Arctic changes have ignited a new Cold War battleground. These alarming world events have converged to create a "perfect storm" that's thrusting the world toward unprecedented economic chaos and global conflict.

In the pages to follow, I will show how this perfect storm is propelling Russian President Vladimir Putin toward his ultimate goal to dominate world resources, especially in the Arctic, and why the invasion of Ukraine is only the start. I will also reveal details about another scientific breakthrough invented by the NRL that could defeat Putin at his own game, boost the global economy, create new jobs, and halt or even decline our planet's carbon footprint. But unless world leaders act now, Putin's plan could plunge the free world into a nightmare scenario unseen since the Great Depression.

In light of Putin's brazen invasion of Ukraine, and the downing of Malaysia Airlines flight MH17 with nearly three hundred souls lost, are we headed toward another potential nuclear showdown? Do we need to buy bomb shelters and cases of bottled water? Hopefully not, but what's unfolding in Europe is only the beginning. The potential for military confrontations over territorial and resource claims is escalating, but most of the fighting will likely occur four thousand miles away from Ukraine. The winners could take all and leave the losers—perhaps you and your family—without jobs, homes, transportation, or even food. Some may scoff at such an idea, but the truth is often hard to hear. The overwhelming evidence of Putin's grand plan that could change the world as we know it has been exposed in frightening detail in the book you're about to read.

Some believe Putin is emulating Adolf Hitler and is focused exclusively on a land grab in Europe, but Ukraine is only the tip of the iceberg. Others are confident that U.S. and North Atlantic Treaty Organization (NATO) leaders will eventually stop him, but the rattling swords are made of rubber. Still others are certain the Middle Eastern oil glut will declaw the Bear and force Putin into subservience, but they're underestimating his tenacity, fortitude, and chessmanship. They are also likely unaware of the unprecedented geopolitical moves Putin is making to undermine the U.S. petrodollar and position Russia as the world's energy leader within the next decade.

Can the U.S. turn the tables on Putin before it's too late? Possibly, but not unless President Barack Obama and his allies act immediately by playing the right cards, just as Kennedy did with Khrushchev during the Cuban Missile Crisis. The problem is, Obama and the European Union (EU) apparently have no idea that the ace they need is right under their noses at an obscure and underfunded NRL lab, or that this revolutionary invention could solve the world's energy needs, add trillions of dollars to U.S. and European economies, and mitigate carbon emissions.

Cold War III reveals what this powerful secret is and how it can also be used to keep Putin from getting his "MacGuffin," which could eventually trigger conventional or even nuclear conflicts. The term MacGuffin was originally coined by Alfred Hitchcock in 1935 when he filmed the popular movie *The 39 Steps*. In every thrilling story, a MacGuffin is the person, place, or thing that everyone wants the most—including the protagonist and the antagonist. It's the Holy Grail, the Maltese Falcon, or the three Elven rings that the Dark Lord Sauron is willing to kill for.

In fact, J. R. R. Tolkien's *The Lord of the Rings* provides us with an excellent metaphor. In this popular story, Sauron fashioned a powerful One Ring that he thought would rule all of the other Rings of Power, including three rings worn by the Elves. His plan failed when the Elves outsmarted him by hiding the rings. Sauron invaded the West to recover the rings but was eventually driven back to Mordor.

Unfortunately, unlike the wise Elves in *The Lord of the Rings*, the Westerners in our story have already handed Putin the first Elven ring. What can the Western protagonists do to stop Sauron from capturing the other two rings? How can they, with the help of NRL scientists, eventually drive him back to Mordor? Moreover, if the Elves fail to defeat the Dark Lord and throttle the Arctic changes that feed his powers, what are the potential consequences for the inhabitants of Middle-earth?

CHAPTER ONE

The Ridge—The First Ring

August 2, 2007 Lomonosov Ridge, Arctic Ocean

natoly Sagalevich's heart thudded as he seated himself inside the tiny submersible. Although the sixty-nine-year-old undersea veteran had trained for this momentous occasion, no amount of preparation could quell the excitement of a journey such as this. A harsh wind whipped across the Arctic Ocean and sent it splashing against the Plexiglas canopy of his *Mir-1* mini-sub. Years earlier, Anatoly had led similar dangerous missions to the bottom of the Atlantic and other seas to explore the murky remains of the *Titanic* and the *Bismarck*. As the department head of Shirshov Institute of Oceanology, his often-perilous job had brought him to the far north. Russia had invested in Anatoly's vast geological and environmental knowledge, and they were counting on him to discover the evidence needed to claim a prize of great wealth.

Russia was also counting on Anatoly's colleague, the sixty-eight-year-old Artur Chilingarov, who was commanding this mission from the cockpit of the *Mir-2* mini-sub. The calm, easygoing polar scientist had been the recipient of Russia's most prestigious Hero of the Soviet Union award after completing several harrowing treks to the South Pole and other treacherous locales. Well known throughout his country, Artur currently served as a deputy chairman for the Russian Federal Assembly.

Artur looked up from his instrument panel, winked at Anatoly, and flashed the okay sign with an O-shaped finger and thumb. Anatoly winked back. The mini-subs housing the two explorers had been lowered into the water from the *Rossiya*, a nuclear-powered Russian icebreaker. While roiling about in the choppy waters, Anatoly focused on his panel and completed a mental checklist. Satisfied that all systems were green, he gave Artur the sign to dive. From his cockpit, Anatoly glanced up at the gray clouds above and watched them disappear, gradually replaced by an ink-black sea. He switched on the forward running lights, but they did little to illuminate the dark. He and Artur would need to rely on instruments and instincts to find their way to the bottom, almost fourteen thousand feet below.

Reaching their destination would not be easy. Water temperatures averaged just below zero degrees centigrade in this region, which could freeze equipment and systems needed to navigate, maneuver, and survive. Even if they reached their destination and found the evidence they sought, returning with the goods could prove impossible. Pushed by ocean currents, ice floes in this region moved often. If the two scientists did not break the surface in their exact original location, they could wind up stuck under a thick pack of ice. Teams from the *Rossiya* would not be able to break through the hard cover in time. Trapped in their vessels, both explorers would soon ache for air as supplies grew thin. Their bodies would eventually be found with faces wrinkled in agony, having succumbed to a slow death by asphyxiation.

Anatoly had little time to ponder this thought as he guided his craft into the abyss, careful to keep an accurate track on his path. An hour passed, then another. Finally, four hours into the journey, Anatoly smiled. He had reached the bottom. He settled onto the rocky floor and received a report from Artur that *Mir-2* had also touched down nearby. Anatoly did a system check, and then extended the mini-sub's retractable robotic arm. The metal hand scooped up soil and rock samples and deposited them into a container. Satisfied that he'd collected enough "proof," Anatoly swelled with pride and excitement. Although gathering samples had been his government's primary goal, Anatoly had risked his life for more than just geological evidence. He radioed his colleague and told him to stand by. Artur acknowledged with an excited voice.

Anatoly retracted the arm and carefully cinched the metallic fingers around a cylindrical piece of titanium. The metal pole was attached to one edge of a small rectangle. He extended the arm and drove the pole into the silt and sand. Beaming broadly, staring at the Russian flag planted on the seabed at a depth of 13,980 feet, he radioed Artur and told him that their mission had been accomplished. The two mini-subs ascended and managed to find their way back to the awaiting icebreaker. Later that day, Anatoly made an entry in his log: "Today we set the flag of the Russian Federation on the floor of the Arctic Ocean."

Back in Moscow, the two explorers were greeted by cheering crowds, red carpets, and brass bands. Both congratulated their teams and all of Russia for "reaching the North Pole of the earth." Sergei Balyasnikov, a Moscow-based Arctic Institute spokesman, told the press, "This is like placing a flag on the moon; this is really a massive scientific achievement."

Anatoly and Artur had a right to be proud. This expedition marked the first plunge beneath the polar ice cap made by manned mini-subs down to that depth. But their pride had little to do with being first, as if this were another space race. This mission was part of a strategic plan to outmaneuver other players on the international chessboard. Knight to Queen's pawn two. Artur Chilingarov was a close friend of President Vladimir Putin. Together, the two had plotted their moves carefully, well aware that to the victors go the spoils.

THE ARCTIC IS OURS

Putin had more than once previously announced Russia's dire need to lock up "strategic, economic, scientific, and defense interests" in the Arctic. Artur had seconded the motion by stating that "the Arctic is ours, and we should manifest our presence." He and colleague Anatoly Sagalevich had done just that. First, they had brought back geological evidence they hoped would secure their claim to a chunk of the Arctic seabed under international law as governed by the United Nations Convention on the Law of the Sea (UNCLOS). Although the law grants countries exclusive economic rights to natural resources discovered in areas extending up to two hundred miles offshore, Russia wanted more. If they could prove that the "natural prolongation" of their underwater continental shelf stretched beyond that two hundred mile limit, they could lay claim to all the riches buried there. All of the area's oil, gas, minerals, food, and more would belong to Russia. They could either extract these resources or sell them to the highest bidders, profiting like pirates who had found the proverbial X on the map. But first, they'd have to win their case.

Six years before the 2007 mini-sub mission, referring to the UNCLOS, Russia had petitioned the UN Commission on the Limits of the Continental Shelf (CLCS). They had asked the UN Commission for exclusive economic rights to the Lomonosov Ridge, a three thousand- mile-long shelf that runs from the New Siberian Islands, past the North Pole, to Ellesmere Island of the Canadian Arctic Archipelago near Greenland. No spot in this icy ocean is shallower than three thousand feet deep. Before recent increases in global temperatures, most of the area lay beneath large chunks of frozen ice. Any resources found there were inaccessible. With the ice melting, and in light of new extraction technologies entering the scene, Russia's interest had escalated.

Unfortunately for Putin, the CLCS voted against the initial petition, stating that Russia did not have sufficient evidence to verify ownership of the ridge. An infuriated Putin then met with an eager Chilingarov to mastermind the plan to find irrefutable evidence that Russia owned the Lomonosov Ridge.

When the two Russian explorers planted their country's flag on that ridge, to them it was more than just symbolic. They intended to make a statement to the world that effectively said, "First come, first served."

"If a hundred or a thousand years from now someone goes down to where we were," said Artur Chilingarov, operator of the *Mir-2* mini-sub, "they will see the Russian flag." While Chilingarov was certainly aware that stabbing a flag into the sand does not necessarily constitute ownership, he likely believed that it set a precedent that could sway CLCS voters to rule in Russia's favor. Also, it would send a clear signal to other nations that Russia was dead serious about claiming large portions of the Arctic.

When asked about this incident, Rear Admiral Robert Kamensky, head of NATO submarine operations, had this to say: "What bothers us is when the Russians send out deep submergence vehicles and plant a Russian flag in an area that used to be covered by ice, but is now mostly ice free, and state that it's part of their territorial shelf. Then they claim that all the mineral resources, including sizable petroleum deposits, are all theirs."

Tom Casey of the U.S. State Department commented on the incident, stating that, "I'm not sure whether they put a metal flag, a rubber flag, or a bedsheet on the ocean floor. Either way, it doesn't have any legal standing." Canadian Foreign Minister Peter Mackay vehemently commented: "This isn't the fifteenth century. You can't go around the world and plant flags." Andris Piebalgs, the European Union's energy commissioner, added his opinion to the mix by saying that he was "not at ease with developments in the Arctic," and that "countries that are bordering the Arctic should be extremely serious about not making conflictual (sic) announcements, because whatever solution is found, it should be between all the countries bordering it."

In Russia, Chilingarov shot back by saying, "We are happy that we placed a Russian flag on the ocean bed, where not a single person has ever been, and I don't give a damn what some foreign individuals think about that." Chilingarov then referred to Soviet Arctic researcher, Ivan Papanin, who led an expedition in the winter of 1937 to a remote ice floe. "Russia [has] always expanded its territory by northern lands...seventy years ago, they would say, 'Bolsheviks have conquered the Arctic.' Now our crew is United Russia. The Russian flag is the point of the North Pole of the earth. Full stop. If someone doesn't like it, let them dive as deep as fourteen thousand feet and try and leave something down there."

Despite Chilingarov's rhetoric, it was obvious that Russia's motivations stemmed from more than just patriotic pride. Putin had invested tens of millions to send his friend on a dangerous mission to the Arctic with a single purpose in mind: to secure the economic rights to a vast storehouse of oil, gas, and other precious minerals near the North Pole. Russia currently has no infrastructure or capability in that region to extract or transport these resources anywhere, so why the urgency? They have an abundance of infrastructure near Murmansk and other areas where large pipes feed Russia's customers in Europe and Asia, so why not focus on expansion and exploration closer to home? What was Putin plotting?

This was the burning question that kept me awake at night as I continued to learn about Russian aggression in the Arctic from various navy and government contacts, including one of the directors of the U.S. Navy's Arctic Submarine Laboratory (ASL), who helped me gain an invitation to ride aboard a nuclear fast attack submarine deep beneath the Arctic ice. It was there that the proverbial lightbulb burned bright and I became compelled to write this book. And it was there that I started to uncover the truth about the dark future our planet is hurling toward that has haunted my sleep ever since.

CHAPTER TWO

Cracking the Ice

The author (center) with the USS *Connecticut* crew in the Arctic

The Arctic is our planet's last great wilderness. No artist's paintbrush or photographer's film can capture the feeling that swells in your chest and mists your eyes when you experience the Arctic's splendor for the first time. Aqua-blue icebergs shimmer and crackle atop crystal clear seas. Massive snow peaks, haunting and majestic, sparkle in the sun. Rivers of once-frozen water carve giant troughs across ice sheets as old as time.

The Arctic Ocean is actually the world's smallest, but it can stop your heart in a matter of seconds. The ancient Greeks named the region after the northern constellation Arktos when Pytheas discovered the frigid sea in 300 B.C. Sheer walls of ice, some hundreds of feet high, loom above the ocean's surface during winter months when temperatures plunge to minus thirty degrees centigrade. Only the native Inuit, polar bears, seals, and other wildlife have dared to call this desolate place home. But now their sanctuary has been invaded by deadly intruders.

One of the most formidable of these is the United States Navy. Every few years they send two nuclear attack submarines to the Beaufort Sea, two hundred miles north of Alaska, to hone tactics and test the latest weapons, communications, navigation, sonar, and fire control systems in icy conditions. The program is called ICEX, which stands for Ice Exercise, and it is now the navy's primary method of maintaining submarine dominance and proficiency in the Arctic region.

To better understand why this program may soon become a critical element in thwarting Russian and Chinese aggression, I petitioned the navy's chief information office for almost a year. I asked them to allow me to join four dozen officers, sailors, scientists, and engineers at the ICEX camp and spend several days aboard a nuclear fast attack submarine. With the help of ICEX Camp Director Jeff Gossett, I finally convinced them to approve my request.

I was excited until the thought of freezing to death, drowning under the ice, or being eaten by a polar bear gave me pause, but there are times when a man must squelch his deepest fears and laugh in the face of danger. The navy assured me this would *not* be one of those times. In fact, they said I'd eat like a Roman, watch B movies in the wardroom, throw snowballs at orange-suited sailors, and play cribbage until midnight. *I can handle that,* I thought. So I girded my loins with wool and prepared for an exciting cruise in the High North.

Prior to my trip, while sitting in my backyard in sunny San Diego, I hadn't given much thought to the changes happening in the northern regions of our planet, or the environmental and political transformations impacting the Arctic. Or why Putin was so interested in this region. When I did read something about the polar ice cap, I nostalgically envisioned a land of bearded explorers bundled in parkas trudging across a desolate white expanse in search of glory. But I soon learned that due to recent Arctic changes, the U.S. might be headed toward serious conflicts in the region.

I started reading articles about how the average winter temperatures in the area had increased by nearly seven degrees Fahrenheit over the past sixty years. I found stories about drastic changes in the seasonal ice pack that brought to mind images of starving polar bears and suffering seals. I read that Arctic sea ice was disappearing rapidly and would likely never return.

For this and other important strategic reasons, U.S. Navy Secretary Ray Mabus called the navy's ICEX in the Arctic "invaluable" and said he hoped the Pentagon would be able to find the funds to keep the program on a two-year cycle.

U.S. Coast Guard Rear Admiral Christopher Colvin is the commander of the Alaska and Arctic district, an area larger than the continental United States. Citing concerns over Russia's increased aggression in the Arctic, including plans to send eight shipments of gas condensate through the Northern Sea Route (NSR), Colvin said, "I'd like to see more U.S. ice camps [ICEX] for longer periods of time in the Arctic. Demonstrating U.S. use and presence is important."

Alaska Lieutenant Governor Mead Treadwell stated publicly that he's worried that, in light of recent Chinese and Russian moves, the United States is not doing enough to prepare for the inevitable challenges. He also said that even though the U.S. had no plans to build more icebreakers, the government had agreed to a draft treaty that divides responsibility for search and rescue among the states that border the Arctic.

I had read that tensions were on the rise between council nations over territorial claims and passage rights, but I did not appreciate the severity or import of these disputes until I boarded the fast attack submarine USS *Connecticut* (SSN-22) and submerged beneath the polar ice cap in the company of our navy's finest.

The English language holds few metaphors that can match nature's palette and describing in these pages what I saw and felt during my journey has been quite a challenge. I hope the following account does justice to the sailors, officers, and civilians who made this experience of a lifetime possible.

ARCTIC DANGERS

My trip began in late March 2011 at San Diego's International airport. I wasn't supposed to be flying from that city, or on that day, but the navy moved my excursion date back by a week. Alaska Airlines customer service representative Sarah Blanchard greeted me with a smile that quickly turned into a frown.

"I apologize," Sarah said with a pleasant British accent, "but there seems to be an issue with your reservation."

"An issue like I'm getting a free upgrade to first class," I said, "or one like I'm sitting on someone's lap for three hours?"

"The someone's lap one," Sarah said. "But not to worry, we'll get it sorted."

Her blue eyes focused on a monitor screen as she typed away. Several nervous minutes passed. My palms started to sweat. Had all my planning, training, packing, and waiting like an excited kid just ended due to a computer glitch? Had the cruel hand of fate stabbed me in the back?

Sarah glanced up and smiled again. "I assume an exit row seat is satisfactory?"

I thanked her profusely, handed her my business card, and said if she'd e-mail me, I'd send her an autographed copy of one of my books. She beamed. I beamed back and jaunted to my gate, wondering if she'd ever send that e-mail.

In Anchorage, Alaska, I met up with a CNN film crew who'd been tasked with doing a documentary on ICEX 2011. The crew's producer, Ken Shiffman, looked to be in his early forties. He had a friendly smile, dark hair, and a medium frame, and was more excited than a kid on his first trip to Disneyland. Kaj Larsen, the tall on-camera correspondent, viewed this excursion as a lot more fun than others he'd taken aboard submarines as a former navy SEAL officer. A master's degree from Harvard and an abundance of charm helped make Kaj, who was in his mid-thirties, the ideal "face man" for this documentary. Twenty-something Toby Thiermann probably could have been a movie star with his wavy hair and boyish smile, but he chose the backside of the camera as a cinematographer. Lieutenant Ed Early functioned as our public affairs officer, and did an exceptional job of guiding us through various requirements related to security protocols.

All of us boarded a plane to Prudhoe Bay, where we met a team from the navy's Arctic Submarine Lab. These guys help run the ICEX camp in concert with the University of Washington's Applied Physics Laboratory (APL). Flat, treeless, and white, Prudhoe resembles a snow-covered oil field in Texas. Alaska Airlines ferries in daily a slew of oil workers sporting red flannel shirts who maintain the Trans-Alaska Pipeline. The navy commandeered a hanger near the terminal, where Charlie Johnson from ASL told us how to keep from freezing our family jewels off at minus-twenty below. I learned that wool makes for the best defense against the ultracold. Cotton can cause you to sweat, and sweat tends to refreeze, which can turn your skin into a Brillo pad.

The secret is layers. First wool, then polypropylene, then more wool, then a jacket, then hand and toe warmers followed by a balaclava and cap, then a scarf, prayer beads, and a gun. The gun is so you can shoot yourself before you freeze to death. Or maybe it's to shoot the polar bear before he rips you apart, I don't recall. Anyway, after transforming into a mash-up of the Stay Puft Marshmallow Man and Pillsbury Doughboy, I waddled out to the single-engine Cessna on the runway, alongside my CNN cohorts. We booted each other in the tail more than once climbing in, and the engine sputtered to life.

I envisioned an ocean, or at least part of one, but saw nothing from the air save a blanket of icy white for a zillion miles in every direction. Now and then a glimmer of grayish blue peaked through to reveal the possibility of a sea, otherwise my mind convinced me that beneath the wings lay the surface of Mars, never before touched by humankind. I tried to imagine how anything might find food here, especially something as large as a polar bear. Then again, that's probably why the sight of a pudgy pink guy seems so appealing to them.

The ICEX camp appeared from nowhere, as if conjured by Houdini. More than a dozen wooden boxes dotted the ground, resembling large rectangular coffins hammered together from plywood. I had been told that the camp was built weeks earlier by a hired construction crew who ferried parts from Prudhoe Bay, and would burn the remains after the April shutdown (rather than haul them back to Alaska). Camp Director Jeff Gossett met us at the plane and ushered us to our quarters—a hooch ironically called Truk, as in the Pacific island near Guam. We veteran navy guys know better than to select a top bunk, so I threw my green duffle bag onto a bottom rack.

After checking into our frigid suite, we briefly met again with Gossett while the CNN crew went to work. While Ken directed and Toby pointed a camera, Kaj asked the first question: "We understand why ICEX was important during the Cold War as U.S. submarines hunted Soviet subs in the Arctic. But why is it important now?"

Gossett eloquently informed us that operating in Arctic waters as compared to other areas, such as the Pacific Ocean, is like the difference between driving a car on a four-lane freeway in Nevada versus a one-lane road on the edge of a cliff in Colorado. In the Pacific, you can run at flank speed for days with little worry of hitting anything. Water conditions make it easier to hide from the enemy, and positioning your sub to fire a torpedo doesn't require an engineering degree. In the Arctic, all that changes, and the nation with the best training, tactics, and technologies to operate in these waters will win the day.

"Arctic waters are not very friendly," Gossett said. "Over time, salt leeches out of the ice and freshwater rivers flow into the ocean here. There's little to no evaporation, or any wave action to mix the fresh with the salt water, and the result is lower density and less salinity."

Kaj Larsen asked how that affects submarine operations.

"Things are a lot more treacherous up here," Gossett said. "As subs move toward the surface, due to water conditions, they can feel thousands of pounds heavier. That makes sub driving much tougher. There are also stalactites—or long icicles—that form keels beneath sea ice when a flow of saline cold water mingles with ocean water. In shallow water, some of these spikes can extend all the way to the bottom. Maneuvering around them can be quite dangerous."

"What about surfacing?" I asked. "Most subs can't crack through thick ice, right?"

"That's right. We only have three submarines of the *Seawolf* class that can safely do that, and only two of them have had ICEX training. The older *Los Angeles* and newer *Virginia*-class boats don't have sails that can crack through hard ice without causing some damage. So if they had a casualty, like a fire, toxic gas leak, flooding, reactor scram, or were damaged by an enemy attack, they'd have to search for a thin ice area to surface. If they couldn't find one quickly, they'd be in serious trouble."

We all wanted to know how subs locate areas with thin ice cover.

Gossett explained that for ice exercises, which last about six weeks, ASL and APL teams install a special set of equipment and systems, and then provide sub crews with guidance and training on their usage. The extra gear includes a low-light, upward-looking camera mounted in the sail. The camera stares at the ice above to help the crew determine ice conditions for surfacing and better assess relative position in relation to a constantly moving ice floe.

A monitor screen in the control room, mounted in a one-foot square metal housing, displays the video captured by the camera. The image looks like a dull white blanket dotted with mud spots, which are caused by ice imperfections and small holes bored into the ice by melting water.

A marine conductivity, temperature, and depth (CTD) sensor on the hull broadcasts data to a customized display to inform the CO and crew about environmental conditions and changes, etc. This can be critical for surfacing as it monitors such things as density changes, which could affect the sub's weight and thus cause issues with the rate of ascent. As Gossett explains, "It's like being able to see an upcoming hill ahead when you're driving a car so you can speed up before climbing."

All submarines have "factory installed" high frequency top sounder and ahead-looking sonar systems, but crews are not trained on how to use these in frosty northern waters. This equipment is more often used to search for enemy mines or anti-submarine warfare (ASW) ships. ICEX personnel conduct training and supervise exercises to teach crews how to repurpose their high frequency sonar to determine ice thickness and look for ice keels to avoid smacking one. The sonar has limited range, only about five hundred yards on either side, so crews need to go slow to avoid ramming something or missing an open area for surfacing.

ASL teams set up shop in a wooden command hut at ICEX, which is chock-full of monitors and systems. During the more than month-long program, they assist subs with exercises to improve under-ice operations; learn how to use the special ASL gear; test communications, sonar, navigation, and weapons capabilities; and practice Arctic operational skills. Gossett assured me I'd soon have the opportunity to observe this firsthand aboard the *Connecticut*.

ARCTIC FLAMES

Later that day, Captain Rhett Jaehn, the number two man in charge of all U.S. Navy submarine operations, gave us a first-class tour of the camp. I spied a large ICEX banner plastered on the side of a hooch that displayed the ASL logo, along with a tagline denoting the camp's fifty-year anniversary. Jaehn explained that ASL and APL combine forces, along with scores of researchers from many other labs, to ensure that U.S. submarines maintain their tactical advantage over potential enemies who operate in the Arctic.

Jaehn said that the need for ICEX had escalated in recent years due to altered weather patterns, which is leading to an increase in mining, oil production, shipping, and fishing inside a region many refer to as the planet's final frontier. These concerns prompted Navy Chief Oceanographer Rear Admiral David Titley, Pentagon Comptroller Robert Hale, Navy Secretary Ray Mabus, and several congresspersons to visit the 2011 ICEX camp.

"It's important for us to continue to train and operate in the Arctic," Jaehn said.

He mentioned that bordering nations like Russia, Denmark, Greenland, Canada, and Norway, along with others such as China and South Korea, are frequently sending submarines and ships into the area and jockeying for position to own mineral and mining rights to vast resource-rich underwater shelves. Melting ice is also opening up two major shipping arteries, and the jump in commercial traffic will increase the need for submarine and Coast Guard patrols, especially across the fifty-six-mile wide Bering Strait that separates Alaska from Russia.

"[The Arctic] is a key potential transit line between the Atlantic and the Pacific," Jaehn said. "We want to be able to demonstrate that we have global reach, that we can operate in all oceans, and that we can operate proficiently in any environment."

Shortly after our tour of the camp, Jaehn issued our first assignment: jump on the back of a sled pulled by a snowmobile and hack up some ice. This just in: ice is hard. My teeth darn near rattled loose every time the sled jumped over a frozen crest and slammed down on the other side. I contemplated filing a lawsuit for whiplash, but then my pain vanished when I saw the edifice in the distance, about a quarter-mile away from the camp. Jutting over ten feet into the air, the ice chunk resembled a freeway slab pushed up from the ground after a massive earthquake. While the top and sides were pristine white, the sun lit up the undersides of a curved archway that glimmered with a radiant blue not seen since Marilyn Monroe's eyes graced this earth.

My jaw dropped, but not for long. The dry cold robbed my tongue of moisture and turned my saliva to sawdust. Now I know what King Tut's mouth felt like after hundreds of years in a tomb. The experience reminded me of why we had undertaken this jaunt in the first place: we needed to chop up some ice with axes and bring back large chunks for our stove pots. Kaj volunteered and had to swing an axe for a half-hour to produce just a few small chunks. Did I mention that ice is hard?

Each hooch came equipped with a fifty-five gallon drum of propane, just outside the door, that fed a small stove atop which sat a large soup pan. Upon whacking up enough ice chunks, we placed one in the pot to humidify the hooch. The Arctic is essentially a desert. It's so dry that the air sucks up all the moisture, resulting in "hard and frozen." Since we didn't want our noses and throats to resemble dried prunes, we ensured our bucket always contained some heated water.

That evening, I followed my new CNN compadres over to the blue-and-white-striped mess tent for dinner, where we were amazed by the cuisine. If not for the plastic tables and chairs, and the ice floe ambience, the dining experience could have easily rivaled a four-star restaurant in Paris. A husband and wife team, Grey and Sarah Wicker, had graciously volunteered for ICEX cooking duty, and all of us were glad they did. I've not had ribs that tasty in Texas.

While consuming my second helping of dessert, I saw something yellow and sparkly through the back window of the kitchen. At first I thought it might be a reflection from the sunset, but I soon realized that this was something far more sinister. No alarms sounded, but those of us qualified on submarines acted on instinct. We darted out the side door, slid around to the back of the kitchen, and stared at the fire leaping from atop the propane tank connected to the back of the stove. Flames sputtered and shot skyward, as if delivered by a giant cigar lighter, nearly scorching the side of the wooden hut. Those "qualified" on this particular system instantly shut valves, flipped switches, checked and rechecked systems, and quelled the situation within seconds. Most people might have been impressed, but I wasn't. All submariners endure frequent fire drills while underway, as "smoke on a boat" can be fatal. For me, watching these submariners handle the situation with calm precision was just another day at the office.

The night brought more cold, but ushered in a blanket of brilliant stars. The Milky Way's galactic edge streamed across the dark sky like an ethereal ribbon of white silk. This episode of "dancing with the stars" was later trumped by the brilliant green glow of a aurora borealis. My first day complete, I stifled a yawn and climbed into my bottom bunk. The stiff wood beneath the thin foam that supported my sleeping bag failed to keep me awake for more than a few minutes.

UNDER THE ICE

Dawn came early, along with the thrill of relieving myself. Nothing compares to the shock of exposing your buttocks to Mother Nature's freezer when it's twenty below, but since the hooch contained no toilet, I had little choice. Outhouses were placed strategically around the camp and offered that "oh so wilderness" feel. No one dared take a shower, which could only be had by chopping up more ice, melting large chunks, and filling something akin to a garden sprayer. Instead, we opted to cleanse with moist wipes. Four layers of clothing later, I was ready to see a nuclear submarine crack through three feet of ice.

Submariners love code names, and that year the ICEX team used the movie *Top Gun* and the game Monopoly as inspirational sources. The *New Hampshire* became "Goose" and the *Connecticut* "Iceman," with their respective surfacing locations named "Waterworks" and "Marvin Gardens." Once the *Connecticut* had received final instructions to surface at Marvin Gardens, a helicopter descended and whisked us away to the rendezvous location. The chopper blades whipped the snow off the ice at our landing spot a few miles away and turned the sky white. A wooden warming hut, no larger than a walk-in closet, sat on the frozen ground next to a couple of bundled figures.

One of the ICEX guys approached and waved us away from the chopper. A fat cigar dangling from his lips, icicles coating his beard, a bright red glow on his Rudolph nose, he said his name was Hector Castillo. He cupped a pair of headphones and called the *Connecticut* via Gertrude—a short-range underwater communications system that uses hydrophones to send open voice messages. "Iceman, this is Marvin Gardens. Media is ready for your surfacing."

Cameras in hand, fingers numb, and hearts thumping, we stood on the polar ice cap and waited. No French horns blew when the *Connecticut* punched through the ice, as they had in the movie *Ice Station Zebra*, but I heard them all the same. I also heard the ice crumble as eight thousand tons of steel cracked through the hard cover and pushed skyward. The ground rumbled like the prescient warnings of an avalanche. Where only nature had once painted the landscape, a dark intruder emerged. Foreboding and mysterious, the monolith inched higher until a black rectangle loomed large. Orange-suited sailors popped up from the front of the mound and attacked large chunks of ice, pushing them over the side. Boulders of white flew from the submarine's sail and crashed to the ground below.

More orange-covered suits appeared, one with a chainsaw dangling from his hand. He resembled a cross between Jason from the horror movie and a pumpkin patch worker. Another sailor came down from the sail and used a line to measure distance from the back of the sail, this to mark the approximate location of the after entry hatch. Pumpkin Jason walked over to the marked spot and brought the chainsaw to life with a roar. As if spewed from a refrigerator gone mad, crunched ice flew into the air while he cut into the snowpack covering the boat. Thirty minutes passed before a glint of sunlight reflected from the black steel of the submarine hatch. Pumpkin Jason completed his sculpture by notching a large square step into the ice just in front of the hatch.

The author aboard the USS *Connecticut* in the Arctic

The spring-loaded hatch opened and a distinct "boat smell" wafted from below. A combination of stored diesel fuel, amine, something electronic, something else deep fat fried, and 160 guys passing gas conspired to create the odor. Those who have served aboard nuclear submarines recall this scent well and are filled with memories whenever something resembling that smell nears our noses. Still bulk-bundled, I climbed down the ladder and landed near the galley. The executive officer (XO) welcomed us aboard and motioned us into the crew's mess. We stripped from our Arctic gear and followed a petty officer to the sixteen-man berthing section, one deck up, where I selected a bottom rack.

The three submarines that comprise the *Seawolf* class were built in the late '90s, but the original design was completed toward the end of the first Cold War, when large Soviet warships and submarines were a major threat. In my book, *Red November*, I discuss the primary missions of fast attack submarines during that time period. Often we were ordered to trail a few dozen yards behind Soviet SSBNs and record sound signatures, sneak into enemy harbors, and take "up-close and personal" pictures, or "wire-tap" communications cables seven hundred-feet down using "saturation" divers. Submarines today still undertake such missions, and this class of boat is well suited to the task.

Meals in the wardroom are formal affairs, and our lunch followed submarine officer's protocol. We stood when the commanding officer, Commander Michael Varney, entered the room, and then sat in our assigned seats. A steward entered from the galley, dressed formally in serving attire, and placed a bowl of soup in front of the captain. Soup bowls clicked atop plates in a counterclockwise direction until everyone had been served. No one ate until the CO consumed his first spoonful. The rich French onion flavor of the soup rivaled recipes found in top New York restaurants. All of our meals aboard the USS *Connecticut* were spectacular, and I was thankful that I brought sweatpants with expandable waistlines.

That afternoon the CO gave us a tour of the boat, starting in the torpedo room. I tagged along behind the CNN crew like a puppy dog, trying hard to "stay out of the damn shot." We were not shown the more interesting areas of the boat, such as the multi-mission platform (MMP), which contains a hyperbaric chamber to allow saturation divers, breathing a helium-oxygen mixture, to undertake clandestine missions. The MMP also has special electronic systems that can be used to capture and record various signals, a splicing chamber for fiber-optic cable tapping, and other interesting espionage equipment. This cadre of gear, which is more prevalent on the USS *Jimmy Carter* (SSN-23) than her two sister ships, is the reason why that boat has earned the reputation of being "Washington's premier spy platform."

Should a troublemaking enemy vessel appear during our time aboard, Commander Varney assured us that the USS *Connecticut* could handle the challenge. This boat and the other two subs of her class are uniquely outfitted with eight torpedo tubes and a fully-automated system to load MK-48 ADCAP (advanced capability) torpedoes and Tomahawk cruise missiles—similar to the ones fired on Libya in March 2011 by the submarines USS *Providence, Scranton,* and *Florida.* The crew demonstrated the loading of a weapon in a tube, sounding off warnings and completing procedures with polished precision. We were told that the *Connecticut* could sink eight warships and be prepared to do it again in less than fifteen minutes. As a former Fire Control (weapons systems) technician, I couldn't help but marvel at this capability, and I admit to drooling a bit when I neared the modern control panels that make such a thing possible. Yeah, I know, it's a guy thing.

That evening we were allowed into the control room to watch the boat sink. Subs don't actually sink, of course, but they do submerge. Within seconds they can become self-contained miniature cities where mammals can actually breathe underwater and eat like pigs. While the crew prepared to dive, Varney pointed to various control stations and explained their functions. Most of this I already knew, and I was overcome by nostalgic memories of my ninety-day jaunts into enemy waters during Cold War I. I also had a twinge of jealousy and wished that the two classes of boats I had served on, the *Permit* and the *Sturgeon,* had been this modern. Digital displays blinked and flickered near the diving stations, which fronted two operators who gripped airplane-like steering wheels. One sailor operated the rudder to go right and left, and the other the bow planes to go up and down. Nearby sat the Chief of the Watch (COW), who is responsible for various operations including flooding the ballast tanks to make the boat heavy enough to dive.

And dive we did. The diving alarm sounded, orders were issued and repeated, and the boat slowly dropped from her icy perch to mingle with the fish below. We leveled off at four hundred feet and were promptly escorted from the control room, but not before I caught a glimpse of the BYG-1 (pronounced "big one") fire control panels.

Back in my day (when I trudged five miles to school in the snow, or at least said I did), my sub's MK113 fire control system took up the entire starboard side of the control room. Refrigerator-sized analog computers clicked away while struggling to track up to four targets at a time. Today, the digital BYG-1 panels resemble large video game consoles and can keep tabs on dozens of contacts without breaking a sweat. My eyes wandered from the "big one" panels to the sonar shack, just forward of the fire control area, where headphone-wearing operators stared at BQQ-10 sonar stacks. With this advanced system, they can practically hear a pin drop (yeah, even underwater) from dozens of miles away.

With our stint in the control room completed, we dined on prime rib and played cribbage in the wardroom with the CO and XO until the wee hours. Later that night, I almost shot the contents of a toilet up my nose.

Defeated in cards, stuffed to the gills, and feeling fat, I climbed into my bottom rack, a tiny thing less than three feet wide. In the middle of the night, while groggy from sleep, I wandered into the head to relieve myself. I missed seeing the signs hanging on the stall doors and started to open one.

A large hand grabbed my shoulder and pulled me back from the precipice. In a deep baritone, the petty officer said, "Not a good idea." My eyes popped open as I read the signs. I flashed a sheepish grin and left the head.

Facilities on a submarine resemble porta-potties, but larger and more complicated. Understandably, they need to be emptied every so often. This is called "blowing sanitaries," and as the term implies, the holding tank is pressurized to expel the contents out to sea. During this time, signs are posted on all head stalls warning users not to pull open any flush valves. More than once during my boat years I heard someone scream in agony when they forgot and pulled, and the contents blew upward into their face. Only by luck did a petty officer warn me in time and save me from making a similar mistake. Submarines are dangerous places. If you don't eat yourself to death, you can commit suicide by amoebic dysentery.

DRILL OR DIE

The following morning, after a brisk run on one of the boat's treadmills (yes, they actually have a few!), I had the privilege of interviewing Commander Varney in his stateroom. What he told me opened my eyes to what's really happening in the Arctic, and why it's imperative that U.S. research labs continue to develop new technologies and systems to fight under-ice battles. Also, for fast attack submarines to learn how to use these systems and practice tactics and maneuvers in Arctic waters.

Varney grew up in Kittery Point, Maine, next to a shipyard that built submarines. Several of his classmates' fathers were submarine captains, and his own dad, a harbor master and a firefighter, had served as a sonar technician on a destroyer involved in the Cuban Missile Crisis. It was natural that Varney grew up intrigued by submarines, their technology, and their missions. When *Top Gun* hit theaters, all his friends wanted to be Maverick, except Varney. "I wanted to be the guy who gets to hunt for *Red October*," he told me.

I then asked him about his assignment in Afghanistan, and how a sub commander got tapped for land duty. He explained that he'd been in the right place at the right time. Before taking command of the USS *Connecticut*, he did a stint at the Pentagon right after his tour aboard the USS *Topeka* as the executive officer. One year into that assignment, the brass asked him to work on the global war on terrorism as a chief of staff supporting our efforts in Afghanistan. Special Forces units were operating reconstruction teams there, and Varney took command of a special unit on the Pakistani border for about eighteen months.

"We had a unique interagency team," Varney said, "with people from the army infantry, Special Forces units like the Navy SEALs, the State Department, the Department of Agriculture, the Army Corps of Engineers, and other agencies. Some of these guys served as far back as Vietnam and were very familiar with counterinsurgency tactics. They understood that to fight terrorists, you needed to improve local governance, which is usually the weak point that allows insurgency to prosper."

Varney told me about an incident that happened during an interview with a film crew from CNN. The crew had embedded with Varney's team to film a documentary on how well the U.S. was doing with reconstruction efforts. Paktika Province had a reputation for being one of the most violent places in Afghanistan. Varney spent a week there, showing CNN all the work they had done to reduce the number of attacks by insurgent forces. Unfortunately, none of that made it past the editing floor. On the last day of filming, while Varney and his team were meeting with the tribal elders, a firefight broke out about four klicks (kilometers) away to the east. Four Apache helicopter gunships fired missiles into the side of the mountain against a Taliban stronghold.

"So while I'm spouting off about how safe this region is now," Varney said, "bright explosions are erupting over my shoulder. The cinematographer swings his camera away from me and starts filming all the action." A few months later, when the CNN piece came out on television, Varney said there were five seconds devoted to the peacekeeping efforts and all the progress made, and five minutes to gunships blasting away at the Taliban.

"I guess no one wants to see a boring documentary on rebuilding Afghanistan when they can see gunships blowing up terrorists," Varney said.

I asked Varney what he had gained from that experience that helped him command a U.S. attack submarine.

"I mentioned that my father was a firefighter," Varney said. "He used to say that fighting fires was ninety-nine percent boredom and one percent sheer terror. I learned something from that, and from my Afghan experience, that I live by today. I believe that it's not how you train that prepares you for the unexpected, but how you live. I think that how an individual or a team performs in combat comes down to what they know instinctively, and not just what they've been taught. When this crew is confronted with the fact that either the enemy dies or they do, that reality can induce tremendous stress. Even the best trained crews can crumble under that kind of pressure. You can avoid that by introducing instinctive behavior into their everyday life."

The author witnessing the USS *Connecticut* surface through Arctic ice

After our interview, Cdr. Varney conducted a few simulated drills to show us how his crew might respond. As a former submariner, I didn't need to ask what the greatest fear might be while submerged; I already knew. The sound of an alarm followed by the word "Fire!" conjures a sub sailor's worst nightmares.

Operating under the waves carries a multitude of risks, but few are worse than a fire. The entire boat can quickly fill up with smoke and rob us of our ability to breathe. Even though we're trained to don Emergency Breathing Apparatus masks with hoses that plug into air manifolds, thick smoke makes it hard to see or operate. If the boat is not surfaced quickly, so that the smoke can be cleared from all spaces, operating effectively can soon become nearly impossible. While in hostile waters, surfacing might not be an option, but at least it's possible. When in the Arctic, if there's no shallow ice nearby, it's *not* possible.

An example of this occurred during an exercise under the ice in 2007 when the USS *Connecticut* conducted an ICEX with the USS *Alexandria* (SSN-757) and HMS *Tireless* (S88). An oxygen generator on the HMS *Tireless*, known as a SCOG, broke down. SCOGs are prone to malfunction when not in pristine condition and the ones on the *Tireless* were tired. Sailors described the machines as "beasts that burned with ferocious violence." When the SCOG on the *Tireless* cracked, the beast exploded.

Thirty-five-year-old Navy Stores Accountant Richard Holleworth recounted the story during an interview. "I was about a meter away when I heard a really loud bang," Holleworth said.

He felt the heat of the blast on his face.

"The room was instantly filled with bright white smoke. I could not see my arm in front of my face, just a glow."

Coughing and blinded by smoke, Holleworth crept into the escape compartment. There he heard twenty-year-old Anthony Huntrod screaming in pain. He also heard the crackling sounds of fire and felt intense heat on his cheeks. Stepping closer, his eyes shot open when he saw Huntrod engulfed in flames.

"He was making noises and I could see he was on fire," Holleworth said. "I put my arm down to grab the fire extinguisher, but it was not there, so I started hitting at the flames with my forearms. Then Tony fell to the floor and I used my feet to put out the flames."

Holleworth tried to kick open the hatch but to no avail. "I thought I would just grab Tony and carry him with me. But it was futile."

When Huntrod stopped screaming, Holleworth heard another sailor, Paul McCann, cry out through the smoke. He reached forward and grabbed McCann's hand. They sat together on the floor and hoped for the best, but feared the worst.

"I had a moment of clarity that I was trapped in there," said Holleworth. "I knew I was going to die."

Barely able to move, Holleworth noticed instrument lights nearby. Thoughts of his unborn son filled him with the will to crawl toward the panel until he found an emergency oxygen relay station. He grabbed a mask and pulled it on. He tried to move back toward McCann, but lost consciousness.

"All I remember is slumping to the floor...I must have just passed out."

Forty minutes later, the crew finally breached the compartment and found him there.

Holleworth survived the day, but operator mechanic Anthony Huntrod died from first degree burns. Leading mechanic operator Paul McCann was poisoned to death by carbon monoxide. The *Tireless* found a suitable location with thin ice so they could surface, but not before two of the crew had perished in the incident.

Sitting in the crew's mess, while an alarm blared and blue-suited sailors all around me raced to put out an imaginary "drill" fire, I thought about the brave men who had perished that day aboard the *Tireless* and hoped that fate never befell any of the crew aboard the *Connecticut*. But should such an unfortunate event ever occur, given the efficiency they now demonstrated, I was confident that they'd survive almost any emergency.

I learned more about Cdr. Varney's view on the importance of crew training during my interview with him. When questioned as to why the *Connecticut* was involved in the 2011 ICEX, Varney explained that this was the sub's fourth ICEX. He felt that without the knowledge and experience gained in these operations, his crew would be at a severe disadvantage if they had to go toe-to-toe with the Russians or Chinese.

Later that day, while gorging myself with the officers in the wardroom, I once again struggled with the obvious mismatch between the importance of ICEX and the limited financial commitment made by the U.S. Government for these operations. How could the congresspersons who had visited the camp not leave with a burning desire to secure more dollars for these programs? How can the navy be expected to protect national security and avoid or perhaps engage in a skirmish in the Arctic without more training and equipment? They can't, I concluded, yet they have no choice.

Having consumed more chow than a linebacker, and having played more cribbage than a blue-haired grandmother, I learned that we were going to spend an extra day aboard the *Connecticut*. Due to a thick layer of fog, the helicopter slated to pick us up had been grounded. Hopefully the weather would clear the following day, but even then, the secretary of the navy and the congresspersons aboard the USS *New Hampshire* (SSN-778) would take priority. Upon hearing this, Varney slapped me on the back, let out a laugh, and said if we missed our window we'd just have to ride with the *Connecticut* back to port. That meant we'd be underwater and out of contact with the outside world for almost a month. No e-mail or voice mail for thirty days? "I'm in," I said.

Varney lost his smile.

He regained it again when the fog cleared the following day. I joined the CNN team in the control room to watch the sub's crew punch a big hole in the ice. Almost two-dozen bodies crowded the small space, mostly shouting and repeating orders while studying readouts, flicking switches, turning wheels, or operating equipment. The CNN boys and I were about to witness the boat's surfacing through three feet of ice, which is always a danger-ous maneuver that requires precise timing and accuracy. Water must be pumped to and from forward and aft trim tanks to ensure the submarine is horizontally level. Should we surface with the back end up a tad too much, we could damage the rudder and/or propeller. We'd then have a tough time going anywhere. Coming up with the bow too high could whack a hole in the sonar dome, taking away the boat's "ears," or worse, rupturing the hull, which could cause flooding.

Thinking about the latter scenario reminded me of a serious collision I'd experienced aboard my last boat, the USS *Drum* during Cold War I, an incident that I'd hinted at earlier. We were hunting a Soviet *Victor III* submarine deep inside Vladivostok harbor. We found one sitting on the surface, and in an effort to gain better photographs, we accidentally slammed into the underside of the Russian vessel. The smack crushed our sail, resulting in a gush of seawater from a leak in a periscope seal. We ran deep and fast for several days while the Soviet Navy chased us out of the Sea of Japan. They dropped depth charges, shot torpedoes, and pinged away with active sonar, but never caught us. Had they, you would not be reading this book today.

Now, standing in the control room of the USS *Connecticut*, I figured that whatever was about to happen couldn't be that bad, right?

I wiped the sweat from my palms and fired up my camera.

Punching a hole through a yard's worth of ice is like trying to crack through a sheet of sidewalk concrete. The *Connecticut* weighs almost eight thousand tons, stretches longer than a ten-story building, and has a hardened sail coated with tough steel. These attributes, combined with upward-looking underwater cameras, advanced high frequency sonar, and intense crew training make vertical surfacing from under the ice almost routine. Still, most submariners whisper silent prayers during the ascent.

Standing next to the XO, I watched the crew issue and repeat orders with the timed accuracy of a Swiss watch.

"All masts and antennas are in the under-ice position," the chief of the watch reported.

"Very well, Chief of the Watch," the officer of the deck said.

"Officer of the Deck, vertically surface the ship," Varney ordered.

"Vertically surface the ship, aye, sir. Dive, vertically surface the ship."

"Vertically surface, aye, Chief of the Watch, on the 1MC, vertical surface, vertical surface, vertical surface."

The COW grabbed the 1MC, and throughout the boat every speaker blared, "Vertical surface, vertical surface, vertical surface!"

A dozen more orders and reports were issued and echoed.

"Diving Officer, one degree up angle."

"One seven zero, point eight, two one."

"Clearing all top sounders."

"Very well, Dive."

"One hundred, one point four, two seven."

I glanced at the monitor on the port side just aft of the Ballast Control Panel. The screen displayed a video broadcast from the upward-looking camera mounted in the sail. I could see the underside of the ice layer, one hundred feet above us, white and dotted with sprinkles of black created by cracks in the ice. I curled my fingers around a nearby stanchion as the hard ice crept closer and closer.

"Chief of the Watch, stand by for ice impact."

"Stand by for ice impact, aye."

"Seven zero, two point one, three eight."

"Ice impact!"

The boat shuddered. Dull thunder boomed. I gripped tighter and held my breath.

More thunder preceded crunching and grinding, but it was muffled as if quieted by a trumpet mute. For the crew, this had been a dangerous maneuver made routine by practice. For me, having never experienced an under-ice vertical surfacing, this had been an "underwear-changing moment."

Later, outside the control room, in the passageway near the crew's mess, I watched the hatch open and felt cold air gush in. Sailors wearing orange pumpkin suits clambered up the ladder and disappeared into a swirl of grey white. I suited up and followed, along with the boys from CNN. My cheeks chilled as I stared again at the barren white, untamed and whisper quiet. Then the fun began. Sailors smoked, joked, and smiled. They lay flat on the snowpack and carved snow angels. Some even joined Kaj, Ken, Toby, and me as we performed funny dance jigs for the camera.

Our helicopter ride finally swooped down from the milky sky with blades thumping. We loaded up our gear and well-fed bodies, strapped in, and lifted off. The chopper pilot agreed to circle the boat a few times so Toby could shoot some downward-looking video. I stared at the black sail beneath us and marveled. While so much of the world endured turmoil and starvation, below me lay proof of mankind's ability to innovate and create. If we can build vessels of hardened steel, powered by nuclear reactors that allow them to cruise for months beneath the polar ice cap and smash through solid walls of ice unfettered, what can't we do?

SILENT SALUTE

Upon our return to the ICEX camp, we stuffed our faces once again and waited. Hours passed and we started to worry. We needed to be in Prudhoe Bay before five p.m. to catch the last flight out. Otherwise, we'd have to stay in no man's land for a night, with no guarantees that we could catch a flight the next day. More hours passed, and we discovered that our delay had been caused by politics. The USS *New Hampshire*, hosting the congresspersons and the secretary of the navy, had also been held up due to the fog.

We didn't grumble, though. We rose to the occasion, accepted our fate, and did what any proud American men would do: we ate cake and played more cribbage. Jeff Gossett finally appeared and said that he had good news and bad news. The good? The Cessna had returned to ferry us to Prudhoe Bay. The bad? We might not make it back in time to catch our flight.

Having a pilot's license to add to his already impressive resume, Kaj convinced our pilot to drop to a lower altitude and trim five minutes off the flight time. We landed, stumbled like walruses to the hanger, pulled off our Arctic gear, and scrambled over to the Alaska Airlines counter. At first I thought they'd never let us on. Not only were we late, but we hadn't showered or shaved and looked and smelled like rugby players. The Alaska Airlines customer service representatives were the epitome of smiling efficiency, however, and quickly handled our ticketing and ushered us through security.

Up in the air, on the way to Anchorage, I gave a silent salute toward an ice floe some two hundred miles north where the USS *Connecticut* slowly melted back into the ice and disappeared. Having witnessed her crew of 160 drill around the clock and efficiently prepare to do battle in a hostile environment under the ice, I couldn't help wonder if their skills would soon be put to the test. With the world apparently hurtling severe resource shortages, I was now convinced that an ice war might be no more than a few years away. If so, what might U.S. and NATO submarines face when they encounter a Russian or Chinese submarine ready to do them harm in the Arctic?

I put that thought out of my mind upon my return to San Diego when I received an e-mail from Sarah Blanchard, the Alaska Airlines customer service agent who had helped me get to Prudhoe Bay successfully. She had inquired about that free book I'd promised her. I said I'd be delighted to give her one, but suggested I sign it in person... over dinner. She agreed.

I proposed to her on Valentine's Day the following year. She said yes, thankfully, and I definitely owe a debt of gratitude to Alaska Airlines for helping make this chapter of my life the most exciting ever.

Still, as global tensions mounted and Putin continued to gain ground in the Arctic, I struggled with what I was witnessing. The puzzle pieces were becoming clearer, but they hadn't yet formed a complete picture.

Then I learned about the chess pieces Putin was placing along a six thousand-mile-long route that had once been nearly inaccessible. Now, given dramatic increases in shipping traffic, this route was poised to become ground zero for the next world war.

Rear Adm. Robert Kamensky and I served together aboard the USS *Drum* (SSN-677) during Cold War I. As the flag officer heading up all NATO submarine operations, he sees an organization that is undergoing one of the most profound command structure reforms in its sixty-four year history, primarily due to recent developments in the Arctic. When I asked him about this topic, he said, "There is a potential for conflict in the Arctic due to natural resources. Conventions are in place, but how are we going to enforce them? That's going to be our biggest challenge. NATO has a very strong concern with this. Up until now we've been focused on Europe because that's where all the sparks are. Meanwhile, things are continuing to fester up in the Arctic region without a lot of national attention."

That statement raised the hairs on the back of my neck, and made me wonder what might happen if the world continued to watch Putin's left hand and completely miss the deadly moves made by his right hand.

CHAPTER THREE

Russia's Routes—
The Second Ring

n 1553, several Russian fishermen near Arkhangelsk watched in terror as a lurking vessel loomed large near the coast of the White Sea. Stubborn sheets of ice and howling Arctic winds had diverted the English warship, commanded by Captain Richard Chancellor, from fulfilling its quest to open a northern trade route with China. Capt. Chancellor had no choice but to cut his trip short and seek harbor in Moscow, where Ivan the Terrible greeted the crew with an uncharacteristic smile.

The "beginning of a beautiful relationship" ensued. Timber wood to build English ships was soon exchanged for Brit-built muskets and small arms. Things went swimmingly for many years until the Russian tsar Alexis I slammed the door on further trade when he heard about the execution of King Charles I in 1649.

Fast forward half a millennium. Russia and the European Union are once again active trade partners, but with tensions running high, will history repeat? Will tsars and kings feud? How are dramatic world changes feeding Putin's powers, and how might they kindle fires that could eventually rage out of control?

The following paragraphs are controversial. When I first travelled to the Arctic to board a nuclear submarine, I was a climate change skeptic. At that time, in my opinion, the science was a lot thinner than the Arctic ice. Four years later, after extensively researching this topic, I have a different opinion, but this book is not intended to be an argument for or against climate change. We are all entitled to our opinions, but unless we have the power to alter world economies or control the movements of entire navies, we are little more than couch quarterbacks in a game where the entire future of our planet is at stake.

What matters is what world leaders—especially Putin and Obama—believe, see and feel about climate change. More importantly, what actions they are taking based on their views and interpretations of the scientific data.

While nearly half of all Americans believe climate change is a hoax, the European Environment Agency is convinced and planning for the worst. They delivered a three hundred-page report on November 21, 2012, full of colorful maps and figures that start at "worrisome" in five years and end with "terrifying" by 2100. The report is essentially a diagramed road map that predicts climate change effects on temperature, drought, fires, flooding, soil quality, sea life, and water and food shortages. Simply stated, the team of scientists who completed the report agree on the prognosis that our planet, and hence all its inhabitants, have the equivalent of cancer that is now irreversible. All we can do is mitigate our pain and suffering until we die, which will be far sooner than previously thought.

The UN weather agency published a report in November 2012 showing an area of northern sea ice larger than the United States had melted away that year. The UN released their report during climate talks in the Qatari capital of Doha, where the World Meteorological Organization warned of record-breaking ice melt caused by climate change that is "happening before our eyes."

In early 2015, during climate change meetings in Geneva, French Foreign Minister Laurent Fabius expressed grave concerns that unless leaders agree on binding global commitments to keep global warming below the 3.6-degree mark, the world could be headed toward disaster.

"Without sounding too grandiose, the survival of the planet itself is at stake," Fabius said to reporters in Geneva. "You have rising sea levels, acidification of the oceans, immigration sparked by climate change, droughts that are much more severe. And then there's an aspect that we don't talk about much: the impact on security. If you have climate degradation, global security as a whole is degraded, there is immigration, and the fact that we fight over resources, be it oil or water."

FIRES AND DROUGHTS

In May 2014, wildfires burned out of control just a few miles from my home in North County San Diego. Over 120,000 people were evacuated from their homes, and I wondered if my house might become a cinder block at any moment. Most of my neighbors packed up and left, but my family and I chose to tough it out. Temperatures in excess of 105 degrees Fahrenheit, coupled with winds gusting to seventy miles per hour, fanned wildfires into frenzies just a few short miles away. Red-orange plumes, some as high as fifty feet and hissing like angry snakes, arced into a night sky filled with smoke and ash.

The fire raged for almost ten days and scorched nine thousand acres of land. Damage and containment costs exceeded $60 million. Captain Richard Cordova of Cal Fire said, "We usually don't see these kinds of conditions until late September. It caught a lot of people off guard."

There used to be a fire season in California. Not anymore. Through most of 2013 and 2014, wildfires have flared up all year long. The sunshine state is not alone. In May 2014, Oklahoma, Arizona, and even Alaska endured the burning lick of the fire tongue, months ahead of normal, if such a word even exists anymore.

In 2013, residents of Colorado stood in awe as they watched a blaze race cross a snow-covered forest in the Rockies. The month was November, not August. In July 2014, an area four times the size of Seattle turned black as a wildfire raced across the typically wet state of Washington. The Carlton Complex wildfire, centered in the north-central part of the state, scorched almost three hundred thousand acres and burned down two hundred homes—making it the largest in Washington's recorded history.

Over the past three years, firefighters in almost every state in the West have been forced to put out a record number of fires—more devastating than anything seen in the past fifty years.

David Cleaves is an advisor to the chief of the U.S. Forest Service and a life-long expert on wilderness fires. He's spent decades helping the service create economic models to forecast the intensity and cost of potential fires. During that time, he saw the average number of acres burned go from three million in the '80s to five million in the early '90s. "Large parts of whole counties in the West were going up in single fires," said Cleaves. "We'd never seen fires like that."

By the mid-2000s, the toll had climbed to more than nine million acres, which equates to almost one tenth of the entire state of California. Desperate to find an answer to the rapid increases, Cleaves examined the data and discovered an undeniable correlation to a rise in average temperatures. Even a slight increase can cause drought, tree and soil drying, and higher infestations of bark beetles and other insects that turn live trees into dead tinder. "I think the result will be that we're going to see an average of maybe ten thousand wildfires burning ten million acres a year," said Cleaves.

Two decades ago, the average number of wildfires was one-fourth that amount.

Nasty weather or not, skeptics side with Dr. Wei-Hock Soon of the Harvard-Smithsonian Center for Astrophysics. In recent years, he has become the "high priest" for this side of the fence, especially when he says that scientists who worry over climate change "are so out of their minds!" and dismisses their research as "crazy."

Believers retort that nearly 90% of climate scientists say climate change is real and caused by humans, and note that Soon received more than $1.2 million in funding from oil giants ExxonMobil, Southern Company, and the American Petroleum Institute. They also point to undisputable evidence from NOAA satellites and other credible sources showing drastic ice abatement in the Arctic.

Skeptics fire back and say this is just Mother Nature temporarily having her way, which she has done since the beginning of time.

Andrew J. Hoffman, from the Stanford Social Innovation Review, says the debate is prompted mostly by "Ideological filters." He says the differences in opinion are not necessarily over the science, which was decided years ago, but "over culture, worldviews and ideology" and the "innate desire to maintain a consistency in beliefs." He says that people tend to "refute views or arguments that are contrary to those beliefs."

Hoffman wrote: "We'll consider evidence when it is accepted or, ideally, presented by a knowledgeable source from our cultural community; and we'll dismiss information that is advocated by sources that represent groups whose values we reject."

Is it possible that both camps are right? Dr. Donald Ross believes this may be the case. Ross was the first person in history to graduate from Harvard University in three years. Yes, he's that smart. Ross is considered one of the "fathers" of modern submarine sonar technology and received an award (the highest one a civilian can attain) from President Nixon for his work in this field. As a skeptical scientist, Ross set out to disprove climate change. After years of research, he formed a decidedly different opinion, but notes that skeptics have a right to question the facts delivered by climate scientists.

"Most climate scientists have a messaging problem," said Ross. "They're confusing people when they talk about climate models, degrees of average temperature variance, salinity saturations, and other mumbo jumbo. When I visually show people four graphs, they instantly get it. Even hardline skeptics raise an eyebrow."

The first graph Ross shows is the earth's average surface temperature since the year 1800. This graph is not from one source, but four, including the NASA Goddard Institute for Space Studies (GISS), the National Oceanic and Atmospheric Administration (NOAA), the UK Hadley Centre—Climate Research Unit (HadCRU), and the Berkeley Energy and Climate Institute (BECI). When overlaid on top of each other, they line up almost exactly and show a modest temperature fluctuation from the year 1800 to about 1950. Ross said this is what we'd expect as normal. The chart then curves sharply upward. Taken by itself, this could just be a coincidence or an act of Mother Nature, but Ross pulls the rug on this theory with his next three charts.

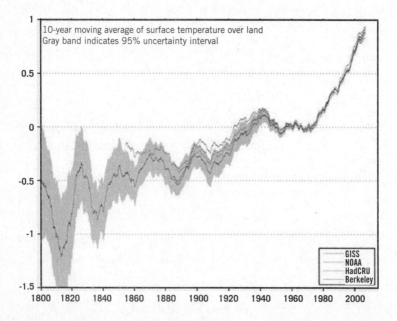

Chart two deals with sea level change and is derived from the University of Colorado and Australia's Commonwealth Scientific and Industrial

Research Organization (John Church & Neil White). This chart shows a moderate increase in sea level from the year 1800, with a more pronounced spike beginning at around 1950. Ross says that in the forty-five centuries up until about 1800, the earth averaged less than one inch in sea level rise. In the nineteenth century, this increased to three inches, and then to seven inches in the twentieth century. In the twenty first century, predominately after 1950, sea level change shot up to almost twenty inches and is now at around one inch per decade.

Ross said, "Many climate scientists focus on the melting ice in the Arctic, which has been quite dramatic. Skeptics are right to question ice melt in one area as proof of climate change. However, it's not just one place, it's everywhere. Glacier ice is melting in Greenland, China, New Zealand, Europe, and even Antarctica. We didn't understand how much the ice had melted in Antarctica until recently because it wasn't that visible on the surface. The fact is, most of the melt has occurred underneath the visible ice due to warmer ocean currents."

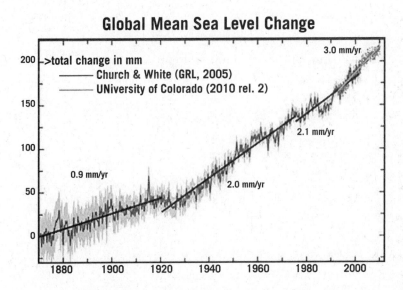

Chart three deals with the infamous carbon monster. Citing data from the Scripps Institute of Oceanography National Climatic Data Center and other sources, Ross shows that across hundreds of centuries prior to 1950, atmospheric carbon dioxide cycled between one hundred eighty and two hundred parts per million. Then, around 1950, it eclipsed the 300 mark. By 1987 the number climbed past 350. Today we're at 400 and we'll easily hit 450 by the year 2035.

"I know some folks want to believe that our carbon increase is normal and caused mostly by Mother Nature," Ross said. "After all, volcanoes and other natural phenomenon spew out lots of carbon. But the data is pretty clear. When it was just Mother Nature in charge, for hundreds of centuries, our carbon content was fairly steady and never moved above two hundred eighty. We're at four hundred and climbing, and that can't be due to natural causes."

Ross believes this point becomes undisputable when he reveals his fourth and final chart showing the world's energy consumption. Here's where it really gets interesting. The graph line is almost flat until—you guessed it—around 1950. Then it heads north in a hurry with oil and coal leading the pack.

"After the war, around 1950," Ross said, "the world's population increased steadily, but more importantly, so did the average energy consumption per person. In fact, energy consumption has increased by fifteen hundred percent. One third of that is due to a population increase and two thirds because people are using more energy. A lot more energy."

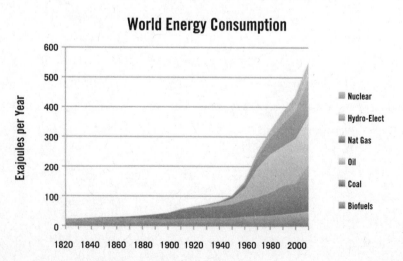

World Energy Consumption

Ross said that our society changed after 1950. We formed more and larger suburbs, started driving and flying more, installed air conditioning units, and most importantly, chopped up far too many trees.

"Skeptics have a right to be skeptical," Ross said. "But we can't deny that carbon has increased dramatically since 1950, alongside energy consumption. This is a clear indication that mankind is at least partially responsible. Many climate scientists point to the burning of fossil fuels, but deforestation is also to blame. For hundreds of centuries, Mother Nature had a built-in way to keep carbon in check. When mankind started cutting down the rain forests, and dumping more carbon into the air, we unseated this balance."

When Ross lays all four charts on top of each other, jaws drop. All four line up almost perfectly and show a direct correlation between temperature increase, sea level rise, carbon escalation, and human energy consumption. All show spikes beginning around the year 1950. He agrees that two charts with nearly identical curves and spikes at the same time could be a coincidence, but not four.

"I empathize with the skeptics," Ross said. "After all, I used to be one. But when the evidence became this clear, I finally decided that I couldn't keep saying the world was flat. That said, I agree that it's not perfectly round either."

In conclusion, Ross believes that a massive increase in energy consumption, human population, and deforestation have altered Mother Nature's natural balancing act and exacerbated climate change. In his opinion, there would have likely been a more modest increase in world temperature, carbon density, and sea level rise, but definitely not three hockey stick spikes that all start in the same year that mankind also dramatically increased energy consumption.

While the ideological battle rages on, a military one is brewing in the Arctic. Due to recent ice melts, the Arctic represents a proverbial warning bell, predicting both demise and delight for millions. Regardless of the cause, no one can deny that, according to satellite data, summer ice in the northern region has declined by more than half over the past four decades.

Many scientists have pointed to this melt as a catalyst for droughts bent on destroying crops in the Midwest, super storms flooding homes along seaboards, and heat waves killing thousands around the world. Conversely, energy firms and shippers see the changes as potential cash cows.

ARM WRESTLING OVER ARTIC ROUTES

The Arctic region comprises only around 6% of the world's surface area, but the U.S. Geological Survey believes the frozen north could yield some 1.7 trillion cubic feet of natural gas, or about 30% of the undiscovered reserves, and over ninety billion barrels of oil, or 13% of the reserves. Like a sought-after bride, the Arctic also promises a dowry of rich veins of precious metals such as uranium, iron ore, gold, and platinum. Engagement ring manufacturers are salivating.

In September 2012, Arctic sea ice reached its lowest level in recorded satellite history, which dates back to 1979. Non-satellite observations made by sea and land travelers prior to the '70s indicate that the record-breaking low has not been seen since the Little Ice Age. The melt is self-perpetuating. As more ice melts, less heat is reflected, causing more ice to melt, and so on. Scientists call this the albedo effect, and note that dry snow reflects over 80% of the sun's radiation, bare ice 65%, and open water only 5%. Each summer, more and more open water areas lead to faster ocean heating resulting in less ice that is thinner and easier to melt the following year. "Less and thinner" has rolled downhill, and current Arctic sea ice volume is now 20% of its 1980 level.

Alarmed by this fact, four scientists hailing from Russia, Norway, and the U.S. recently wrote a paper wherein they said, "The long-term outlook is disturbing. Our view is that a seasonally ice-free Arctic Ocean might be realized as early as 2030."

The Arctic's reflectivity decline is concerning because "it plays a role like a thermostat in regulating global climate," said Martin Jeffries, an Office of Naval Research Arctic scientist. Jeffries intimated that as brighter areas decline, even temporarily, they are replaced by darker heat-absorbing areas and "that has global implications."

If all these scientists are correct, the results may be catastrophic for global weather patterns, but compelling for global transport companies. Formerly treacherous sea-lanes have become more traversable, offering the promise of far shorter routes and less expensive ocean transport. Again, what's important here is not whether skeptics believe these changes are only temporary or believers think global demise is just around the corner. What we should all be concerned about is what Putin believes and what's he's doing about those beliefs.

PUTIN'S MONOPOLY BOARD

Shipping is critical to our world economy. In fact, seaborne trade represents 90% of the world's total, with such transport comprised mostly of fossil fuels, natural gas, dry goods, raw materials, equipment, parts, and various other container-housed cargo. Trade between Europe and Asia is escalating in importance and frequency, creating high-seas bottlenecks through the Strait of Malacca and Suez Canal, increasing the risk of collisions and slower transport times. More time at sea translates to more cost, which translates to higher prices for goods.

Melting Arctic ice now allows shippers to shorten sea time by shipping goods through the Northern Sea Route (NSR), past Russia, or through the Northwest Passage, which winds around Canada. Icebergs and harsh weather prevented Capt. Chancellor from sailing all the way through the NSR in 1553, but more modern commercial ships have no such limitations.

Less than a decade ago, virtually no ships traversed the NSR. With the recession winding down, ocean trade is rebounding, and melting ice is becoming a catalyst. By early 2013, twenty massive merchant ships were traversing the Arctic's "great circle route" each day, humping goods between Asia and North America along the twelve hundred-mile Aleutian chain. Hundreds of tankers will soon be hauling goods between Asia and Europe while cutting their journey times and costs by 40% as compared to travelling through the Suez Canal. The Chinese are doing summersaults. They estimate that up to 15% of their trade will go through the NSR and save them over $500 billion per year.

In the summer of 2014, Mitsui O.S.K. Lines, Ltd. and China Shipping Development Co. Ltd., in Japan and China respectively, announced the start of a regular service to carry Siberian natural gas across the Arctic Ocean to East Asia. The two companies will ship natural gas, by way of the Arctic NSR, from Russia's new $27 billion Yamal LNG facility in Siberia to harbors in Japan and China.

China Shipping Development and Mitsui O.S.K. jointly plan to spend almost $1 billion to have South Korea's Daewoo Shipbuilding & Marine Engineering Co., Ltd. build three new icebreaker-equipped LNG carriers by 2018.

Cargo ships hauled more than one million tons through the NSR in 2012, most of it consisting of toxic fuels and gas condensates. Waterborne travel between Europe and Asia through the NSR only takes thirty-five days as compared to forty-eight days via the Suez Canal. That's one reason why experts project that by 2020, forty million tons of oil and gas will cross the NSR each year, and that fact has quite a few environmentalists worried while some government officials are smiling—especially Putin.

At an international forum in Arkhangelsk in September 2012, Putin announced Russia's plan to transform a main Arctic waterway into a moneymaker. "I want to stress the importance of the Northern Sea Route as an international transport artery that will rival traditional trade lanes in service fees, security, and quality," Putin said.

Melting ice makes the NSR the shortest path between Europe and Asia—two regions with long histories of robust trade appetites. Buoyed by energy profits, Russia's investment possibilities have expanded, and Putin seems eager to own more Monopoly properties and place more hotels on the game board. Russia owns a vast majority of the NSR's coastline and is uniquely positioned in the region, so if anyone wants to "roll logs down the river," they'll need to pay tariffs to Russia. Such fees pay for icebreaker assistance, safety patrols to thwart piracy, rescue efforts when needed, and resources to clean up any ecological spills that may occur. At least that's the byline spewed by Russia, but much of this hype is not yet deliverable.

While Moscow has invested in NSR infrastructure, they have a long way to go and will need to escalate their efforts by an order of magnitude over the next decade. They must rebuild or upgrade aging seaports and equipment. They own twenty-five icebreakers today, and seven are nuclear powered, but most are turning geriatric. Russia has embarked on plans to build three more nuclear and six diesel-electric hybrid vessels, but each one costs $1 billion and can take a decade to finish. Current and future icebreakers will be stationed at ten Arctic aid centers, which also cost a pretty ruble, and should be completed by 2015.

Despite the high cost of their "speakeasy facelift," Russia must lower their cover charge. Current fees for navigation and icebreaking services often eclipse the economic benefits derived by some states and private firms when choosing between southern routes and the NSR. Russia is at least trying to comply. On January 28, 2013, the new NSR headquarters opened in Moscow. The state-owned organization has jurisdiction over tariffs and regulations regarding "navigation safety and the prevention, reduction, and control of pollution in the marine environment," according to the State Duma law passed in July 2012. But costs are not the only problem. Russia will find it hard to demand the tariffs needed to be profitable when today they can offer only inefficient and spotty service arrangements to customers. While many of Moscow's top brass understand well that investing in the Arctic can reap substantial gains, they are fighting internal and external battles to make headway.

Internally, several of Moscow's departments are not yet on the same page. Some provinces are squabbling over jurisdictions, and typical government bureaucracies and inefficiencies abound.

Externally, it's even worse. Russia's sovereignty claims in several straits along the NSR are disputed by almost all of the Arctic Eight and other counsel and ad hoc member states. For now, Putin may need to set aside the argument of who owns what and be content with his "wilderness guide fees." One country that's hoping for such an attitude adjustment is China. As the world's premier negotiators, they have huge resource needs, big ships, tons of experience, and above all, an abundance of desire. Norway also appears hopeful that they can continue to cut deals to send fossil fuel tankers through the NSR. The Norwegian oil giant Dynagas sent the first large liquefied natural gas tanker across the NSR in late 2012. Norway would obviously like to continue with this practice but may be conflicted to do so if Russia keeps invading other countries and continues to fly warplanes over Norway's front yard.

THE BREWING FEUD

Emboldened by new dollars flowing in from oil and gas sales, Russia has more frequently spread its military wings and breached protocol by flaunting its might and toying with the defenses of several NATO countries. Just a few years ago, Putin stated that Russia would resume sending their jets near bordering Arctic countries to test defensive responses, thereby thrusting the region back to the days of Cold War I. Norway has responded by scrambling NATO-supplied planes in pursuit of Russia's fighters whenever they've flown too close to a national border. NATO jets flew after almost ninety Russian bombers in 2008 alone, and Russia has repeatedly conducted naval exercises near Norwegian gas and oil drilling platforms in the North Sea. They were even so brash as to send bombers on a test run to simulate an attack on the Norwegian northern command center, Bodo, in 2007.

Concerned over Russia's renewed aggressive posture in the Arctic region, Norway's General Sverre Diesen was quoted as saying, "Under certain circumstances there is undoubtedly room for the possible use of military power."

Russia and Norway have long been feuding neighbors, but unlike the Hatfields and McCoys, they haven't yet strung each other up or fired volleys across fence lines. That said, in relation to shipping through the NSR, let's imagine that Norway's "McCoys" need to float their logs down a river that runs across ocean areas that Russia's "Hatfields" claim as their own. The McCoys disagree with the claim. To keep the peace and make money, the Hatfields drop the argument but offer low-cost services to guide and protect the McCoys' logging rafts. The McCoys reluctantly agree, as the shorter route will shave 40% off their transportation costs.

Years later, citing an increase in infrastructure costs, the Hatfields double their tolls. Furious, the McCoys refuse to pay and look for services elsewhere while continuing to roll logs down the northern route. The Hatfields get angry and restate their territorial claims. The McCoys say the claims are baseless and continue to use the river. Finally, the Hatfields decide to block the waterway with boats and guns. Do the McCoys give in and pay or do they turn to an ally, namely NATO, for help?

Putin has already begun building a series of military bases along the NSR. He has also beefed up Russia's warship presence and slated several new *Borei*-class ballistic missile and other attack submarines to patrol the area. A more open NSR could upend the naval balance in the Pacific. Russia's Atlantic and Pacific fleets may soon be able to reinforce each other with greater ease and speed, resolving the two-front problem that has plagued Moscow since 1905 when Japan destroyed two-thirds of the Russian fleet in the Tsushima Straits.

If the U.S. and Europe allow Putin to gain complete control of this route, Russia could start acting like a Chicago gangster, demanding fees for ice-breaker escorts, whether needed or not. They could become a dirty cop, deciding who gets to save 40% on transport costs and who does not, perhaps depending upon who bids the highest. They could also try to block the U.S. from shipping oil and gas to Europe to thwart competition and maintain their energy monopoly.

The Western Elves stand duly warned: Putin is after your ring. He wants complete control of the NSR, regardless of the fact that most of the Arctic ocean areas are technically in international waters. He will use his military bases, icebreakers, warships, and submarines to patrol, police, and plunder the region as he pleases. The only way he can be stopped is if the Elves figure out a way to keep the NSR open and free for all. To accomplish this, perhaps they need to crack a history book and brush up on the meaning of "freedom of the seas."

ARCTIC REGION

U.S. government photo courtesy of the Central Intelligence Agency

CHAPTER FOUR

The Peanut Hole— The Third Ring

I n the seventeenth century, a Dutchman named Hugo Grotius became the founder of international maritime law. Grotius postulated that a sea could belong to no man or nation, which prompted the term "freedom of the seas" in the eighteenth century. During that time, Cornelius Van Bynkershoek, also a Dutch jurist, contended that a bordering state could lay claim to an area extending beyond the coastline equal in distance to the average range of a fired cannonball—or about three nautical miles. This definition remained until 1958 when, during a Geneva Conference, efforts were made to better define the Law of the Sea and create legal guidelines related to internal waters, territorial waters, contiguous zones, exclusive economic zones, continental shelves, and international waters.

The conventions did little good, as most nations disputed the definitions. Arguments continued for another two dozen years until the United Nations

Convention on the Law of the Sea (UNCLOS), which defines the term "sea" as any watery area containing salt (such as an ocean, a gulf, or a strait), was adopted at Montego Bay, Jamaica. Another dozen years passed before the agreement was signed by all 158 of the industrialized nations involved, with the exception of the United States.

For nations who did accept the guidelines covered in the agreement, internal waters were henceforth defined as all waters or waterways found on the landward side of the baseline of a coastal nation. Baselines draw divisions between land-based territories and maritime territories, and each state is given leeway to create their own baselines. If one follows the rules, baselines must traverse low-water lines—or the farthest points where waters recede. This can be altered for indented coastlines, impinging islands, or for coastal instability, in which case each nation can use a ruler edge to draw straight lines.

Territorial waters are found between baselines and exclusive economic zones. This is where a two hundred nautical mile rule comes into play, granting states the right to resources found within that range. This does not supersede the traditional territorial definition of twelve nautical miles, which governs geopolitical disputes involving foreign vessels or aircraft that might "cross the line." Most nations guard their territories with fervor. Conflicts and even wars have almost started when a ship or plane has crossed over or skirted these invisible but highly protected lines.

That said, some ships are often granted the right of "innocent passage" through a state's territorial waters, including commercial and military vessels, so long as they are quick about it and do nothing that might be considered "prejudicial to the peace, good order, or the security" of the coastal nation. Territorial waters are subdivided by coastal inner bands, known as archipelagic waters, which extend twelve miles beyond the furthest island. The next concentric band, also out to twelve miles, is called the contiguous zone, wherein a state has jurisdiction over such things as illegal immigration or smuggling. Beyond these zones are the exclusive economic zones and continental shelves.

The term international waters, also known as the high seas, is defined as sea areas extending beyond the economical two hundred or maximum three hundred fifty nautical mile limit, in accordance with continental shelf and coastal baseline prolongations. No nation owns these waters and no "keep out" signs can be posted here, so anyone can motor or sail through these areas unfettered by angry landlords. Still, one must obey traditional laws that govern crime and environmental protection. Drug runners and litterbugs beware.

UNCLOS defines how oceans can be used or governed. Unfortunately, the guidelines in this treaty are often incomplete and difficult to interpret, which opens the door to arguments and conflicts. When drawing lines around Arctic assets, verifying which areas belong to which government could escalate disagreements beyond international courts, with winners decided by muscle and might rather than by lawyers and judges.

THE ARCTIC EIGHT

Since fingers of the Arctic Ocean touch upon the shores of the United States (Alaska), Russia, Norway, Canada, and Denmark (Greenland), these states comprise the "Arctic Five" bordering nations. The wider Arctic region is roughly the same size as the African continent and covers around 8% of the earth's surface. This area cuts across Iceland, Finland, and Sweden, which combined with the Arctic Five, create the Arctic Eight voting council members. There are also twelve permanent observer states on the Arctic Council including France, Germany, the Netherlands, Poland, Spain, Great Britain, China, Italy, Japan, South Korea, India, and Singapore. Ad hoc observer states, which do not have permanent seats or voting rights, include Turkey and the European Union.

The council formed in 1991 when the Arctic Eight signed the Arctic Environmental Protection Strategy (AEPS). The Ottawa Declaration of 1996 certified the Arctic Council as a forum to promote coordination, cooperation, and interactive discussions between the Arctic states, along with indigenous populations, regarding such issues as trade routes, the environment, natural resources, and development. The Arctic Council is an international body commissioned to conduct various studies on oil and gas, climate change, and Arctic shipping. Council chairmanship rotates every two years, with Canada in the hot seat until the ministerial meeting in May 2015. The U.S. will chair from May 2015 through May 2017. While the council discusses Arctic issues, members do not govern or enforce any laws, but instead defer such matters to the United Nations.

A UN Commission on the Limits of the Continental Shelf (CLCS) has been appointed as the adjudicator in this northern court, but its gavel has largely been silent. CLCS members have done little to carve out territorial guidelines or resolve disputes, instead choosing to just say "no" to virtually every claim filed, save for one key submission submitted by Russia for ownership of an area called the "Peanut Hole," which has caused steam to rise from under several collars.

What's causing all the arguments? Until recent years, extracting Arctic riches had been almost impossible. Much of it lays hidden beneath thousands of feet of ocean shrouded by miles of ice pack. But with the ice now receding, that changes the game for everyone. Many nations have already invested millions over the past few years to collect geological and bathymetric data to verify their economic rights to drill, dig, or sell. Although most of the parties launched these quests with visible smiles and concealed daggers, smiles are fading and knives are being stabbed into the wood atop negotiating tables.

RUSSIA'S ARKTIKA EXPEDITION

In the wake of the *Mir-1* and *Mir-2* expedition of 2007, the Russian Federation expressed bitter disappointment over the unexpected denial of their territorial claims delivered by the CLCS. Five years later, on November 7,

2012, the Russian newspaper, *Izvestia*, reported that the federation would never settle for "no" as an answer from the UN to prove once and for all that Russia had sole economic rights to the Mendeleev and Lomonosov Ridges, they sent a unique submarine called the *Kalitka* to the bottom of the Arctic Ocean to gather soil samples. These samples, they surmised, would ultimately verify to the CLCS that the underwater ridges had the same geological "DNA" as their parent continent, Russia.

As part of the special *Arktika* (Arctic) 2012 expedition, the deep-diving *Kalitka* submarine spent twenty days on station to explore the entire ridge area. Submariners aboard the *Kalitka* nicknamed their odd-shaped vessel, which sported a multispherical hull, the *Losharik*, in reference to a character in a poem written by Genrikh Sapgir, a popular Russian poet. The children's cartoon character depicted by Sapgir is a toy horse consisting of small spheres. The name is a portmanteau of *loshad*, which means horse or donkey, and *sharik*, meaning small sphere. The *Losharik*'s special design allows her to deploy on repetitive dives to the bottom of the ocean, over ten thousand feet deep.

Powered by a nuclear reactor and hardened by a unique titanium hull, the *Losharik* mini-sub is carried on the back of an adapted Project 667 *Kalmar* submarine—a former *Delta III* ballistic missile boat with its launching tubes removed. Since its introduction in 1973, the *Delta* class once formed the backbone of the Soviet strategic deterrent fleet during Cold War I. They carried sixteen R-29R (SS-N-18 Stingray) nuclear ballistic missiles equipped with multiple warheads. Fortified with Arctic-hardened capabilities, as well as improved electronics and noise reduction, *Delta III*s gave U.S. attack submariners heartburn by hiding under the polar ice cap, which made them hard to detect. The subs could quickly fire a volley of missiles from their relatively safe positions in the Arctic Ocean and hit targets up to 4,780 miles away. Four *Delta III*s are still in service, but will soon be replaced by newer *Borei*-class missile boats.

A source at the Russian Ministry of Defence told the *Izvestia* newspaper that the *Delta III*-carried *Losharik* assisted the on-station *Kapitan Dranitsyn* and *Dikson* diesel-electric icebreakers in their efforts to pinpoint exact locations to drill for the desired samples. During the expedition, crews onboard the icebreakers drilled three wells at two sites and collected soil samples from a depth of almost two miles down. The Russian Ministry of Natural Resources and Environment intended to use the samples to convince the UN CLCS of Russia's ownership of the two ridges in question.

"The joint effort resulted in a substantial amount of geological material," the Ministry of Defence source said. "More than five hundred kilograms of classifiable rocks were selected. The results of the survey will underlie Russia's application to the UN Commission on the Limits of the Continental Shelf, to allow extension of Russia's continental shelf—the initial application having been rejected because of a lack of geological evidence—and grant Russia the priority right to develop the deposits located on the shelf."

The *Mir* mini-subs used in 2007 operated on batteries that died after less than seventy-two hours underwater. In contrast, the *Losharik* is a nuclear-powered craft capable of operating without surfacing for several months. Crews can work and live in a self-contained environment that includes a recreation room, workrooms, and a mess hall. The air and water regeneration systems are as good as those installed in the international space station.

The Russian Ministry of Defense source stated, "We are in need of such machines. Besides *Losharik*, only *Mir* deep-sea stations are capable of working at depths of two to three kilometers [up to two miles]. We used both *Mir* stations during the previous expedition led by Artur Chilingarov, but the operations we performed recently were even more complicated and took more time. *Mir* stations can't support themselves that long, so we decided to use *Losharik*." He went on to say, "The *Mir* stations are pleasure bathyscaphes rather than research machines—they have weak manipulators with limited mobility, and you can't install deep-sea sounding equipment on them."

Putin undoubtedly watched this operation with a great deal of anticipation. Geological experts had estimated that the reserves extractable from the 1.2 million square kilometers of territory could add almost six billion tons of oil equivalent, as well as 426 billion cubic meters of natural gas to Russia's kitty. The expedition did indeed bring back a bevy of sediment and other samples that were subsequently submitted to the CLCS as "proof" that Russia owns the ridges.

RIDGE GRUDGE

Russia is not alone. Canada also has its heart set on large sections of the Lomonosov Ridge. They are adamant that it is connected to their North American territory. Like Russia, they too sent a couple of mini-subs on long-range missions under the Arctic ice to find evidence that contradicts Putin's claim.

Denmark spent millions on geological and mapping experts who created a large map that, arguably from a biased perspective, verifies that the

Lomonosov Ridge is theirs. After all, the shelf runs down from the North Pole and eventually connects with upper portions of Greenland, a territory owned by Denmark.

The U.S. would prefer to see Russia lose the ridges, but without a seat on the CLCS, they have only limited influence and any effort at this point is probably too little and too late. Rear Adm. Kamensky, even before the Crimea invasion, hailed the Arctic as a "top priority" that has been mostly ignored by world powers. Russia is concentrating its submarine force to dominate the Arctic and its resources, NATO is not. Russia and 158 countries signed the UNCLOS agreement that dictates how ocean resources can be claimed, the U.S. is the only nation that did not sign.

The heretofore "ostrich in the sand" approach by the U.S. and NATO, which appears likely to continue, could allow Lord Putin to gain his Arctic Rings and leave the free world little choice but to gear up for confrontations over natural resources. Potential conflict-sparking scenarios abound. If the CLCS surprisingly votes against Putin to grant him ownership of the Lomonosov Ridge, will he follow through with his threat to use his navy to act as a guard dog over the bones? What might happen if the other Arctic Five countries were to challenge Russia's claims?

What if the U.S., China, or Japan insists that portions of the ridges are technically still in international waters and therefore open for exploitation? What sparks might fly when Russia starts shipping oil and gas from the Lomonosov Ridge, through the Sea of Japan, to feed China?

RAISING THE STAKES

If the promise of a massive resource payoff on the Lomonosov Ridge isn't enough to fight over, perhaps we need to raise the stakes. The Peanut Hole is an even more hotly contested area, and represents the third Ring of Power sought by the Dark Lord Sauron. It's a thirty-five-mile wide by three hundred-mile-long area in the Sea of Okhotsk that Russians refer to as "a real

Ali Baba's cave" because it contains over one billion tons of oil and two trillion cubic meters of gas.

Putin's maneuvering to control resources in the Peanut Hole was nothing short of brilliant, not to mention ruthless. Putin had the world focused on his left hand in Ukraine, while four thousand miles away, with his right hand, he grabbed an Arctic area the size of Switzerland and secured the rights to all its oil and gas. This invasion required no guns, rebels, tanks, or planes, yet has a far greater impact on world power than the cessation of Crimea.

Using sleight of hand, in similar fashion to the card tricks he employed against Obama in Syria, Putin created panic over the mundane issue of pollock fishing in the Sea of Okhotsk to influence the seven-member CLCS subcommission to expedite the decision. Of course, Russia's track record flies in the face of any real environmental concerns.

Recall that Putin arrested over two dozen Greenpeace activists who were peacefully protesting near one of Russia's offshore oil rigs. The activists asserted that the rig lacked a contingency plan in the event of a spill. Russia threatened the activists and their U.S. ship captain with seven years in prison, despite the fact that the rig suffered no damage or operational setbacks.

Over half of Russia's fresh water is no longer potable, and around three-fourths of its surface water has become seriously polluted. The country's air is barely breathable with over 85% of the population subjected to intense smog, and two major cities are consistently on the world's top ten most polluted list. Clouds of poison are so bad in Dzerzhinsk that the *Guinness World Records* book rates it as the planet's worst, and no one who resides there is expected to live beyond the age of fifty. In 1993, Russia callously dumped nuclear waste in the Sea of Japan—not far from the Peanut Hole. Yet we're expected to believe that Putin is concerned for the environmental safety of a fish in the Sea of Okhotsk?

Regardless, Putin intimated that if the UN did not do his bidding by voting positively for his territorial submissions, he would be "forced" to use Russia's naval fleet to prevent foreign vessels from transiting across the Sea of Okhotsk, but of course, only to protect the precious Pollock. Perhaps swayed by this threat, the UN subcommittee gave Putin what he wanted.

Experts believe that Russia may again corruptly use undue influence on CLCS members to gain the needed votes for finalization of the Peanut Hole submission in 2015, when the entire committee ratifies the subcommittee's vote. If so, and the U.S. and NATO countries cry foul, tensions in the region could escalate.

The fact that Putin is investing vast amounts of resources, time, and effort to further his Arctic plans, at a time when the entire world is hammering him about his "illegal" European conquests, speaks volumes about Russia's ambitions and priorities. Putin has placed several submissions before the members of the UN CLCS, but none more important than the two concerning the Peanut Hole and the Lomonosov Ridge.

Referring to the CLCS positive vote for the Peanut Hole, Sergei Donskoy, Russian minister of Natural Resources and Environment, said: "This water area of the Sea of Okhotsk has many biological and natural resources, which have not [been] considered as the main income source of the country's economy and now we can consider and include it in our long-term plans." Donskoy described the area as "a real Ali Baba's cave in terms of resources" that will eventually drive "enormous opportunities and prospects for the Russian economy."

Putin plans to employ every means at his disposal, from a legal, economic, and military standpoint, to secure Ali Baba's cave—the third ring he needs to keep his One Ring fully charged.

Just two weeks prior to the CLCS vote, Putin announced the construction of a "united system of naval bases for ships and next-generation submarines in the Arctic" to defend Russia's interests in the region.

During a Russian Security Council meeting, he called for "strengthening of the naval component of the Federal Security Service (FSB) border guard group." He also said, "Russian oil and gas production facilities, loading terminals and pipelines in the Arctic must be protected from terrorists and other potential threats. It makes sense to create a body similar in status to the state commission with broad authority, as it was previously done for the Russian Far East."

One week later, U.S. Defense Secretary Chuck Hagel warned of a "dangerous potential for conflict there." He further said that "the melting of gigantic ice caps presents possibilities for the opening of new sea-lanes and the exploration for natural resources, energy and commerce, also with the dangerous potential for conflict in the Arctic."

While the entire world was focused almost exclusively on Putin's manhandling of Ukraine, the master magician was pulling strings behind the curtain. We were mesmerized by the show unfolding in Europe while Putin had been heavily investing time and rubles to capture three Rings of Power in the Arctic, and it appears that two of the three may already be well in hand.

If Lord Sauron manages to secure all three rings without a fight, how will that impact Western nations, and most importantly, all of their citizens?

CHAPTER FIVE

Invasion

Unarmed soldiers, shaking in their boots, stared down the barrels of AK-74 rifles as Russian armored vehicles and ground forces assaulted a Ukrainian airbase in Crimea on March 21, 2014. Tensions escalated to the breaking point when pro-Kremlin militia blasted through the main gate with an armored personnel carrier and stormed into the Belbek air base near Sevastopol. Two more armored carriers rolled up behind the first while soldiers tossed stun grenades toward the terrified Ukrainians and fired automatic weapons into the air. When the commotion finally died down, several of the captured Ukrainians fought back the only way they could: by singing their national anthem and stomping their feet in defiance.

Ukraine's local defense ministry spokesman, Vladislav Seleznyov, typed a message on Facebook for the entire world to read: "The base has been surrounded by (Russian) special forces."

Vladimir Putin used the pretext of protecting ethnic Russians from a fascist government in Kiev as his excuse for invading Crimea, and arrogantly defied harsh warnings to grab his prize with no more than a few shots fired. "We went to a knife fight with a baguette," said Andrew Wilson, a senior policy fellow at the European Council on Foreign Relations. U.S. President Barrack Obama responded tepidly in action and words by simply saying, "There's no expectation that they [the Russian military] will be dislodged by force." He went on to say that the world was limited to legal and economic pressures. "It would be dishonest to suggest that there is a simple solution to resolving what has already taken place in Crimea."

Crimean rebels, along with Russian forces, now control over half of Ukraine's Black Sea military bases and around one-third of the active navy. Frank-Walter Steinmeier, Germany's foreign minister, while threatening to wield his country's economic might to slap Putin on the wrist, warned that the entire future of the continent might be at stake.

"The referendum in Crimea," said Steinmeier after meeting with Ukrainian Prime Minister Arseniy Yatsenyuk, "is a violation of international law and an attempt to splinter Europe."

Canadian Prime Minister Stephen Harper commented that Putin had "undermined international confidence" by violating a 1994 agreement wherein Ukraine turned over its Soviet-era nuclear weapons in return for sovereignty guarantees from several Western states.

"By breaching that guarantee," said Harper, "President Putin has provided a rationale for those elsewhere...to arm themselves to the teeth."

Susan Rice, Obama's national security adviser, summed up the free world's only viable response to Putin's obvious breach of international law: "Our interest is not in seeing this situation escalate and devolve into hot conflict. Our interest is in a diplomatic resolution, de-escalation, and obviously economic support for Ukraine, and to the extent that it continues to be necessary, further costs imposed on Russia for its actions."

Although Defense Secretary Chuck Hagel was given assurances by Russian Defense Minister Sergei Shoigu that Russia did not intend to do a "land grab" beyond the borders of the Crimea region, U.S. military commanders harbored serious doubts.

General Philip Breedlove, U.S. and NATO forces commander in Europe, expressed concerns about the massing of tens of thousands of Russian troops along Ukraine's eastern border near Moldova. Russia swore they were only conducting exercises, but the apparent next move was an incursion into the eastern part of Ukraine where pro-Russia sentiments remained strong.

What appeared to worry Breedlove and Obama the most was the potential for Western sanctions to backfire. Russia had shied away from selling Iran S-300 advanced air defense systems that could easily thwart Israeli or U.S. aircraft from pounding Iranian nuclear or missile facilities. What if Putin decided to make the sale out of spite? He could also pull the rug on his support for the P5+1 negotiation meant to throttle Iran's nuclear program. If Russia jumped ship while the other countries involved were trying to finalize a resolution, little opposition would remain to Iran's ambition to build weapons of mass destruction.

Politicians and media pundits branded Putin as a dictator with ambitions that mimicked the most malevolent leaders of the past, including Adolph Hitler and Genghis Khan. However, an examination of Putin's real motives and obvious long-term goals reveal a more calculated and strategic plan that could be even more devastating to the U.S. and its allies than the takeover of Europe by Germany's führer in World War II.

Putin's personality makes him strong, confident, and controlling. It also drives him to be a valiant protector of his family. As the leader of his country, his "family" now includes *all* Russians. It's obvious that he will not hesitate to use whatever means at his disposal, whether diplomatic or military, to secure the well-being of his family. The calculated moves and investments Putin is making in Europe and remote regions of the world leave little doubt that he is plotting a checkmate, but what is the grand prize and why is he so motivated to gain it?

PUTIN'S PAST

Putin was born into the Leningrad home of Vladimir Spiridonovich Putin and Maria Ivanovna Putina on October 7, 1952. Maria worked in a factory and Vlad Sr. was a submariner in the Soviet Navy. Putin Jr. was by no means a silver-spooner and endured a humble and difficult life in a communal apartment in Leningrad. Putin's meager beginnings allowed him to understand well what it means to lack life's basic necessities, including adequate food, water, shelter, and gas for heat.

Young Putin was a strong-headed and rowdy boy. By the time he reached the fifth grade, his defiant behavior denied him membership into the coveted Pioneers organization at his school. He found a release for his anger by learning how to take down opponents in the boxing ring. He traded his gloves for a judo and karate belt, and eventually won his city's sambo championship by besting the reigning world judo champ.

When Putin turned sixteen, he imagined himself as a James Bond secret agent or a KGB officer on exciting undercover assignments. He went so far as to set up a meeting with the KGB directorate to find out what it might take to join their ranks, and was told to get a law degree and never call them again.

He acted on the advice, signed up for law school in Leningrad in 1970, and graduated five years later. He did not contact the KGB. Instead, they recruited him in 1975, and at the age of twenty-two, he was finally living his boyhood dream.

Putin completed his training as a KGB officer and was eventually recruited by the first chief directorate to monitor U.S. and other foreigners and consular officials in Leningrad. He later accepted an undercover assignment as a translator and interpreter at the KGB station in Germany. Part of his job entailed recruiting other undercover agents to become spies stationed in the United States.

Putin ended his KGB career in 1991 after attaining the rank of lieutenant colonel. He was then selected as the head of the Committee for

External Relations in Saint Petersburg, where he was responsible for promoting international relations and foreign investments. During that time, he became embroiled in a $93 million foreign aid scandal, but his cunning abilities allowed him to avoid losing his job. Instead, he effectively got a raise by employing strong negotiating skills to maneuver his way into various promotions within the government at Saint Petersburg.

President Boris Yeltsin appointed Putin as deputy chief of presidential staff in March 1997. Yeltsin later made Putin head of the Federal Security Service (FSB), the replacement agency for the KGB. Yeltsin then propelled Putin into the position of acting prime minister of the government of the Russian Federation and announced that he wanted Putin to be his successor. That same day, Putin declared his decision to run for the presidency.

His odds of winning did not look good. On August 16, 1999, the State Duma approved Putin as the prime minister of Russia, but an election poll taken that month gave him less than 2% of the votes for president. Yeltsin tipped the scales by resigning in December 1999, more than six months before the scheduled election. That forced an earlier election and allowed Putin to ride a wave of popularity garnered from his tough war policies in Chechnya. He surged from 2% to 53% of the votes and won the presidency.

Putin served his first term as the Russian president from 2000 to 2004, and won a power struggle with the Russian oligarchs by negotiating a "grand bargain." They got to keep their powers and Putin got their undivided support. He wanted that support for several reasons, but none more important than energy. He knew that any resurgence in Russia's prosperity would not be possible without exploiting the country's vast reserves of natural resources, and the oligarchs were in control of most of these.

Wresting that control away from the oligarchs, and placing it under his thumb, was the first step in Putin's plan. His initial target was Mikhail Khodorkovsky, the most prominent and wealthiest of the lot. The outspoken businessman had amassed over $18 billion from oil profits and had made it no secret that he hated Putin. Through a series of questionable and essentially illegal tactics, Putin eventually seized all of Khodorkovsky's bank accounts and holdings and tossed the man in jail at the culmination of a kangaroo court.

By August 2003, Putin was well on the way to bringing Khodorkovsy's Yukos oil company under the complete control of the Russian government. Less than a year later, he forced the firm's largest enterprise, which accounted for a majority of its oil production, onto the auctioning block. Russia's oil firm, Rosneft, eventually gained complete control of Yukos, thereby tripling its oil production. Within the week, Rosneft became Russia's third largest oil producer and Putin became one of the wealthiest men in the world, with an estimated net worth of over $70 billion.

Now rich, Putin was overwhelmingly elected to his second term in March 2004. A year later, he confirmed his commitment to his Russian "family" by backing reforms in education, health care, agriculture, and housing. During his reign, Putin led Russia through an unprecedented economic transformation. Wages tripled and real incomes rose by 250%. Poverty and unemployment were cut in half, and the self-assessed life satisfaction of the average Russian in Putin's "family" shot toward the stars.

Putin served in his second premiership between 2008 and 2012. During that time, reality hit him square in the face when the Great Recession delivered low blows to the Russian economy. Under his leadership, Russia waged war with and defeated the state of Georgia, then a NATO ally. Putin helped maneuver Russia through its economic crisis by leaning on the reserve Stabilization Fund of the Russian Federation, which had been accumulated in large measure through lucrative oil and gas exports.

The World Bank praised Putin and his advisors, stating that "prudent fiscal management and substantial financial reserves have protected Russia from deeper consequences of this external shock. The government's policy response so far—swift, comprehensive, and coordinated—has helped limit the impact."

Having come from meager beginnings likely provided Putin with the will and the wits to survive rough waves. One need only visit the Russian continent once to witness the toughness and resolve of its people. Most have endured lives of hardship that few in the U.S. or most European countries have seen or understand. As their leader, Putin has repeatedly demonstrated his resolve to ensure his people, his *family*, are fed, clothed, and warm.

When Putin ended his rule as Russia's president in 2008, Dmitry Medvedev took charge and increased the presidential term to six years. Medvedev stepped down after only one term, and lit the path for Putin to step back in as president. When Putin once again took the presidential oath on May 7, 2012, he knew he could potentially stay in power until 2024. To ensure that his throne remained unchallenged, Putin abolished the regional governor direct elections, and instead "trimmed their claws" by downgrading them to nothing more than Kremlin appointees. From that viewpoint, Putin saw Ukraine's Yanukovych as a state appointee who deserved to be removed, rather than as the elected president of a sovereign nation.

In 2014, Putin no doubt smiled like a Cheshire cat when Obama folded his hand and walked away from the Syria negotiating table. Obviously emboldened by the West's lack of will to thwart Russia's egregious actions, Putin moved forward with his plan to dominate world resources by invading Crimea.

While Madeleine Albright described Putin as "delusional," and Germany's Angela Merkel said he was "living in another world," the Russian president's actions display calm confidence, decisive action, and intelligent planning. Perhaps Putin fashions himself in the image of Peter the Great as he glances at the czar's portrait near his desk. Or perhaps, as he wrote in his autobiography, he does not think of himself as a power-hungry control freak, but rather as a patriotic protector of his people. From that viewpoint, almost any means justifies the end, as evidenced by the merciless brutality Putin displayed during the 1999 Chechnya incident.

When Chechen rebels attacked Russian cities, instead of negotiating for peace, Putin resorted to all-out war. He later commented in his book that to do otherwise could have resulted in the collapse of Russia. This kind of thinking may have prompted Putin's invasions of Georgia, as well as Ukraine years later.

Putin's actions underscore his propensity to view any challenges to his authority, or potential threats to his country, as intolerable. Perhaps this mind-set comes from his days as a young KGB officer while serving in Dresden, East Germany. He watched in horror as the West tore down the Berlin Wall and stabbed a dagger deep into the heart of the Soviet Union. This signified the beginning of the end for Soviet power. Putin described this event as "the greatest geopolitical tragedy of the twentieth century." He blamed Moscow's leaders and lamented that their behavior signified "a paralysis of power." He intimated that more decisive actions could have prevented the collapse of the Soviet empire. Putin's swift actions in Georgia and Ukraine may have been prompted by a deep-rooted desire to protect his homeland and ensure that history did not repeat. No doubt he is also trying to prevent scenarios where all of his hard work to turn around the Russian economy will not be undone in a fortnight.

All that hard work is definitely paying off. Since 1995, Russia's GDP has jumped from $195 billion to over $2 trillion. Per capita GDP skyrocketed from $1,320 to $14,800. Inflation was throttled from around 37% to less than 7%, and government debt was trimmed to 8% of GDP from almost 80% previously. In contrast, the U.S. economy appeared to be on life support with a meager 0.1% GDP gain in the first quarter of 2014. President Obama's approval ratings plunged to almost 40% while Putin's ratings shot up to 80%.

On March 18, 2014, in a speech delivered to the Russian parliament, Putin exposed what truly drives him by proclaiming to be the protector of the ethnically Russian people. It's important to note that he used the term "Russkii," which means the Russian *people*, or more accurately, Putin's

Russian *family.* He did not say "Rossisskii," the more broad term that simply refers to those who reside in Russia.

To what ends will Putin go to protect his Russkii family? Apparently to the ends of the earth, where massive underwater shelves may underscore devastating battles that could one day spell the difference between human survival and demise. Where the third Cold War is about to turn hot within the next few years.

THE THIRD COLD WAR

The first Cold War began in 1945, shortly after the conclusion of World War II. That long and expensive conflict dragged on for forty-six more years until the Soviets finally ran out of money and the will to fight.

While some believe Ronald Reagan was largely responsible for ending Cold War I, this isn't exactly true. As revealed in my *Red November* book, intelligence derived from the most daring, decorated, and dangerous underwater spy missions ever conducted gave the U.S. a huge advantage that eventually helped break the Soviet's backs. What also helped was the ineptness displayed by Soviet leaders in properly managing their large stash of natural resources.

Instead of investing in more exploration, extraction, and infrastructure, the Soviets spent everything they earned to improve their standard of living and maintain a political façade. When the world's oil prices dropped after the Arab oil embargo, Soviet oil production declined by more than half. By 1989, the economic hit made "keeping up with the Joneses" impossible. Russia could no longer afford to keep pace with U.S. military spending and their financial wheels eventually fell off.

With the Soviet Union on the ropes, China soon became the new number one enemy on the block for all NATO countries, and in my opinion, the second Cold War swept across the globe like a frigid fog in the night. Although not as hostile or costly as the first Cold War, the Eagle displayed as much fear and mistrust toward the Dragon as it once had toward the Bear.

The U.S. reignited tensions with Russia and dragged them into Cold War II alongside China on August 12, 2000, when the Russian submarine *Kursk* was lost in Arctic waters. Russia presented evidence that the USS *Memphis* attack submarine collided with the *Kursk* and sent her to the bottom (outlined in detail in a later chapter). The U.S. denied any involvement, but the incident eventually incited Russia toward an increase in military spending made possible by a subsequent surge in oil and gas exports. President Vladimir Putin was criticized for his handling of the affair, but his anger toward the U.S. was undeniable, possibly exacerbated by the fact that his father had served as a Soviet submariner.

China fanned the flames high into the air when President Obama was holding high-level talks in Beijing on November 9, 2010. On that cold California night, the Chinese unexpectedly launched an unarmed ballistic missile from a submerged *Jin*-class submarine, not more than thirty-five miles off the coast of Los Angeles. More on this incident later.

Again in my opinion, Cold War III was ignited long before the Russian invasion of Crimea in March 2014. Several years prior, the U.S. and EU began investing billions in a Ukraine destabilization project. They had hoped to convert Ukraine into a NATO country and thereby gain control of the majority of the gas pipes that feed Europe.

In mid-December 2013, Victoria Nuland, then U.S. assistant secretary of state for Europe and Eurasia, bragged that the U.S. had "invested five years' worth of work and preparation" to help "build democratic skills and institutions." Reportedly, she engaged in a "tough conversation" with Ukrainian President Yanukovych where she made it "absolutely clear" that the U.S. wanted him to take "immediate steps" to "get back into conversation with Europe and the IMF."

Such meddling by the Western Elves left Lord Sauron with little choice but to invade and conquer Crimea and continue to force his hand in

Ukraine. He then made it clear he would use his weapon of mass reduction by truncating supplies of gas to Europe if NATO or U.S. forces interfered. Given the EU's dependence on Russian resources, delivered via pipelines that cross Ukraine, European leaders could do little more than huff and puff and turn a blind eye.

Unlike Sauron in *The Lord of the Rings*, Putin is not motivated solely by blind ambition or an evil heart, but instead by something—that if unbridled—can be far more frightening: *blind passion*. His actions speak volumes about his intentions to ensure that his Russkii family is allowed to sit first at the table. Lord Putin is passionately convinced that as long as he can keep his One Ring of Power fully charged, they will.

CHAPTER SIX

Putin's Pipes: The One Ring

Wikimedia Commons photo of Vladimir Putin aboard a Russian submarine

I n *The Lord of the Rings*, Sauron's One Ring served as the foundation for all of his power. In like manner, Putin's energy supply lines—including his pipes—hold the key to Russia's primary sources of income and therefore Putin's One Ring of Power. Without the necessary infrastructure, he cannot deliver oil and gas to Europe or Asia. Lacking the profits derived from Russia's energy exports, Putin may well become just another wannabe dictator with no muscle to back up his bark.

Russia controls around one-third of Europe's gas supply, and half of that passes right through Ukraine. The Russian Federation is now the largest exporter of natural gas and oil to the European Union, and Putin has leveraged this reality to place European leaders in an energy stranglehold. Germany counts on Russia for more than 25% of its gas. For Poland, Austria, and Slovaka, it's almost 60%. The Swedes, Fins, Czechs, and Baltics are on the hook for almost 100% of their gas (*Stansberry's Investment Advisory*, Vol. 15, Issue 3, March 2014). For nearly all of these countries, many of their citizens could freeze to death if Russia decides to cut off supplies.

Gazprom is Russia's energy giant and the world's third largest company, responsible for 17% of global gas production. Nearly all of the company's gas is piped in from sources located in the Arctic region. The term "company" is actually a misnomer, as Putin established government control over Gazprom in June 2005 by orchestrating several shady stock manipulations.

© Iskander1 | Dreamstime.com - Gazprom Building in Moscow Photo

Like Rosneft, Gazprom was a pebble in the ocean when Putin took the company under his wing and helped turn it into a dominate energy player. By 2009, Gazprom was servicing its European customers through a dozen pipelines. Ronald Reagan led efforts during Cold War I to block construction of those pipes. His efforts obviously failed and the pipelines were built, but they ran through several unreliable countries along Russia's western border.

Three pipes directly feed Estonia, Finland, and Latvia. Four run through Belarus and feed Lithuania and Poland. A majority of the pipes, with nine inputs and six outputs, run through Ukraine and connect to Hungary, Romania, Poland, and Slovakia. Another pipe, the new South Stream line, was under construction until recently and ran right past the southern tip of Crimea.

Delivery infrastructure is crucial to Putin's plans to dominate world energy markets, hence the construction of new pipelines in Europe and Asia that do not run through risky backyards. Unlike older pipes, such as a 40-inch diameter by 930-mile-long one that runs through Ukraine, Gazprom's newer European pipes are designed to bypass unreliable countries. "We are at the beginning of a long road of redirecting transit gas volumes from Ukrainian territory to our subsidiary Beltransgaz and our new undersea export routes," said Gazprom spokesman Sergei Kupriyanov in 2012.

The new undersea pipeline Kupriyanov mentioned is called Nord (North) Stream, which takes gas from Russia to Germany along a 759-mile journey through the Baltic Sea. It's the world's longest underwater pipe and it came online in 2012 at a final cost of $20 billion. Although the new pipe makes European delivery of gas more secure, it does not feed all of Gazprom's customers. Ukraine's pipes are still strategically important, and the U.S. and EU are learning the hard way that Putin will not stand by and watch his pipes fall under NATO control.

In 2006, and again in 2009, Ukraine started stealing gas from the pipes that feed the EU. In response, Putin used Gazprom to manipulate Ukraine by turning off their natural gas spigot. At the behest of Russia's president, Gazprom reduced supplies to Belarus in 2010 and threatened the Moldovans in the fall of 2013 with similar tactics if they didn't pay their bills or if they signed a free-trade accord with the EU. A Russian deputy foreign minister grinned as he said to the Moldovans: "We hope that you will not freeze."

Jeffrey Mankoff, a Russian expert at the Center for Strategic and International Studies, was quoted as saying: "One big difference between the U.S. and Europe on this issue is energy. The assumption that, because of the energy relationship, Europe was not going to risk a major confrontation over Ukraine was surely part of Russia's calculations."

The Ukrainians buy more than 50% of their gas from Russia's Gazprom and after the 2006 and 2009 Russian manipulations, Ukraine's then-elected president, Viktor Yanukovych, vowed to become energy independent by 2020. In deference to his Russian leanings, he made a down payment on that promise in 2013 by agreeing to a $10 billion shale gas exploration deal with Chevron, an American energy company. Imagine how thrilled Putin must have been when he heard the news. The natural gas that Chevron planned to extract is located in Crimea.

Yanukovych then failed to pay his gas bill in March 2014. At the time, Ukraine owed Gazprom almost $2 billion. Alexey Miller, the head of Gazprom, told reporters: "Today, March 7, is the deadline for making a payment." Putin used this as an excuse to escalate tensions by stating that he intended to raise prices (which he did anyway after the invasion) and constrict the flow of gas to Ukraine. Memories of 2006 and 2009 caused serious unrest amongst Ukraine's citizens.

Putin then marched troops into the Crimea region shortly after Yanukovych signed the deal with Chevron, and right before he was about to sign a trade agreement with the EU. Putin had previously warned Yanukovych not to sign either by stating that it would be bad for Russia's security interests.

The Crimean region contains one of the largest gas deposits in the Black Sea, where production increased by over 40% in 2013. Gazprom's new South Stream pipeline was slated to come online in 2015 and connect to those fields. In November 2014, Putin announced that Russia had abandoned completion of South Stream. Many analysts assumed Putin had simply thrown in the towel due to push back from some European countries. They obviously have not been paying close attention.

Putin originally pushed hard for the South Stream construction because five pipes run through Ukraine, a decidedly unstable partner. He needed an alternate pipe to service those customers. Since the invasion of Crimea, reports of Russian-backed forces mounting offensives against Ukrainian troops have emerged almost daily. If Putin is stepping away from South Stream, it can only mean that he is convinced Ukraine, along with its five pipes, will soon be under Russian control.

It's all about the pipes, and it's apparent that most European countries are loathe to stand in Putin's way and risk the consequences that befell Ukraine—including supply constriction and potential military invasion. This is not surprising given that Russia signed an agreement on January 18, 2008, with Bulgaria that splits the gas spoils fifty-fifty. Russia signed similar agreements with Serbia, Hungary, and Greece in early 2008, and one with Slovenia on November 14, 2009. Croatia followed suit in March 2010 as did Austria one month later. Despite current contentions, all of these countries will have a difficult time walking away from lucrative gas profits. EU officials turn their heads to one side and call for a plan to wind down the Moscow gas spigot, and then turn back toward Russia's state-controlled energy giants to cut new deals.

At $15 billion per year, Germany is Gazprom's largest customer. German officials have been less arrogant than their geopolitical neighbors, but nonetheless acknowledge that Russia is a reliable source of gas and will continue to invest big in maintaining a steady flow. Germany's BASF, the world's largest chemicals company, by way of its Wintershall subsidiary, became a key partner in South Stream. Germany is by far the EU's economic kingpin. Anton Börner, president of BGA, Germany's main trade group, expressed deep concerns that $15 billion generated by over six thousand German businesses are connected at the hip with Russia and will suffer economic harm if sanctions against Russia escalate.

UK Prime Minister David Cameron implemented sanctions against Moscow after the invasion of Crimea but that's not stopping Centrica, the parent company of British Gas, from honoring its 2012 contract with Russia. Centrica signed a three-year gas deal with Gazprom, with a start date in October 2014. When Centrica executives were challenged by the Anadolu Agency after the invasion, they stated that there would be "no change" to the agreement.

ENI's Scaroni proclaimed that the toothless actions of the EU in the wake of Putin's Crimea invasion and subsequent actions in Ukraine could only be viewed as new low points for Europe's energy security.

"This is by far the toughest time for European energy security that I have seen," Scaroni commented to the *New York Times*. He added that the EU's disjointed energy policies and reluctance to untether from Russian energy control seem almost schizophrenic.

"The EU cannot have its cake and eat it, too," Scaroni said. "I just tell them that you cannot keep on shouting and being inconsistent between what you say and what you do."

To date, Putin appears unfazed by the timid actions taken by the U.S. and EU. He is well aware that at $370 billion per year, Russia is the EU's third-largest trading partner behind the U.S. and China. Of the 485 billion cubic meters of gas burned by Europeans each year to stay warm, Gazprom supplies 160 billion. With only $26 billion in trade, the U.S. holds almost no trading cards or leverage.

Russian Natural Resources and Environment Minister Sergei Donskoi warned of serious repercussions should Western energy firms implement sanctions. On April 24, 2014, while conferring with journalists in Birobidzhan, he said, "It is obvious that they won't return in the near future if they sever investment agreements with us, I mean there are consequences as well. Russia is one of the most promising countries in terms of hydrocarbons production. If some contracts are severed here, then, colleagues, you lose a serious lump of your future pie."

NO WAY NORWAY

Despite coming up dry more often than not, the Norwegians are trying to help avoid that serious lump by turning up the dial on Arctic oil and gas exploration and provide an alternative to Russian energy sources. Norway currently derives 20% of its GDP from the energy sector, but it's still highly dependent on Russian oil and gas. Norway has embarked on a plan to sell licenses for fifty-four blocks in the Barents Sea to the highest bidders in late 2014, much to the chagrin of the country's environmental agency.

Norwegian waters offer the enticing combination of being shallower, less icy, and more temperate as compared to other Arctic areas. For Norway, the eight billion barrels of oil equivalent under those calmer waves could total more than 40% of the country's undiscovered reserves. In light of the Ukrainian hostilities abounding with Russia, and the tight energy noose Putin has placed around the EU's neck, Norway could have emerged as a knight on a white horse carrying oil and gas to European countries.

Unfortunately, that now seems unlikely.

Today, the only oil field pumping out crude is Statoil's Snohvit in the Barents Sea. Another field, the Goliat, may soon come online and will employ a new cylindrical, floating production facility. Statoil is launching additional projects to meet its goal of growing production by 3% through 2016. Competitors include Valemon, Gudrun, and Vilje South in the Norwegian continental shelf, but the more concerning blocker in Statoil's way is the Norwegian government. Shortsighted thinking, coupled with obvious greed, prompted the Norwegians to raise oil and gas taxes in May 2012, which made several regional projects unattractive to energy firms. In light of recent events in Ukraine, perhaps they'll repeal the taxes to help release Putin's grip on Europe, but even so, projects started today will not yield results for many years to come.

Even if Norway does encourage more exploration, Norwegian energy firms have been vexed by a lack of infrastructure, rising extraction costs, and a host of unfruitful exploration results. Experts believe that Barents Sea drilling will hit a record high in 2014 with only a dozen producing wells. If things don't pan out soon, energy companies could curtail their capital spending by pulling up roots and moving on to more promising areas in the Arctic.

"There are dark clouds gathering on the horizon because of rising costs and investment cuts by energy companies," said Norwegian Minister of Petroleum and Energy Tord Lien. "This could be a critical year for projects in the Barents Sea." He added that "Costs are rising too high and too fast and the Norwegian costs have increased a bit more than elsewhere."

Dry oil wells and light gas discoveries in the area, and the lack of pipeline infrastructure, make delivery problematic and uneconomical.

"The cost per produced unit [of oil and gas] in Norway has increased dramatically, by tenfold over the past ten years," said Bente Nyland, the director of the Norwegian Petroleum Directorate. "The problem is that we have a lot of small discoveries but no means of getting out the gas."

Unlike Russia, Norway has virtually no Arctic pipelines so the only way to transport gas is to leverage Statoil's liquefied natural gas plant on Norway's northern tip. However, that facility is already at capacity and may remain so for the next few decades. Statoil will not be motivated to expand until the region produces more gas.

"This is a Catch-22 situation," said Grethe Moen, CEO of Petoro, which manages the Norwegian government's direct stake in oil licenses. "Given the current high cost level it's difficult to see new infrastructure built."

Potential problems could arise if the sector decides to shift its focus toward Norway's border zone with Russia. This part of the Barents Sea was recently opened, but has no gas or oil infrastructure. A great deal of work and investment would be needed, but the larger concern is the potential to anger the neighboring Bear and trigger an undesired conflict.

Given the motivation to stop throwing good money after bad, and avoid pissing off Putin now that he's channeling Sauron, it's no wonder several energy firms are balking at further investment near Norway. That potentially takes one Western Elf out of the game, and given the realistic options available, leaves only a handful of others to potentially bail out Europe and do an end run around Putin's pipes.

UNSETTLED SYRIA

The Russian energy firm, Soyuzneftegaz, signed a $90 million deal with Syria's oil ministry in December 2013. The agreement allows Russia to explore more than eight hundred square miles of ocean in the Mediterranean for oil and gas. Some experts believe Putin is backing Assad because he likes the guy, or just wants to be on the other side of the table from Obama. The truth is, if Assad loses control of Syria, the new kids on the block might flood the market with cheaper Qatari gas, which would be a bad thing for Russia's Gazprom.

Moreover, Putin understands that keeping a leash on Syria allows him more control and influence on other Middle East players. Conflict in the region is Putin's friend, as long as Assad doesn't wind up losing. A continuing civil war delays any pipeline building and keeps Gazprom in the driver's seat to escalate Europe's energy dependence.

The Europeans, now hooked and happy, are also not eager to see their supplier lose ground, even if it means saving money. Russian gas has been dependable and affordable. When Obama threatened to attack Assad for his war crimes, calmer heads in Europe warned him of the potential for unintended energy supply consequences. Perhaps these admonishments played a part in Obama's eventual decision to back down. In any case, Syria is too unsettled at present and Putin is too clever to allow that country to become much of a competitive threat anytime soon.

INDIFFERENT ISRAEL

A long-standing joke that Prime Minister Benjamin Netanyahu likes to retell is: "Moses led his people through the desert for forty years and found the only place in the Middle East with no oil." That was a true statement until about fifteen years ago. Before then, Israel spent 5% of its GDP on oil imports—usually from nearby countries it really didn't like. In the year 2000, Israel struck black gold by finding trillions of cubic feet of natural gas just off its coast.

The jury is still out as to whether the Israelis can economically extract all that booty, but lips are already being licked by a horde of suitors knocking on Israel's door. None more so than Gazprom, which is now at the head of the line. They signed a twenty-year deal with Israel's Levant LNG Marketing Corporation for exclusive rights to all the gas in the Tamar offshore field. It will take years to actually start the ball rolling, but Gazprom has already set up an Israeli subsidiary in partnership with Trading Switzerland.

This is very bad news for the U.S. and EU. Until recently, Israel was a key strategic partner in the region. Unfortunately, instead of befriending Israel and strengthening the partnership, Obama did just the opposite. The Israelis have made it no secret they do not trust Obama, especially after what they believe were serious missteps made by Secretary of State John Kerry during the 2014 Hamas conflicts and the 2015 Iran negotiations. Any remaining clout the U.S. had with Israel will fade quickly once the gas starts flowing and Russia becomes a closer bed partner.

Israel will also see Russia as a potential protector of its newly discovered resources. In late 2012, the Israeli Defense Forces moved ahead to buy four new warships at a total cost of $3 billion. These ships will be used to thwart terrorists, pirates, and competitors who may want to undermine Israel's gas trade. For example, Hezbollah could get frisky again and lob missiles onto offshore gas platforms. Should such threats loom, Israel might open the door and allow Russia to waltz in with subs and ships and play the role of the bouncer in the bar.

The Europeans might still have some hope of dealing with the Israelis directly to buy gas, but given that many European countries are a part of NATO, and Obama has rubbed Israel the wrong way in recent years, and Putin is way ahead of everyone else in the energy game, the EU should probably consider Israeli gas and Russian gas as one and the same.

UNLIKELY U.S.

Russia launched the world into the petroleum game in 1846 at the base of the Caucasus Mountains on the west side of the Caspian Sea. It was here, on the windswept Absheron Peninsula, where the first modern oil well chugged to life at Baku and quickly replaced manual shoveling and hand drilling. Thirteen years later, the revolution rolled into a small Pennsylvania town called Titusville. Edwin Drake dug the first oil-only well down to seventy feet and fanned a fever that spread across the globe.

Up until 1876, when the first four-stroke engine sputtered onto the scene, petroleum's purpose was to lubricate, light, and heat up things. Gasoline was considered too flammable and dangerous for commercial use. With automobile and other engines playing a larger role, demand ignited and the world changed.

By 1950, given the postwar economic boom, gas consumption eclipsed production and the U.S. had to start importing to keep up with demand. More than 50% of U.S. oil was coming from foreign sources when the Vietnam War ramped up in 1972.

A tonne of oil equivalent (TOE) is a unit of energy equal to 7.4 barrels of oil equivalent (BOE). So 100B TOEs equals 740B BOEs. Around 86 million BOEs of crude oil are produced worldwide each day, with Americans gobbling up 19 million BOEs. China is actually in second place behind the U.S.; however, the U.S. government predicts that by 2020, Americans will consume 2 million BOEs less oil per day due to an increase in engine efficiencies and the use of electric and hybrid vehicles.

Today, the U.S. imports around 9 million BOEs per day, with over 5 million coming from Middle East and OPEC sources. Over 75% of U.S. oil consumption is used for transportation, with almost 70% of that for personal automobiles. Due to such high consumption, and a lack of production, the U.S. has not been an energy competitor to Russia, but that position could change.

Since the days of Richard Nixon, every U.S. president has barked about energy independence. With the discovery of new oil and gas deposits, such as those in the Arctic, this heretofore "pipe dream" is now closer to reality. New figures show that America has become the world's fastest-growing producer of oil in just the past few years. Citigroup analysts are hailing the U.S. as the new Middle East, and the Energy Information Administration believes that American oil imports could decline by 20% by the year 2025. British Petroleum made the bold prediction that U.S. oil imports will be cut in half and domestic energy production will climb from 77% today to 89% by 2030.

Citigroup experts are even more optimistic and believe that North America could achieve energy independence, and maybe even become an exporter, by 2020. In fact, Citigroup energy strategist, Seth Kleinman, thinks that the U.S. might one day actually export more oil than it consumes and create four million new energy industry jobs along the way.

The U.S. has increased crude oil production by 15% over the past decade, and new technologies have been a huge contributor. In 2000, Texas oilman George Mitchell brought to market a new gas-drilling technology known as hydraulic fracking that extracts previously unrecoverable natural gas. Using horizontal drilling techniques combined with water, sand, and chemicals to pull gas from rocks, the inventive technique dramatically improves yields over traditional "straight down" drilling. In recent years, Mitchell's approach was adapted to oil drilling, and the results have been dramatic. Due to fracking, which makes "tight oil" extraction from shale and tar sands more affordable, experts agree that oil production could jump by 33% between 2014 and 2017.

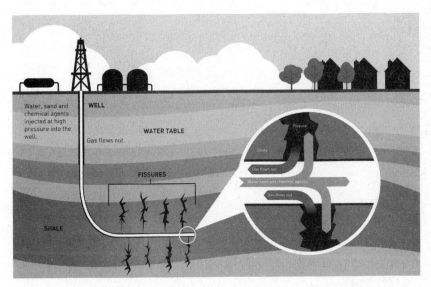

© Jaddingt | Dreamstime.com - Gas Fracking Infographic Photo

As we can see, the above-noted changes in demand, approaches, and prices are escalating interest in oil and gas in the Arctic and other untapped regions. The cost to find and remove these resources in the past was too high, but extracting black gold from regions like the Arctic is becoming more economically feasible. Economists are encouraged by this news. Chris Lafakis, energy economist at Moody's Analytics, says that reducing the amount America pays to foreigners to import oil by $400 billion each year could act like a giant tax cut.

"A third to forty percent would be my guess," Lafakis said. "At forty percent, that's one hundred sixty billion dollars a year, and that's massive."

To spur exploration and reap the economic benefits, former Alaska governor Sarah Palin pushed through a new law to do away with the onerous progressivity system and charge energy producers a flat 35% tax. The lower tax rate prompted British Petroleum to increase Arctic investments by 25% in 2014 to $1.2 billion. BP may also throw another $3 billion into Alaska's Prudhoe Bay and Milne Point fields to boost production by forty thousand barrels per day. ConocoPhillips, emboldened by the new tax law, plans to add another rig to the Kuparuk field, which is currently North America's second largest. They also plan to drill two more exploratory wells in the Arctic region.

"The Arctic is one of the world's largest remaining regions of undiscovered conventional oil and natural gas resources," said Rex Tillerson, chief executive officer of ExxonMobil during the Moscow World Petroleum Congress in the summer of 2014.

Tim Dodson, a senior executive at Norwegian group Statoil, who also attended the conference, said the Arctic "is one of the very few remaining areas with the potential to make huge discoveries." He went on to say, "To unlock the full potential of the Arctic and also to make Arctic projects commercially viable and globally competitive, we need new technology and innovative business models."

Oleg Mikhaylov, vice president for oil and gas production at Russian group Bashneft, agreed with Dodson when he said that the Russian Arctic "will require significant support from the Russian government in addition to investments by private corporations." While speaking to the conference attendees, he said, "If you envision full-scale development of the Arctic you have to envision moving millions of tonnes of supplies to one of the most remote regions of the world."

The promise of pearls, combined with the complexity of extracting those spoils, has promoted otherwise combative nations to cooperate, even when one of them is violating international law. For example, the French firm Total has been working closely with Gazprom for years to tap the huge Shtokman gas field in the Barents Sea. Events in Ukraine and subsequent sanctions did not dampen this partnership one bit.

President Barack Obama stated that U.S. and EU sanctions were "designed to have maximum impact on Russia while limiting any spillover effects on American companies or those who are allies."

The "spillover limitations" appear to be making many of the sanctions meaningless. In February 2013, the head of Russia's Rosneft, Igor Sechin, and the president of American ExxonMobil signed an agreement to jointly explore the Russian Arctic shelf. This deal grants the U.S. access to seven sectors totaling six hundred thousand square kilometers in the Chukchi, Kara, and Laptev Seas. In exchange, Russia gets to acquire 25% of the Point Thomson project on one of Alaska's largest fields.

Dmitry Alexandrov, head of the Department of Analytical Research of the Univer Capital investment group in Russia said, "The main task for Rosneft is to find a partner experienced in similar projects. It is important for Rosneft to have both a financial and technological partner for developing its own resources. For ExxonMobil, this means access to very rich resources." He went on to say that participating in the Point Thomson project lets Rosneft benefit from the latest technologies for resource exploration in harsh climatic conditions.

ExxonMobil is the largest oil company in the U.S. Even after the downing of the Malaysia Airlines jet in Ukraine, and while the EU was clamoring for more sanctions, the oil giant moved ahead to pull their West Alpha oil rig all the way from Norway to Russian Arctic waters. Like miners with gold pans, they appeared hopeful for a big strike in the Kara Sea. If this occurs, Russian partner Rosneft will obviously share in the booty. The fact that a top U.S. firm is economically backing Putin has not gone unnoticed.

"It's a bit discordant with the message that the United States government is trying to send, having this long-planned summer drilling season go ahead right now," said Elizabeth Rosenberg, energy program director at the Center for a New American Security, and a former Treasury Department sanctions adviser.

In response, ExxonMobil stated via e-mail: "We are evaluating the impact of the sanctions and don't have anything further at this time."

The West Alpha rig is actually owned by Seadrill, a Norwegian firm with a reputation for being the largest supplier of offshore rigs. ExxonMobil is renting the rig until late 2016.

Energy program director Rosenberg intimated that companies that move forward with drilling and other joint projects risk the ire of the U.S. administration. "You'd be missing the point if you took one drilling season, what is ultimately at this point a pretty limited joint venture activity, and weighed it quite heavily against the president of the United States."

Will joint explorations between NATO countries and Russia dissolve in the wake of more aggressions on the part of Putin? Even worse, will he turn those bellicosities toward the U.S. and EU member nations if they force companies from their respective countries to shut down joint projects with Russia? Or if the U.S. steps in to lend a hand to the EU by helping them to wrest free of Putin's energy power grip? When ExxonMobile and Rosneft start pumping gas out of the Arctic, or Total and Gazprom begin shipping liquefied natural gas, who will be allowed to buy it? Will current sanctions be a factor . . . or not?

Who will, or can, help the EU break free from Russian energy dependence? With Norway apparently sucking wind, and projects in other areas already locked up by Putin, the closest point on the map from Europe to a near-term oil and gas rescue may be Alaska by way of the Arctic NSR, which skirts Russia's coastline. The total distance from Alaska's northern shore to ports in Europe is around 3,700 miles—a little farther than Seattle to Miami. Is this a viable option?

As part of the deal with Saudi Arabia forty-plus years ago, when the petrodollar was created, the U.S. agreed to ban oil producers from exporting crude oil. Ernest Moniz, U.S. Secretary of Energy, recently hinted that the energy world we live in today has changed dramatically since 1975 and thus a review of the ban is in order. Citing the need to unravel Putin's control over European energy sources, oil company executives are encouraging Moniz to lift the ban and allow exports. However, there is no such ban for natural gas.

In September 2014, U.S. regulators approved the construction of two plants to export natural gas to Europe and Asia. The two permits, for facilities in Louisiana and Florida, were awarded to a subsidiary of Sempra Energy.

Said Debra L. Reed, CEO of Sempra Energy, "Today's decision marks the last major regulatory hurdle for our Cameron LNG liquefaction-export project, clearing the way for construction to begin on the largest capital project in Sempra Energy's history. This landmark project will create thousands of jobs and economic benefits for Louisiana and the U.S. for decades to come, while delivering natural gas to America's trading partners in Europe and Asia."

Environmental groups like the Sierra Club argue that increasing exports will exacerbate "dirty and dangerous" fracking, but the American Petroleum Institute argues that Obama's Secretary of the Interior, Sally Jewell, has stated that regulated fracking is safe and gas exports could add $31 billion to the U.S. economy while creating up to 155,000 jobs.

Former treasury secretary Lawrence Summers voiced his opinion in a speech at the Brookings Institution by saying: "The question is whether we are going to organize our public policies in a way that enables that natural gas to be shared with the rest of the world so that it can do there what it has done here [to] permit the displacement of coal, or whether we are going to seek to horde that natural gas here and allow coal exports to continue on a substantial scale. I cannot see a rational argument for the latter course."

Kate DeAngelis, an environmentalist with Friends of the Earth, countered by saying: "In supporting liquefied natural gas exports, President

Obama is treating climate change like a game of peekaboo, opening his eyes to the harmful impacts of carbon but closing them to the devastating disruption potential of methane."

Should the U.S. government lift the ban on crude oil and encourage those exports alongside LNG? Perhaps, but more infrastructure will need to be built in Alaska and other locales to support exports, including gathering systems, liquefaction plants, conditioning facilities, and pipelines to loading structures. While the investments for these items are not astronomical, and if expedited, the time requirement is reasonable, the U.S. appears to lack the political will to execute. This is not without good reason. Exporting crude oil would effectively end the "ban" agreement with Saudi Arabia and turn the U.S. into an unfriendly competitor rather than a friendly consumer. Doing so could bolster Putin's plan to further dominate world resources and unravel the petrodollar. In validation of his grand plan, Putin is expanding his reach into Asia, and may soon have the Pacific Rim under his thumb as well.

PUTIN PROFITS FROM THE PACRIM

On May 21, 2014, in the city of Shanghai, Russia and China inked a $400 billion, thirty-year gas deal. It took a decade, but Gazprom finally got the agreement signed and will supply the China National Petroleum Corporation with thirty-eight billion cubic meters of gas every year starting in 2018.

According to Putin, Russia will invest over $50 billion and China will toss in another $20 billion. The plan is to build a big pipe from the Sakhalin gas fields near Vladivostok and the Sea of Japan to China's northeast line. This pipe will also feed North Korea and Japan.

"Without any overstatement," said Putin, "this will be the world's biggest construction project for the next four years." Alexei Pushkov, head of the International Affairs Committee, said "The thirty-year gas contract with China is of strategic significance. Obama should give up the policy of isolating Russia. It will not work."

There are three operations at Sakhalin. ExxonMobil owns 30% of Sakhalin-1, which primarily drills for oil. Shell owns 28% of Sakhalin-2 and Gazprom owns 50%. Sakhalin-3 is poised to become one of the largest regional producers in the near future, and will be one of the primary projects slated to supply Russia's Asian partners.

Russia's Rosneft owns 75% of the Veninsky block of Sakhalin-3 and the China Petroleum & Chemical Corporation (Sinopec) owns 25%. The 3,180 square mile block is located in the Sea of Okhotsk not far from the Peanut Hole. ExxonMobil and Chevron were granted rights to develop the area in 1993 but Russia revoked their licenses in 2004. The average sea depth in the area is about 250 feet. The field is estimated to contain almost five hundred million tons of oil.

On the gas side of the equation, the Kirinskoye gas field is located seventeen miles northeast of Sakhalin Island and is 100% owned by Gazprom Dobycha Shelf. The area is covered by ice six months out of the year and is estimated to contain around seventy-five billion cubic meters of gas. The field produced its first gas in October 2013 and is expected to pump out almost six billion cubic meters of gas each year. Russia's gas deal with China starts in 2018 and will use up thirty-eight billion cubic meters per year. If Sakhalin-3 can only pump out six billion, Russia will need another thirty-two billion from other fields. Sakhalin-1 contains around five trillion cubic meters, but much of that production feeds current customers. Russia will need additional sources of gas, preferably new fields, to keep up with demand.

As for oil, in 2001, Russian oil company Yukos proposed a bold plan to complete the Eastern Siberia Pacific Ocean (ESPO) oil pipeline, the longest and most expensive extent. The ESPO allows Russia to diversify its oil delivery by servicing customers throughout the Pacific Rim. The project consists of a pipeline from Angarsk, where Yukos has a refinery, to the city of Daqing in northern China. An alternative project to pipe oil from Taishet in Irkutsk Oblast to the Far East port Kozmino near Nakhodka was also proposed.

Putin decided to combine the two in May 2003 and signed a construction agreement with China that same month.

Work started in April 2006 and the first stage of the pipeline was completed in December 2009. Russia signed another agreement with China that year to build a line to supply the Chinese with fifteen million TOEs of oil per year for twenty years. Russia started pumping oil to China on New Year's Day 2011.

JAPAN JUMPS ONBOARD

Japan is next in line for Putin. According to Chief Resource Analyst Karim Rahemtulla, the recent $400 billion natural gas deal between Russia and China is without precedent, but it's just the start. Japan and Russia have also been working on a gas deal for more than a decade.

Devastated by the Fukushima nuclear plant disaster and subsequent shutdown in March 2011, Japan has seen half of its nuclear power capacity wiped off the table. Prospects of that changing any time soon have dimmed due to far more stringent nuclear standards going forward. The unfortunate nuclear incident has left the Japanese much more dependent upon imported liquefied natural gas. In 2013, Japan imported almost ninety million metric tons of LNG, costing more than $70 billion. Less than 10% of that came from nearby Russia.

To rectify this problem, Japan and Russia have banded together to finalize the construction of a big pipe to connect the two countries. Putin and Japan's Prime Minister, Shinzo Abe, in a late 2014 meeting, are committing almost $6 billion to link Japan's Ibaraki Prefecture, northeast of Tokyo, to Russia's Sakhalin Island. LNG from Gazprom will be routed via the Sakhalin-Khabarovsk-Vladivostok pipeline, which is fed from sources in the Arctic.

Japanese officials are licking their lips in anticipation of a sweetheart gas deal like the one Putin gave China. Even though it will take between five and seven years to build the pipeline, the eventual price tag for Russian LNG imports should be far lower than the cost of transporting gas via tankers from Qatar or similar locales. Once at capacity, Putin's new pipe could supply up to 17% of Japan's gas needs.

Another country, another noose.

ARCTIC OIL AND GAS EXTRACTION

Sakhalin-3 represents a technological step forward in the extraction of Arctic gas. To avoid the issues that Shell faced when trying to extract oil from wells that float on the surface of the ocean, Gazprom has developed the first Russian subsea production facility that uses a manifold connected to several high-pressure pipelines mounted on a single foundation. The manifold sucks in the gas mixture produced by the field wells and sends it through the under-ocean pipeline to a treatment processing facility onshore.

A new type of construction process ensures that the manifold and wells are tightly secured and will not sway during an Arctic storm. This makes it possible to extract oil and gas in harsh environments without the need to construct a platform. Gazprom made the subsea facility nearly bulletproof with the ability to withstand earthquakes registering up to nine on the Richter scale.

No doubt Putin plans to leverage Sakhalin-3's cutting edge technology to eventually tap into all that oil and gas in the Peanut Hole and allow Russia to meet its customer demand for decades to come. Remember, Ali Baba's cave holds over one billion tons of oil and two trillion tons of gas. When Putin gets his hands on all that bounty, thanks to the "yes" vote granted by the UN CLCS, he will have nearly all the "rings" he needs to manipulate the world's energy markets.

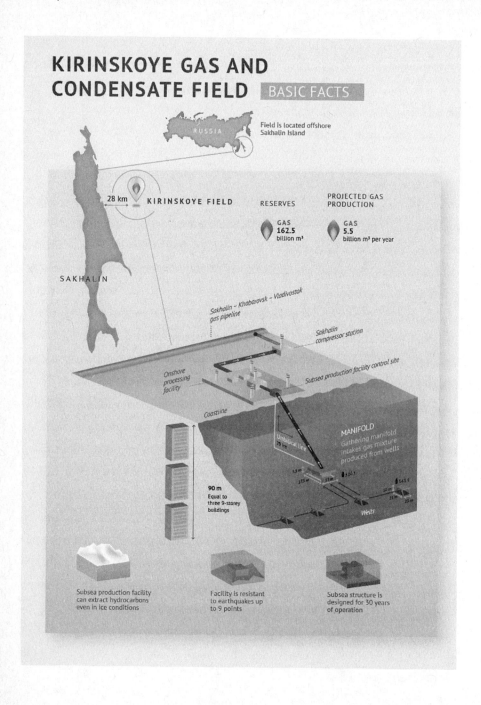

Inforgraphic courtesy of Gazprom

DOLLARS OR RUBLES?

There are three significant issues the U.S. and EU must pay close attention to regarding Putin's Asian energy dealings. First, Putin's ability to maintain an aggressive world posture is directly related to his economic might, which is directly related to his energy profits.

Second, the amount of oil and gas that will be supplied to China, Japan, North Korea, and other Pacific Rim partners will be massive, for gas alone it could be around fifty billion tons per year. While the Sakhalin fields still have lots of reserves, the increase in demand will create a big dent in Russia's current supply, and Gazprom will need new sources to service its customers. Where will Russia obtain more oil and gas to supply its new Asian partners?

The Peanut Hole. It's in the Sea of Okhotsk, just a stone's throw away from Sakhalin Island. The undersea extraction technology used at Sakhalin-3 will set the stage to allow access to the oil and gas in Ali Baba's cave. This is why Putin strong-armed the UN CLCS into granting him the exclusive economic rights to the entire area, and why the U.S. and EU must find a way to reverse or at least delay the ratification of this vote. They must also put the brakes on approval by the UN CLCS to give Russia exclusive rights to the Lomonosov Ridge, which contains almost as much bounty as the Peanut Hole.

Third, and most important, what currency will be used between Russia, China, Japan, North Korea, and other Asian countries to buy and sell gas? Rubles? Yuan? We're talking about hundreds of billions and the U.S. dollar will likely not be invited to the party. If, or more likely *when* this happens at the start of the China deal in 2018, it could spell the end of the petrodollar as the world's currency standard. If so, this move by Putin will deal a massive hammer blow that could cripple the U.S. economy. More on this later.

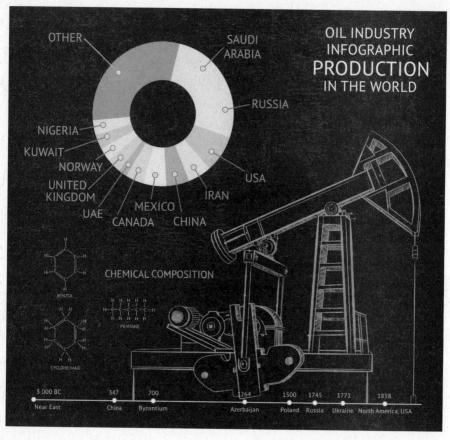

© Andrey Kotko | Dreamstime.com

PUTIN'S VISION

What's Putin's next move in Ukraine? All indications are that Putin prefers a docile government in Kiev with no allegiance or ties to NATO. He will continue to fuel a civil war to that end. He needs the five pipes that funnel half his gas to Europe to remain intact and unfettered by Western hands. With control of the Crimean Peninsula, he ensures his Black Sea fleet has continued use of the Sevastopol port, and his pipelines are protected from foreign meddling. Lastly, control of Ukraine provides a warm and fuzzy buffer between mainland Russia and NATO countries.

The battle for Ukraine is far from over. Russia escalated its support of the rebels in early 2015 by providing more weapons and assistance. This motivated Ashton Carter, Obama's new pick to run the Pentagon, to consider offering the same to Ukrainian fighters. Carter pointed to "a clear violation" by Putin to abide by the 1994 Budapest Memorandums that "provided for Russia to respect the territorial integrity of Ukraine, which it's obviously not done."

Justifying his opinion to better arm the Ukrainians, Carter said the U.S. also committed in 1994 to "respect but also assure . . . the ability of Ukraine to find its own way as an independent country. That is at stake today."

If Carter is successful in convincing the powers that be to authorize direct military assistance to the Ukrainian fighters, in effect, the U.S. will be at war with Russia. Although fought by "proxies," larger armies supplied by the U.S. and Russia will be pitted against each other on bloody battlefields in Ukraine, and the fighting could last for many years to come.

ARCTIC BATTLES

On the other side of the world, in the Pacific Rim, Putin has his fingers in several more pies, which could soon ignite even more battles in the Arctic. It appears that demand for Russian resources is about to skyrocket. Despite a temporary oil glut, big gas and oil deals with the Chinese and Japanese will fill Putin's pockets, and as we have seen, other countries like the U.S., Norway, Syria, and Israel are not poised to mount much competition anytime soon. On the downside for Putin, all these wins place more straws in the middle of Russia's dwindling energy supply cup.

Russia's current oil and gas fields, most of them discovered during the Soviet years, may run dry within the next few decades. The western Siberia fields that supply Europe are becoming depleted. A statement to this effect can be found on page seventy-five of the *Energy Strategy of Russia for the period up to 2030* document: "Depletion of the main gas deposits in the

Nadym-Pur-Taz district of the Tyumen Region" has led to the "necessity of developing new gas-producing centers on the Yamal Peninsula and continental shelf of the Arctic and Far Eastern seas, in the Eastern Siberia and Far East."

According to the Ministry of Energy, the country's oil production levels, which have also contributed greatly to Russia's dramatic economic turnaround, will drop from five hundred million to four hundred million TOEs by 2030. Scattered across the region are 257 oil wells, but most fields are yet to be explored.

The petroleum industry accounts for 20% of Russia's GDP and 43% of its budget revenue, which grants Putin the economic ability to continue playing the role of a thug. As such, he is highly motivated to keep his pockets and pipes full. He plans to do so by forcing the UN CLCS to grant Russia exclusive rights to two large resource locations in the Arctic. Should the Western Elves allow this to happen, Putin will be in the economic and energy driver's seat. On the other hand, if Lord Sauron fails and is driven back to Mordor, Russia could see a severe oil and gas production decline within the next few decades. They will be unable to keep up with demand, which could take a big bite out of the country's GDP and limit Putin's ability to mimic Hitler.

The Russian Arctic shelf is estimated to contain over one hundred billion TOEs of natural gas and oil. That's *billions,* not *millions.* This is why Putin is focused on the Arctic, and has already made giant strides toward owning and defending the region. The Western Elves have idly stood by and watched, and may soon pay a heavy price for doing so.

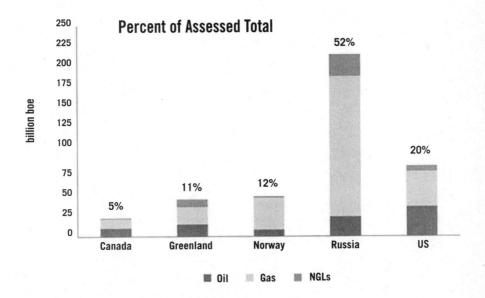

Percent of Assessed Total

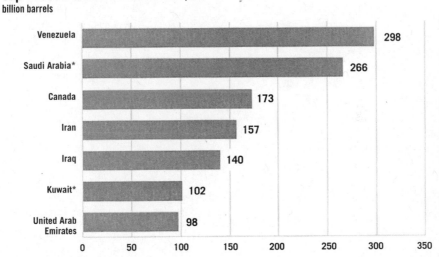

Top Proved World Oil Reserves, 2014
billion barrels

Source: *Oil & Gas Journal*
* Does not included Partitioned Neutral Zone

CHAPTER SEVEN

The Wild Card

Photograph of Chinese Jin-class ballistic missile submarine provided to
CRS by Navy Office of Legislative Affairs, December 2010

No part of the Arctic touches China, but that hasn't deterred the Chinese from referring to their country as a "near-Arctic" state. In March 2010, retired Chinese Navy Rear Admiral Yin Zhuo declared, "The Arctic belongs to all the people around the world as no nation has sovereignty over it." He went on to say that China "must also have a share of the region's resources." Strong words in light of the fact that experts believe China now has submarine-launched nuclear missiles, has started sending attack subs to the Arctic, and owns the world's largest icebreaker.

China is not one of the Arctic Eight nations, so they are not compelled to send mini-subs to the North Pole to plant flags. They are, however, masterful negotiators and were recently granted a permanent observation seat on the Arctic Council. They are also an enigmatic dichotomy. They want to maintain a low global profile, but are motivated to innovate, control, and defend. They desire success as a nation, but don't want to brag about it, lest they draw too much attention to themselves.

Unlike Russia's leaders, who often act like bullies fighting over marbles, China prefers to bargain behind closed doors. Rather than beat you to a pulp and take your bag, they'll trade you two worthless cat's-eye marbles for that valuable chrome-plated steelie and make you believe you got the better deal. That said, if you try to take that steelie back, they'll bloody your nose.

Expressing concerns about potential Chinese aggression, NATO submarine flag officer Rear Adm. Robert Kamensky said, "Who has a very large appetite for new fisheries opening up in the Arctic? China. So what do they have up there in force right now? A lot of fishing vessels harvesting and taking their catches down to China. So there's a potential for conflict in that area over natural resources."

The Arctic Council, made up of the Arctic Eight and a few other nations, granted China and India "observational" seats on the council in May 2013. The two nations can observe what goes on, but have no voting rights. China petitioned the council for years for that seat, and has been an active player in the High North over the past decade.

Resource-starved and highly motivated, China has negotiated with Denmark to lock up a deal for a copper mine in Greenland, and have their eyes set on some of the world's largest deposits of rare earths, which are key ingredients for smart phones and green tech. China is now one of Greenland's largest mining investors. To that end, China's Sichuan Xinye Mining Investment Company has forged a partnership with London Mining to sniff for iron ore in the Arctic.

Not long after Russia tried to lock up the Lomonosov Ridge in 2007, China convinced the Canadian province of Nunavut to allow them to mine for uranium ore. Of course, the Chinese had to promise not to use any of that radioactive material to produce nuclear weapons. Upon crossing their hearts and pledging a scout's honor, China sent ships and miners to the small province located in northeast Canada near Greenland's Baffin Bay. To get there, they had to sail through the Bering Sea and go right past Alaska and Siberia. When they did, the U.S. and Canada took notice.

During the summer of 2012, Chinese ministers visited Iceland, Sweden, and Denmark to offer lucrative trade deals. High-level diplomats also knocked on doors in Greenland, where Chinese companies have increased mining operations and are delivering five thousand Chinese workers to an island that houses only sixty thousand residents. Chinese interests are also looking to exploit mineral deposits near Canada's Baffin Island as the world's purest iron vein resides in this region.

The Defence Policy Research Centre of the Academy of Military Sciences of the People's Liberation Army highlighted the Arctic region as a key interest in their 2014 strategic assessment. An excerpt, published by the official China News Service, stated, "The Arctic region has rich oil and gas resources and quick and convenient shipping conditions, which has important meaning for ensuring the sustained development of China's economy. The Arctic region could become an important supply base in the future for China's overseas oil. China will . . . open cooperation with Arctic countries with energy supplies.

"China sits in the northern hemisphere and has important strategic interests in the Arctic region," the report said, "which relates to national economic development sustainability and national security."

China is now the world's largest economy, and although the country was responsible for half of the planet's growth in oil consumption for 2011 (Source: U.S. Energy Information Administration), they have limited production capabilities. They see the Arctic as a potential way to level the playing field and become less dependent upon Russia, especially in light of recent deals they inked with Putin. Canadian Prime Minister Stephen Harper called Canada an emerging "energy superpower" and said that his country needed to diversify energy exports by shipping more to Asian customers and less to the U.S., especially in light of Obama's feet-dragging on the Keystone Pipeline.

In December 2012, Harper approved a $15 billion bid by Beijing-based CNOOC Limited to acquire Nexen. The result was the largest foreign acquisition by a Chinese company in history. The deal affords the state-owned firm a share in Canada's largest oil-sands project, along with a majority position in the UK North Sea Buzzard oil field. The China National Offshore Oil Corporation also forged a partnership with Eykon Energy in Iceland to sniff for oil in Arctic waters.

Shorter sea routes are almost as important to China as Arctic oil, gas, and minerals. As we learned earlier, dozens of commercial ships travelled through the NSR in 2013 as the new route shaves nearly 5,200 kilometers and nine days off the traditional European excursion, which typically requires going through the Suez Canal and Malacca Straits.

Wang Hexun, director of the Donghai Navigation Safety Administration said, "More than ninety percent of China's international trade is carried out by sea, so once the route is completely open, it will significantly facilitate the cargo shipping and trade sectors in China."

Chinese ambitions for the NSR have encouraged the development of an NSR route guide, published in July 2014, which provides a "comprehensive, practical, and authoritative" informational document to help Chinese cargo ships navigate the NSR to Europe. The guide comes complete with nautical charts, icebreaker hotlines, sailing suggestions, geographic data, climate information, and even the laws and regulations of foreign lands that crews will pass along the way.

China's strategic report noted that the country's growing involvement in Arctic affairs is motivated in part by the desire to prevent a handful of Arctic Council nations from gobbling up all the riches. Also, China has long harbored supply chain fears, given that a bulk of their supplies must travel through the narrow Malacca Strait, which connects the Indian Ocean to the Pacific. Recent posturing by China's navy to exert control over various sea-lanes, coupled with massive increases in defense spending, have U.S. and NATO military leaders worried.

While becoming the world's number one economy, China has dramatically increased its weaponry, technology, and capabilities to do serious harm to its enemies. Most troubling are recent improvements in nuclear submarine warfare, especially with the launch of new *Jin*-class ballistic missile submarines. These boats are reportedly only armed with conventional weapons, but experts believe that China now has underwater nuclear missile launching capabilities.

China has at least three *Jin*-class boats, operating alongside a *Xia*- class SSBN, as well as two *Shang*-class and four *Han*-class SSN attack submarines. With a range of nearly eight thousand miles, the JL-2 missile fired from the *Jin* class can hit targets across most of the continental U.S. from north of the Kuril Islands, which is just south of the Arctic Ocean.

CHINA'S WARNING

On November 9, 2010, China came out of the closet and sent a clear statement of their missile-launching capability to the U.S. and the world at large. That Monday night, less than thirty-five miles off the Los Angeles coast, a *Jin*-class submarine shot a missile into the night sky. The launch was caught on camera by KCBS's camera crews and broadcast to millions across Southern California. Reporters at KFMB radio called the U.S. Navy and Air Force to inquire about the missile trail, but were shunned by government officials. The station then showed the video to former U.S. ambassador to NATO Robert Ellsworth, who was also the former deputy secretary of defense.

Ellsworth viewed the footage and said, "It's spectacular.... It takes people's breath away." He later called the projectile "a big missile."

A navy spokesperson finally admitted that it wasn't a U.S. missile, stating that there was no navy activity reported in the area that evening. Another navy official said, "We've checked and confirmed—this is not associated with any navy operations."

Colonel David Lapan, a Pentagon spokesman, said that none of the military or DoD agencies that might have launched a missile "have come up and said they were involved in this. So we're still trying to find out what the contrail off the coast of Southern California was caused by."

Later, inside sources revealed that the contrail came from a Chinese-launched ballistic missile test. What's interesting about this event is the timing. The incident occurred while President Obama was in China and right after the Federal Reserve had made a unilateral move that angered the Chinese government. Experts believe China decided to have one of its *Jin*-class nuclear submarines, deployed from its secret underground base on the south coast of Hainan Island, launch an intercontinental ballistic missile from international waters off the California coast in protest.

The Chinese move came as a double blow to President Obama. The day after the missile firing, China's leading credit rating agency, Dagong Global, downgraded the sovereign debt rating of the United States to A-plus from AA. The missile demonstration, coupled with the downgrading, represented a military and financial show of force on the part of Beijing toward Washington.

The missile firing came in the wake of a Federal Reserve move made on November 3, 2010, when the decision was finalized to buy U.S. debt from China with the debt-based notes that the Fed creates in its private vaults. The U.S. government was not involved in this decision. The timing of the launch also came on the exact same day, three years earlier, when a Chinese submarine surprised the U.S. Navy by suddenly surfacing alongside the USS *Kitty Hawk* aircraft carrier, which was conducting exercises in the Pacific. Somehow, without warning, a near-silent *Song*-class diesel-electric sub managed to sneak through the carrier's destroyer escort net and close to within torpedo and missile firing range. Needless to say, this angered several U.S. Navy admirals and caused quite a stir in the anti-submarine warfare (ASW) community. Until that time, the U.S. was completely unaware that China's submarine navy had advanced far enough to pull off such a stunt.

In early 2014, Admiral Sam Locklear, Commander, Pacific Command, was quoted as saying "China's advance in submarine capabilities is significant. They possess a large and increasingly capable submarine force."

The Chinese navy has strayed well beyond its littoral patrols of the past by deploying nuclear submarines in the Indian Ocean. The deployments showcase their ability to position subs within nuclear ballistic missile range of the U.S. and its allies. The Chinese have embarked on a program to build four new, improved variants of the formidable Type 093 *Shang*-class nuclear attack submarine while expanding their diesel-hybrid fleet. Navy experts believe that ASW forces will have their hands full within the next few years chasing Chinese subs off the east and west coasts of the U.S.

In its annual report, the U.S.-China Economic and Security Review Commission stated: "While the United States currently has the world's most capable navy, its surface firepower is concentrated in aircraft carrier task forces. China is pursuing a missile-centric strategy with the purpose of holding U.S. aircraft carriers at high risk if they operate in China's near seas and thereby hinder their access to those waters in the event of a crisis."

The panel responsible for writing the report added: "Given China's growing navy and the U.S. Navy's planned decline in the size of its fleet, the balance of power and presence in the region is shifting in China's direction." That will give China an "increasing number of opportunities to provoke incidents at sea and in the air that could lead to a crisis or conflict."

Perhaps these concerns, coupled with worry over the growing economic partnership between Russia and China, prompted Obama to begin talking with Chinese President Xi Jinping about more open communication and cooperation between their military forces.

Nevertheless, a bipartisan commission in Washington, D.C., remained skeptical and cautious. "With a few exceptions, the U.S.-China security relationship deteriorated" in 2014 while China continued "increasingly bold and coercive actions toward its maritime neighbors," with "turmoil in the East and South China seas" a "key driver of this downturn."

According to China Military Online, China Defense Minister Chang Wanquan tried to diffuse any concerns by noting that the country's location and size "places the Chinese military under heavy pressure in securing the country and its border areas. There is therefore a pressing need for China to strengthen its national defense and armed forces."

To counter the growing threat, the U.S. Navy plans to deploy sixty-seven warships and submarines in the area, up slightly from the fifty units in place today. It's a far cry from what's needed as China will have 351 missile-firing surface ships and submarines in the region. Their fleet will be equipped with the DF-21D anti-ship ballistic missile, which can take out an aircraft carrier from over the horizon, and sub-launched missiles that are almost as lethal. No wonder navy admirals are lying awake at night with worry and pounding on political doors during the day to secure more funding. If China and Russia joined forces, and it appears they are moving in that direction, U.S. forces could be outgunned.

CLIMATE COLLABORATION?

Environmentalists are calling it historic. Skeptics are calling it a farce. Barack Obama and Chinese President Xi Jinping announced a climate deal in late November 2014 that promises to truncate carbon emissions. If one believes that reducing carbon emissions worldwide will help save the planet from climate change destruction, the agreement is cause for jubilation. After all, China is responsible for 26% of the world's carbon dioxide production while the U.S. comes in at 16%. Unfortunately, a closer look at the fine print reveals a half-empty glass, or perhaps no glass at all.

The "deal" requires the U.S. to double its carbon slashing to meet a more restrictive mandate by 2025. In return, China will continue to crank out more carbon for the next sixteen years and then "think about" cutting back. According to the Lawrence Berkeley National Laboratory, China will likely slow its carbon emissions around that time anyway due to natural urban decline.

China lights off one new coal plant almost every week. Even if the U.S. shuts down every coal mine in West Virginia, Kentucky, and elsewhere, the planet would still be hurtling toward a black tar death. As noted earlier, most of the coal plants in the U.S. are aging out anyway, so nothing would be achieved save an economic decline.

While the agreement also includes a promise by the Chinese to use non-carbon sources for 20% of its energy by 2030, the country was already on track to do this, but not due to climate change. The Chinese are literally being choked to death in several major cities due to pollution, so nuclear, wind, solar, etc., were already on the docket. In short, Obama has committed the U.S. to slash its energy wrists while the Chinese do the hokey-pokey and turn themselves around. By 2030, the U.S. will need to cut its greenhouse gas emissions by almost 30% while the Chinese will actually be allowed to *increase* their emissions by 20%.

In the meantime, the U.S. continues to borrow money from a communist country that's using the interest collected to fortify its navy so it can harass Japan and other U.S. allies and tighten its grip on sea-lanes and locations with natural resources. Given China's escalating interest in the Arctic, and closer economic ties with Russia, has the stage been set for Cold War confrontations deep beneath the ice?

ALARMING ALLIANCE

Not long after the Russian invasion of Crimea in March 2014, Obama scheduled an Asian tour, in large measure to assure allies that the U.S. would step up to the plate should conflicts arise with China. "What we can say after seeing what happened to Ukraine is that using force to change the status quo is not acceptable," said Japanese Prime Minister Shinzo Abe.

Japan, Malaysia, South Korea, and the Philippines are all worried about China. Several analysts commented that events unfolding in Europe could encourage Chinese leaders to overstep boundaries. They may question

Obama's mettle to make good on his security pledges after reneging on his promise to launch a military strike against Syria, and after again showing a weak hand against Putin in Ukraine.

"The heavyweights in the region got very scared by the Syrian decision," said Douglas Paal, a U.S. diplomat in Asia and the vice president of the Carnegie Endowment for International Peace. "They've never seen anything like that."

Administration officials, including Defense Secretary Chuck Hagel and other administration officials, have wagged fingers at China and issued warnings over the use of military force against Japan and other countries in relation to South China Sea territorial disputes. However, the U.S. has stopped short of officially taking sides over who owns the islands in question.

With world affairs unraveling in Europe, and Putin greedily scooping up Arctic resources, and China cutting deals and flexing muscles, the motives and scenarios for conflict seem endless. Bad decisions and actions on the part of certain states could ratchet up tensions to the breaking point should one party take a swing at an opponent, make an inciting move, position military assets aggressively, stiffen naval forces to ensure security, or over-react to a perceived threat.

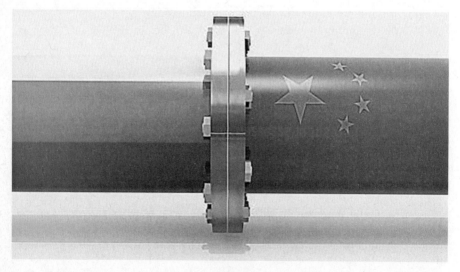

© FabioBerti I Dreamstime.com - Gas Tubes with Russian and China Flag Photo

AVERTING WORLD WAR III

There is little doubt that the Russians and Chinese have escalated their economic alliance and are highly motivated to control the Arctic to obtain the critical resources they need to ensure the survival of their populations. They want to own the Arctic and they are way ahead in the game. While Russia is gaining approval to lock up massive energy-laden shelves, and China is negotiating deals to grab the oil, gas, and minerals they need, the U.S. and EU are sitting on their hands.

If the worst should occur, what can the U.S. Navy and NATO forces do to ensure that attack submarines operating in the Arctic don't wind up on "eternal patrol" at the bottom of the ocean? What ace card can Obama and NATO play to avert a catastrophe that might escalate into World War III?

In *The Lord of the Rings*, Sauron could not be defeated until his One Ring of Power was destroyed. This is also the case in our story, at least metaphorically. The U.S. and the EU need to "destroy" Putin's lock on European and Asian energy supplies and the resultant economic gains that fuel his power, and that of his new ally, China. To this end, the Western Elves must play an ace card. If they continue to fold, hand after hand, Sauron's empire will stand triumphant, and the West may be forced to choose between freezing to death or starving to death.

What is this miracle ace card?

CHAPTER EIGHT

The King and Queen

As fires burn, sea levels rise, oceans turn acidic, hurricanes and tornadoes blow, and the ice melts, fear and panic will likely rise and cover humanity with the force and destruction of a massive tsunami. People will want answers from their leaders, but most of all, they will demand the basic necessities of life.

Food, water, minerals, and energy will trump everything. Countries that have stored up acorns for the winter will survive, and the ones that "lived for the day" will not. Conservatives will die alongside liberals and no one will care about the color of your skin. Governments will have no choice but to do whatever it takes to feed their masses, and the "have-nots" will fight tooth and nail to obtain the resources they need from the "haves."

Remember 2008, when the price of oil surged worldwide? Angry protestors wielded signs and marched down streets shouting demands at government officials to defy the laws of physics and economics and return prices to normalcy. In Spain, tens of thousands of truck drivers used their eighteen-wheelers to block roads and strangle traffic along the French border. Drivers in France, Italy, and Portugal did likewise, creating a near-economic crisis. Violence broke out in other countries, like Indonesia, where policemen were forced to quell crowds with truncheons and water cannons. Similar incidents erupted in Malaysia, Haiti, and Nepal.

Oil wasn't the only cause for panic. Worldwide supplies of rice dropped to a thirty-year low, resulting in uproars and violent mobs in Yemen, Uzbekistan, Haiti, and Morocco. Robert Zoellick, president of the World Bank, further frightened the masses by stating that "thirty-three countries around the world face potential social unrest because of the acute hike in food and energy prices." The UN Food and Agriculture Organization added logs to the fire by predicting even more dire scarcity for the foreseeable future, and perhaps for many years to come.

Professor John Beddington, Britain's chief scientist, predicted similar ominous consequences in March 2009, stating that the planet might soon face several "perfect storm" shortages for energy, water, and food within two decades. During a sustainable development conference, Beddington proffered "a very gloomy picture" in the near future and warned that "things will start to get really worrying" in the wake of weather pattern changes and unabated population growth.

Many Americans believe we live in a world of endless abundance, and that our government should act like Superman, easily vanquishing bad guys and even controlling the weather. A world of want is inconceivable. Virtually none of us, save for a few immigrants from socialist or third world countries, have ever stood in line for hours for a roll of toilet paper like they once did (and sometimes still do) in Russia. When we turn on the faucet, we expect clean water. If our electricity goes out, we fume until it's returned. We feel entitled to our abundance. We expect, even demand, cozy lives void of want.

Those who experienced a week without water, electricity, or even a roof over their heads after super storm Sandy ripped across the Northeast received a glimmer of what can happen in a world where shortages and severe weather patterns are commonplace. While most Americans dismiss the prognosticators of a dark future bereft of abundant oil, natural gas, food, water, or other necessities, we can't argue that the population demand line will someday cross above the resource supply line.

When that day comes, and many experts believe it's not far off, how many of us will demand that our government use its might to secure the bounty we need? And how many of us realize that much of it has become accessible only within the last few years? Or that the Dark Lord Sauron, as the protector of his Russkii family, is about to seize control of all the Elven rings he needs to fuel his One Ring of Power and leave the rest of the world wanting?

In *The Lord of the Rings*, the Western Elves hid their three rings to keep Sauron from capturing the "mobile phone charger" he needed to keep his One Ring "iPhone" powered on and dialing up death and destruction. We've learned that in our case, the three rings are the Northern Sea Route, the Peanut Hole, and the Lomonosov Ridge. Now we'll learn that the West's potential play against the evil Lord Sauron actually consists of three miracle cards: a queen, king, and finally, the ace.

THE QUEEN: FILLING THE NETS WITH FISH

When it comes to choosing which way to die, most may argue that freezing to death is preferable to starving to death. If that's true, then the stakes over who controls the Arctic may have more than doubled in the wake of an unexpected find that has lifted eyebrows around the globe.

In the summer of 2010, a group of scientists aboard a Coast Guard icebreaker were cruising the Arctic's remote Chukchi Sea in search of gems. However, they were not interested in diamonds or sapphires, but in something far more valuable. Kevin Arrigo, a biologist and oceanographer at Stanford's School of Earth Sciences, together with Donald K. Perovich of Dartmouth College and a team of researchers, wanted to find phytoplankton to study. These undersea microscopic plants are a potential source of food for people and ocean life.

Off the Alaskan coast, at the edge of the sea ice, the scientists discovered something unusual. Instruments showed a massive bloom of tiny plants that were clouding the otherwise clear water. The bloom of plankton was doubling in size daily and was so thick that the ocean was transforming into a green sea that resembled a large batch of pea soup. The bloom, located some two hundred miles west of Alaska, spanned an area greater than sixty miles under the ice. Arrigo's team determined that the plankton was thriving due to a melting and thinning polar ice cap, which had occurred due to the melting of the sea ice in the region. When water from the melted ice pooled, this made it easier for sunlight to filter its way into the ocean, which acted like a catalyst to help the plants thrive. Essential nutrients like phosphates, nitrogen, and other elements are abundant in the Chukchi Sea and further stimulate rapid growth.

Marine life in the area, which forms the foundation for the entire food chain, thrives on this plankton. Fish, whales, walruses, seabirds, and other creatures consume these organisms to survive. Scientists and other experts speculate that this massive bloom might spur large fisheries that could eventually feed millions. Politicians and military experts agree and know well that countries laying claim to this bloom could feed large populations for decades to come.

This is the queen card that Obama and the EU can play. While Khrushchev feared a nuclear holocaust, Putin fears losing control and causing his "family" of Russians to starve. He perceives energy domination as the way to avoid such a catastrophe, but people can't eat oil. If the Western Elves invest in creating large fisheries and other sources of food in the Arctic, not only can they ensure the nourishment of their own citizens, especially in light of increasing crop failures due to weather pattern changes, but they will now have a bargaining chip against Sauron and his allies.

Putin is continuing to tighten the screws on the EU by leveraging Europe's oil and gas dependency. He may soon also exploit his energy ties with China to play bad cop against NATO. Can the West use abundant and possibly inexpensive sources of Arctic food as a way to balance the scales? Perhaps when food becomes more precious than oil and gas, Russia and China may be forced to cooperate and trade. They will eventually need greater and more economical ways to feed their people. If Putin controls the majority of the Arctic's energy *and* food supplies, he will have no motivation to sit at the table with anyone. However, if the Western Elves exploit the Arctic food resources right under their noses, and invest heavily in innovative ways to increase yields and lower extraction costs, they can likely beat Putin at his own game. He'll have no choice but to negotiate and perhaps lower gas costs for Germany and the UK in exchange for ships full of fish to feed the masses in Vladivostok.

THE KING: REBUKE THE WIND AND THE WAVES

A grand bargain for fish, or any other Arctic resource, may not be possible as long as the U.S. refuses to play cards and sign the UNCLOS treaty. Until they do so, the other 158 nations who did sign, including Russia and China, have a distinct advantage.

"We don't have a seat at the table right now," Navy Secretary Mabus said. He also intimated that until the U.S. signs, it can't stake any claims to its own Arctic continental shelf. Alaska Governor Treadwell said that not signing could open up oil production to outsiders like China on shelves that should belong to the U.S., or at the very least, prevent America from defending against claims made by other countries in open sea territories.

The U.S. needs to play its king card by joining the UNCLOS. They need to stop being the only country out of 158 without a seat. Obama's administration needs to work closely with the Arctic Eight nations to ensure that Russia does not receive a ratification of the vote from the UN CLCS to own the Peanut Hole—at least not entirely. Also, they need to block a favorable CLCS vote in 2015 to hand Russia the Lomonosov Ridge. Rather, these resource-rich areas need to be divided amongst all the bordering nations so that all can share in the energy resources. This will ensure that Putin has at least some competition for the oil and gas he wants to export to Europe and Asia, and makes him more agreeable in relation to the situation in Ukraine. After all, his supplies are dwindling while his demand is increasing. If no one stands in the way of his supply, he will continue to use that demand to ensure the EU is powerless against his continued aggression in Ukraine and elsewhere.

If the EU truly is motivated to extricate its representative countries from Russian energy shackles, they must encourage their U.S. ally to get their head in the game. If the U.S. and Canada can thwart Putin from winning his bids to control the Peanut Hole and Lomonosov Ridge, they can turn down his energy spigot. They could then pull large amounts of gas and oil from the Beaufort Sea in the Arctic and ship these resources by way of the now more open NSR to European ports. This transitory path is the only feasible route as going in the other direction, through the Northwest Passage past Greenland, is longer, more expensive, and somewhat more treacherous. Problem is, the NSR is mostly controlled by Russian naval forces, and Putin may not take kindly to competitors selling their wares to his customers and using his backyard to get there.

Putin is obviously a master at playing geopolitical chess, and has probably thought about this scenario at length. That may have been a factor in recent investments to beef up Arctic bases and place more ships and subs on the board. The potential for competition probably also lit a fire under Putin to push even harder for control of the Lomonosov Ridge. Given the recent pressure he applied on the UN subcommission to vote in his favor for the Peanut Hole, and the expected follow-on coercion to cast "yes" votes for the Lomonosov submission, Russia could secure economic rights to the ridge by the end of 2015. The U.S. and EU must prevent this from happening.

Also, the U.S. needs to invest in icebreakers, submarines, and naval facilities to ensure the east and west passages in the Arctic are open and free for transit. If Putin is allowed to control all of the NSR, or if Canada remains schizophrenic about allowing transit through the Northwest Passage, getting precious resources to where they need to be will become problematic. The U.S. also needs to invest in the infrastructure required to transport oil and gas from Alaska to pipes that feed the EU. If the U.S. fails to do this, the Russians will increase their European energy domination and continue to invade, conquer, and annex.

SAVING OUR PLANET

Whether we'd like to admit it or not, everything revolves around energy. Without large sources of energy, most of us would likely freeze or starve to death. Dinosaur juice is a required down payment to cultivate, farm, produce, package, ship, refrigerate, and distribute our food. Despite advancements in electric and hybrid cars, it will be decades before every car, truck, airplane, ship, and other gas engine can be replaced. Without fossil fuels, everything plastic goes away, along with most of our clothing.

Like your iPod, iPad, iPhone, Android, PC, Mac, or whatever? Your TV, favorite shows, radio, Internet, etc.? Color them all gone without hydrocarbons. Perhaps the recent hit television show, *Revolution*, provides a glimpse of a potential bleak future without energy. This science fiction program depicts what could happen should all of the world's energy sources suddenly "switch off." No more computers, air conditioners, cars, planes, ships, mobile devices, or microwave ovens. Within a few years, anarchy takes over and previously law-abiding citizens become hungry killers, murdering neighbors in search of food and water. While this scenario seems extreme in a world governed by laws and morals, and is arguably an exaggerated work of fiction, it does point to probabilities we'd all like to avoid, but that are not out of the question.

We may idealistically wish we could eliminate carbon-producing energy overnight and replace it with wind, solar, nuclear, or whatever, but all those alternate sources of power require time to build and huge investments in capital to get off the ground. Where's the money going to come from? As we've just read, without a vibrant energy economy—literally fueled by the oil and gas industry—we're just this side of broke.

Unfortunately, things are going to get a lot worse before they get better. Around two-thirds of the world's population is so poor that the word "energy" holds little meaning for them. They don't chat, tweet, call, text, watch, or drive. But someday many of them will, and that day is coming soon. How will a global population of ten billion power everything they own? Windmills? Doubtful. We'd need trillions of them to power one city. Nuclear power? Not in Japan, or many other countries with neither the funding or stomach to build reactors. It's hard to get one approved in the U.S. The same environmentalists who insist we should destroy every refinery on the map also firmly block research to build clean, efficient, and safe fusion reactors.

That's our quagmire. Most of us want to save our planet but not starve or freeze along the way.

President Obama, in an address delivered in June 2014 to eight thousand graduates of the University of California, Irvine, said, "Today's Congress is full of folks who stubbornly and automatically reject the scientific evidence. They'll tell you climate change is a hoax, or a fad. One says the world might actually be cooling." This came on the heels of his announcement to invest $1 billion in a plan to help communities to develop better ways to rebuild or plan for infrastructure to combat climate change.

Skeptics say Obama's plans and prompting to mitigate climate change are either unneeded, or too little and too late. They insist that even the most aggressive moves, at this point, would only slightly cut greenhouse emissions (which are mostly comprised of carbon dioxide) from current levels while proving to be devastating to the U.S. economy. In fact, they say even if the "greens" successfully park every car and shut down every major energy project in the U.S. including the Keystone Pipeline, fracking in California, every coal plant, and virtually every drilling platform and refinery, it would barely make a dent in the world's carbon footprint. That's because a vast majority of the world's CO_2 is coming from China, and as we've just read, despite the "historic" deal they signed with Obama, the Chinese are not motivated to take their foot off the proverbial gas pedal anytime soon.

Claims by experts that massive initiatives in the U.S. could cut CO_2 emissions by 30% sound hopeful, but they're not realistic or economically feasible. In 2013, power plants accounted for almost 40% of CO_2 emissions in the U.S., and if these were shut down overnight, almost half the country would freeze to death. Also, Obama's 30% is misleading in that it overstates the cuts. The "cut clock" started in 2005, and in the decade since, the U.S. has already seen a large move away from coal. At that time, power plants accounted for 2,402 million metrics of CO_2, and a 30% reduction equals 721. But in that decade we already shaved off almost half, so we're really down to only 15%, not 30%. The average coal-fired plant is forty-three years old, so the problem is really going away on its own as the plants age out.

Coal's share of electricity generation has already declined from 50% in 2005 to 39% in 2013, and the EPA estimates it will fall to 31% by 2030. Cleaner natural gas's share increased from 19% to 27% and will rise to 32% by 2030.

All this simply means that even the most aggressive plan to trim CO_2 emissions in the U.S. will not save our planet. That's not to say we shouldn't try, say those who've crunched the numbers, but it does little good to get so radical that we all wind up homeless with an economy worse than the Great Depression. Conversely, environmentalists argue that massive energy cuts won't harm the gross domestic product (GDP), but that does not coincide with the facts.

In the U.S., the overall economy, measured in terms of the GDP, grew by a meager 1.9% in 2013. In contrast, the Chinese economy leapt forward by almost 8%. All five states with the highest growth owe their good fortunes in some measure to the energy sector. North Dakota, for example, led the pack with a rate of almost 10%. They had the lowest unemployment rate at just 2.9%, and since 2010 they've been the fastest-growing state in the nation. They grew by 20% in 2012, and nearly all of that growth is attributable to the state's oil boom, thanks to fracking in the Bakken shale formation. Wyoming and Virginia saw booms thanks to coal mining and natural gas, and Oklahoma filled its coffers with oil profits.

In April 2014, the Obama administration announced that the GDP had crept along on life support for the first quarter at only 0.1%. Over eight hundred thousand Americans left the workforce in April, and although unemployment fell, it was mainly because a large number gave up and stopped looking for work. That same month, the North Dakota and Montana Bakken Shale oil field hit one billion barrels. Fox News Channel raised an eyebrow and asked: What happens to the U.S. GDP if you subtract the gains contributed by the energy sector?

The answer? Poverty and starvation.

POLLUTION OR POVERTY?

The nonfarm economy, according to Gene Lockard of Rigzone.com, has declined by over three million jobs since January 2008. That year, oil production was declining and chugged along at only five million barrels per day. Thanks to the shale revolution, instead of heading toward four million barrels, the industry did a U-turn and shot up to almost twice that amount in 2013. The result? For every one job created by the oil and gas industry, which expanded by 26%, another seven were created in other sectors. Like the proverbial pond-rock-ripple effect, every dollar spent on an oil field magically turned into seven dollars spent elsewhere—dollars that created more jobs and kept the U.S. economy afloat.

Let's say by some miracle Obama approves the Keystone Pipeline. Some will argue that spills could occur, pollution might increase, or more gas burned by automobiles will advance climate change. All are plausible arguments, but given track records and global realities, the odds of disaster may unfortunately be outweighed by the economic gains, at least for the immediate future. That's because blue-collar workers in Steel Town will be needed to make the pipes, truckers will need to deliver them, and construction workers will need to lay them. Again, seven jobs and dollars for every one.

Still, when the frackers show up to do their thing, the earth rumbles as though enduring an earthquake. Massive equipment pumps jets of chemical-laden water down big holes. People worry about land abuse and tainted water, and fear the damage done to our precious planet. All understandable concerns, but again history shows limited consequences in relation to major economic gains. The sand used for fracking is transported from Wisconsin. Much of the equipment is built by Caterpillar or GE Industrial Solutions. Caterpillar alone pulled in almost $5 billion in 2013 for this type of equipment. Hundreds of trucks parked at oil fields are built by General Motors or Dodge or Ford. Chevron claims to have spent $2.7 billion with small businesses in 2014.

An ICF International study estimates that over the next two decades the oil industry will spend $641 billion for infrastructure alone. Another $125 billion will pay for shale-related chemical plants. What happens to the U.S. economy if the energy sector is gutted overnight by well-meaning environmentalists? Perhaps our weather improves over the course of decades, but in the meantime, how many children are left starving?

For certain this is a difficult situation. It's not too unlike the worker who hates his boss, and knows that the stress may one day result in a heart attack, but he can't afford to quit as he needs to feed his family. What's the right answer here? Even the oil companies are starting to capitulate. After spending more than $23 million on climate denial groups to sway public opinion, ExxonMobil now reports "rising greenhouse gas emissions (GHG) pose significant risks to society and ecosystems."

British Petroleum switched sides recently and now cites the Intergovernmental Panel on Climate Change report as evidence of global warming. ConocoPhillips says burning fossil fuels can lead to climate disruption. Chevron, Hess, BHP Billiton, and Total share these concerns. (John H. Reaves & Len Hering, *San Diego Union Tribune*, 8/22/14.)

In June 2014, President Obama continued his battle to win hearts and minds, and perhaps votes, by demanding a reduction of 25% in greenhouse gases over the next fifteen years. He said, "As president, and as a parent, I refuse to condemn our children to a planet that's beyond fixing."

To that end, he pledged to fight fossil fuel production, despite the obvious hit to the economy, and fund more solar and wind generation—which requires a substantial investment by taxpayers. Nevertheless, some of these measures may offer relief through innovation and incentives related to ocean fertilizing to help seawater absorb more carbon, sunlight reflection research, and carbon sequestration.

The EPA remains skeptical that the wrist-cutting measures will pay off. Their assessment states that "some additional climate change and related impacts are now unavoidable" given the amount of greenhouse gasses hanging around in our atmosphere. They further claim that "if emissions stopped increasing, atmospheric greenhouse gas concentrations would continue to increase and remain elevated for hundreds of years." Also, "Surface air temperatures would continue to warm." An article printed in the Proceedings of the National Academy of Sciences backs up the EPA's opinions by concluding that climate change as a result of carbon dioxide buildup is "largely irreversible for one thousand years after emissions stop."

In short, the prevailing thinking on the part of the experts appears to be that we could opt to endure chemotherapy treatments, puke up our meals every day, and lose all of our hair, but it will not offer the cure we hope for. We must, at this point, accept our fate and find a way to adapt and mitigate rather than focus on drastic measures to eradicate our disease. In fact, the 2014 IPCC press release mentions "mitigation" only once as compared to "adaptation" a dozen times.

Prodded by public opinion, some politicians continue to throw spears at the energy sector for being the culprits of climate change, but they can't ignore the fact that without profits and jobs created by oil, gas, and coal companies, the U.S. economy could actually collapse overnight. In short, at least for now, we have no choice but to dance with the devil. Whether you believe in climate change, or simply believe in reducing pollution, reducing carbon emissions by stabbing ourselves in the back will likely cause us to bleed to death. If we want to battle the carbon beast, we either need to adapt, find innovative ways to reverse the effects, or invent alternatives to dinosaur juice.

As providence would have it, an obscure research lab has found a way to do exactly that, and despite the fact that they may have a viable and economical way to pull the wind out of Putin's sails and shutter the doors on carbon increases, the government that funds them apparently has no idea what's right under their turned-up noses.

CHAPTER NINE

The Ace

© Fotoeye75 I Dreamstime.com - Ace of Spades Card on Wood Photo

CHANGING WATER TO WINE

The infamous Comte de Saint-Germain came to light in the early 1700s. He reportedly spoke almost every language known to man and demonstrated mastery in a variety of disciplines including music, art, science, math, and alchemy. He helped Mesmer invent the science of magnetism and removed flaws from diamonds for King Louis XV. He warned Marie Antoinette about the fall of the French monarchy, conducted secret spy missions for King Louis, traveled incognito, and could apparently dodge death with nimble ease. He was said to be a Grand Master of the Knights Templar and a Freemason. Casanova called him *der Wundermann* after watching the mysterious count turn ordinary lead into gold as easily as Jesus transformed water into wine.

History is replete with such tall tales of alchemists and saints transmuting the molecular structure of one form into another; a variety of myths and miracles apparently witnessed but never proven. Until now.

Three-fourths of our planet is covered by oceans. What if there was a way to take a large bucket of this ordinary saltwater, wave a magic wand, and convert it into something that could actually power a combustion engine? Impossible?

"This is present shock, not future shock," said Vice Admiral Philip Cullom, Naval Operations for Fleet Readiness and Logistics deputy chief.

Along the banks of the Potomac River, just south of the Washington Monument, you can spy a smattering of old buildings that seem to have stepped out of a 1950s black-and-white military training film. The lime-green paint on these structures has peeled and cracked, and the sidewalks are covered with geriatric age lines that resemble the face of a centenarian. Inside, however, is something far more modern, cutting edge, and perhaps even revolutionary.

"We've done it," said Dr. Heather Willauer, lead scientist at the Naval Research Laboratory in Washington, D.C. With a PhD in analytical chemistry and years of experience working in this field, Willauer is revered as one of the world's leading experts on the science of "fuel creation."

"We can convert ordinary seawater into designer fuel that lets us fly that thing." Willauer pointed to a small hobby airplane hovering above her desk. The radio-controlled P-51 model of a legendary Red Tail Squadron airplane sported a single propeller powered by an unmodified two-stroke internal combustion gasoline engine. Willauer and her team had successfully, on several occasions, flown the model plane using a pint of their alchemist's brew.

"A lot of people have made this a reality," said Willauer. Her eyes twinkled underneath a pair of thick scientist glasses. She smiled and held up a test tube of golden elixir and twirled it between two fingers. "I came to NRL in January of 2002 and joined the program in the latter part of 2006. Before

I joined, we had a researcher, Dr. Dennis Hardy, and our former director of research, Dr. Timothy Coffey, who had already brainstormed this as early as 2000 and filed a patent for the process in 2002. Dennis was nearing retirement, and I came onboard to carry on the work. It's a fascinating science, and it's been fun to see it progress."

So far, that progression has taken more than a decade and a tremendous amount of unwavering support by NRL's upper management over the years, including current Director of Research Dr. John Montgomery, Associate Director of Research Dr. Bhakta Rath, and former branch head Dr. Frederick W. Williams. The snail's pace is due in part to the complexity of the science, but in larger measure due to a lack of funding.

"We only have a small team right now," Willauer said. "If we had just a few more people, we could go a lot faster."

A lot faster toward what? Energy independence? A way to diffuse Putin's powers? Perhaps. Or at the very least, a way to power the U.S. Navy's fleet and maybe, just maybe, a fleet of ordinary cars on America's freeways. And the best part?

"This process has, essentially, a zero-carbon footprint," said Willauer. "In fact, maybe even a negative carbon footprint."

What does that mean, exactly? Well, every time we turn the key to start our car engines, or the navy lights off a ship's diesel engine, or a truck driver barrels down the freeway, we're spewing carbon dioxide into the atmosphere. A vast majority of the world's climate scientists, in fact almost 90% by now, are convinced that humans are the major cause of carbon exacerbation. Whether one believes them or not, it's hard to justify driving a gas guzzler when you know in your heart of hearts that you're polluting the planet. Who among us thinks it's safe to hold our nose over the exhaust pipe of an eighteen-wheeler for eight hours?

Climate scientists have expressed concerns that one of the most harmful things those diesel trucks are doing to the planet is causing our oceans to become more acidic. As saltwater absorbs more CO_2, the acid level goes up and the ocean life goes down. But what if there was a way to take more of that bad CO_2 out of the ocean than we put back in? Could we save the fish along with ourselves?

"To make fuel," Willauer said, "we first need carbon. When we started the program, one of the long poles in the tent was where to get that carbon. The navy operates at sea, so that made more sense than trying to get it from the air. It turns out that CO_2 is 140 times more concentrated in seawater than it is in the air, on a weight-per-volume basis."

Two to three percent of the CO_2 in seawater is dissolved gas in the form of carbonic acid. Around 1% is carbonate, and the remaining 96% to 97% is bound in bicarbonate. It's this bicarbonate, which is essentially carbon combined with hydrogen, that NRL needs for their process. But an energy-efficient way to extract carbon and hydrogen in quantities large enough to create fuel did not yet exist less than a decade ago.

In 2009, while serving in the Offices of Naval Research Reserve Program 38, Lieutenant Commander Felice DiMascio had a brainstorm. The PhD electrochemist had been working on wastewater treatment using electrochemical technology. Another P-38 officer working on the NRL program, Captain (ret) Kathy Lewis, met DiMascio at the annual ONR-RC 2009 Winter Program Review and after a brief conversation, convinced him to join Willauer and her team.

"DiMascio brought that idea to us," said Willauer. "Working with him, we configured a way to electrochemically remove CO_2 from the bicarbonate seawater and simultaneously produce hydrogen, so it was a 'two for one' process. That makes it only one energy penalty for two feedstocks."

By feedstocks, Willauer is referring to the building blocks needed to create what she calls "designer fuel." This includes liquid natural gas (LNG), compressed natural gas (CNG), F-76 (military diesel fuel), JP-5 (jet fuel), and even ordinary nonleaded fuel we can pump into our automobile gas tanks.

"The fuel we create is plug-and-play compatible," Willauer said. "It's synthetic, but it's essentially identical to current fuel and will power almost any kind of unmodified engine. We're very excited because we're actually taking seawater and making fuel that works."

How is this possible? We'll start with a simplified layman's explanation. While NRL doesn't actually boil anything, for our purposes, let's imagine we're boiling some water. Rising from the top of that water is a white cloud of steam. Now imagine that you've created a way to turn ocean water into two different kinds of "steam," one blue and one red. The blue one is carbon, which is created by pulling CO_2 out of the water. The red "steam" is hydrogen (H_2), made by stripping away the oxygen (O) from the water (H_2O). You now have the building blocks, which Willauer calls feedstocks, to synthesize, or design, ordinary fuel. But first you need to combine the two hydrogen and carbon feedstocks together to create what scientists refer to as an "olefin."

"To create olefins," Willauer said, "we first needed to extract the carbon and hydrogen, and that required a scientific breakthrough."

Basically, a miracle.

NRL synthetic fuel. DoD photo by Jessica L. Tozer/Released

Willauer explains that the biggest breakthrough came from visualizing a new type of electrochemical process, and then designing a mechanism that could power the process. NRL calls this the electrolytic cation exchange module (E-CEM). The process, and the module, are now patented, and have transitioned from a laboratory-scale module (5.5 x 14 x 2 inches) all the way up to a 5 x 5 x 3-foot mobile skid that houses one E-CEM along with an array of gauges, panels, tubes, pipes, and snaking cables. While the skid is self-contained, it still needs a power source, so part of the "magic" is ensuring that this input power is renewable and not from fossil fuels. Impressively, NRL has already demonstrated the ability to remove both dissolved and bound CO_2 from seawater at 92% efficiency.

"We've come a long way, but we're not yet ready to operate aboard a warship," said Willauer. "Still, we've gone from a technology rate level (TRL) of only three to around six."

To get there, and to actually create olefins that can be turned into jet fuel, the NRL team needed a catalyst. Oil companies classify the dinosaur juice they pull out of the ground as a "hydrocarbon," which basically means that it consists of various molecular combinations of hydrogen and carbon. As described above, NRL uses their patented E-CEM to extract the hydrogen and carbon they need from ordinary ocean water, because the ocean contains an abundance of both. These two chemicals now need to be "run over" some kind of catalyst to create a liquid hydrocarbon via a recombination process to get the hydrogen and carbon to "dance with each other" in unison.

"We can make almost any kind of hydrocarbon," said Willauer. "Jet fuel, diesel fuel, liquid natural gas, automobile fuel, you name it. What we make depends on the transition metal in the catalyst, such as copper, nickel, cobalt, or iron. It's truly amazing."

Willauer and team chose jet fuel as their initial brew. After all, NRL's ultimate customer is the U.S. Navy, and while a *Nimitz*-class aircraft carrier is nuclear-powered, they carry up to around ninety aircraft during a typical deployment. To power these fighter jets, they also need to carry around three million gallons of JP-5 jet fuel, which only supports about two weeks of continuous air operations. The carrier then needs to load on more fuel, which makes them vulnerable to supply shortages.

"We developed an iron-based catalyst," Willauer explained, "to show how we can make JP-5. The technology did not initially exist to make our system modular in nature, so we started working on a prototype for a continuously stirred tank reactor. We were then able to move that design to a fixed bed that allowed us to scale up to a modular type of technology."

Using the 5 x 5 x 3-foot skid described earlier, NRL can now take the volumes of hydrogen and carbon dioxide that are extracted from the E-CEM, run those volumes of gases over an iron catalyst, and convert them into olefins. These olefins can then be used to create JP-5 or other kinds of hydrocarbon fuel. The skid resides at Key West, Florida, where it pumps out a small amount of hydrogen and carbon dioxide on a daily basis. The overall process does not yet make much fuel, certainly not enough to power a fighter jet or ship for more than a few seconds.

"The navy needs around 250,000 gallons of fuel per day to power an average battle group," said Willauer. "We're nowhere near that amount yet."

Dr. Heather Willauer shows NRL's synthetic fuel at the 2014 Sea-Air-Space Exposition in National Harbor, MD. (DoD photo by Jessica L. Tozer/Released)

"Nowhere near" is not an understatement. Today, it takes around 23,000 gallons of seawater to produce one gallon of gas. NRL can only process about a half-gallon of seawater per minute with the current technology. They hope to scale that to seventeen gallons per minute in the near future. Even then, they will only produce about one gallon of fuel per day per module, so they have a long way to go. Some of the constraints are due to what's currently available in the industry. To keep costs and dimensions small, and energy efficiency high, NRL wants to use as many off-the-shelf components as possible, which poses some limitations.

Willauer feels confident in NRL's ability to scale up carbon and hydrogen extraction capabilities using the E-CEMs, but needs the industry to help out a bit by making more modular reactors for the catalytic olefin creation part of the process. The commercial companies NRL is working with on that end include Huntington Ingalls Newport News Shipbuilding and Ceramatec. The former is involved in designing a fuel-producing ship around the NRL technologies, and the latter with making modular reactors to create the olefins.

"We're using one-and-a-half-inch diameter tubes to make fuel today," said Willauer. "The industry, I believe, will soon have tubes almost twice that size, so that will help us scale. If we have wider and longer tubes, we can make more fuel in the same amount of time."

One might ask if tubes the size of howitzer muzzles will be needed to make 250,000 gallons of fuel per day, but NRL is looking more toward supplementation rather than replacement. While the navy is certainly motivated to help save the planet, the current primary goal has less to do with energy efficiencies or economies and much more to do with logistics and strategies.

"What is just absolutely revolutionary...is that, if you no longer have to worry about where that oiler is, you remove so much of the vulnerability that we have at sea," said Vice Adm. Cullom.

Every adversary knows how to exploit the Achilles' heel of a naval battle group—you cut off their supply lines. Many modern warships are nuclear powered, but many are not. Also, everything aboard a modern aircraft carrier—from the tractors to the winches to the airplanes—runs on diesel or jet fuel. Without it, you have nothing more than a useless floating flattop. According to Cullom, the navy gobbles up around 1.25 billion gallons of fuel every year, and the supply line ships and trucks that comprise the Military Sealift Command are often easy targets.

"Adversaries look to the last conflicts to figure out future conflicts," said Collum. "So if you remove one of those 'soft targets,' then you don't even have to figure out how to protect [them]."

Collum learned this fact the hard way.

"In 1998, I was in the Adriatic, and I was there for the Kosovo conflict. Every X number of days, I would have to leave my station to go out into the Mediterranean where it was safe, to be able to rendezvous with the oiler to get my fuel. When I had to rendezvous out there, I was nowhere near the position where my Tomahawk missiles were valuable. That's why this matters. If you could get the fuel where you're at, you don't have to go to the oiler."

Vice Adm. Cullom is hopeful that the navy can start using more "drop-in" biofuels at a cost approaching $4 per gallon within the next few years.

"We need to reinvent how we create energy," said Cullom. "How we value energy and how we consume energy."

NRL would like to help with that goal, but unfortunately, their contribution may not be viable for another decade. Why so far away? Funding and manpower. Despite the obvious benefits to the navy, and the world at large, the powers that be have kept a tight rein on the purse strings.

"We need backing to do the research because we are not appropriated," said Willauer. "We are not getting money from Congress. We have to look at venture capitalists and people who are willing to invest in the project, and by people, that could also be other government entities."

NRL has also invented a more energy-efficient, low-current system that pulls CO_2 out of seawater, but it does not extract hydrogen to create hydrocarbon fuels. Such a system might be useful to catalyze algae growth for food sources or provide CO_2 for manufacturing processes, as an example.

"This is really good for the navy to be able to work on this," said Willauer, "because just like the space program, the ancillary effects are unfathomable. They're priceless."

Perhaps they are, but how can this technology solve our current problems? How can NRL's "PetroConverter" technology muzzle Putin's European aggression and perhaps slow climate change at the same time?

The author with Dr. Willauer at NRL in Washington D.C.

MUZZLING CARBON

Let's set aside our beliefs about climate change for a moment and agree that, unless you are a proponent of lung cancer, breathing in carbon is a bad thing. That said, how can we reduce the world's carbon footprint without decimating entire economies, which today are reliant upon profits generated by the energy sector?

The oil and gas industry is essentially grouped into three major segments: upstream, midstream, and downstream. The upstream segment is involved with looking for and eventually removing hydrocarbons from

Mother Earth. In short, exploration and extraction. This is the arm that environmentalists rile against due to concerns over potential damage to the planet from processes like fracking.

The upstream segment spends the bulk of its time searching for crude oil and natural gas fields, whether underground or underwater, such as those found in the Arctic. They employ large teams over many months or years, which use expensive scientific equipment and extensive analysis to make educated "guesses" as to where the dinosaur juice might be buried. Drilling and fracking teams then take over and construct oil rigs or inject water into the ground to bring the bubbly brew to the surface.

Upstream in the U.S. is highly lucrative. The value of U.S. merger and acquisition opportunities in this sector nearly tripled between 2009 and 2013, hitting a record high of $135 billion.

The midstream portion of the oil and gas industry revolves around the transportation of all that smelly stuff, either by truck, tanker, train, or pipeline—such as the hotly debated Keystone Pipeline blocked by the Obama administration. These methods of transport deliver "black gold" from production fields or wells to refineries, where it can be turned into something suitable for a gas station.

Downstream is generally focused on processing and purification of the raw stuff found in the ground, as well as the distribution and marketing of final products, such as cans of oil or gallons of gas. As we discussed earlier, the U.S. Navy is a major downstream customer for jet fuel, military diesel fuel, petroleum, LNG, lubricants, asphalt, and many other hydrocarbon-based products. They're not alone. Virtually every person and company on the planet relies on energy products in some fashion for survival. We learned earlier that without the oil and gas sector, the U.S economy would likely be "in the tank," so to speak.

So here's the multibillion dollar question: Why would the oil and gas industry embrace, rather than try to block, NRL's PetroConverter technology?

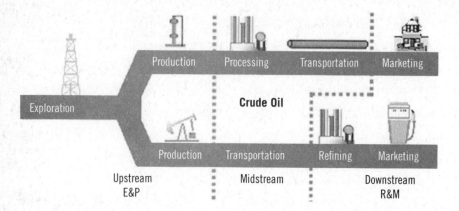

Haven't we all heard the rumors about the one hundred-mile-per-gallon carburetor or super-efficient automobile batteries that the energy sector bought the patents for and then buried? Haven't they been the purveyors of dozens of scientific reports from scientists like Dr. Soon that dispute climate change? Why wouldn't they slam NRL to the mat rather than actually help them bring this invention to fruition?

Oil and gas companies have amassed billions in profits over the past decade, and most of their executives did not come riding into town on turnip trucks. They are constantly at war with environmentalists who are blocking pipelines, fracking, coastal drilling, and Arctic exploration. Still, why embrace rather than entangle NRL? Because the fuel produced by NRL's PetroConverter is plug-and-play compatible. Unlike virtually all other energy alternatives, including wind, solar, batteries, etc., a PetroConverter is still creating ordinary fuel. The oil and gas sector can view this as an augmentation to their upstream extraction operations in the short term, and a more economical replacement to operations over the long term. Instead of spending tens of billions to find new sources of hidden hydrocarbons, and battle environmentalists every step of the way—which is also expensive—they can build nonpolluting PetroConverters off the coastline of every country in the world and have an endless source of olefins from which to make fuel.

Of course, some upstream players will lose out. Explorers and drillers will no longer be needed, but such is the price of technological advancement throughout history. If we operated on the basis of blocking change to preserve every current job, we'd still be riding horses and farming with plows. The key to the adoption of NRL's PetroConverter, the one that makes this ideal for the energy sector, is that it does not require any major changes to midstream or downstream operations. Everything can essentially remain the same. The products supplied to customers, whether Joe Citizen or the U.S. Navy, are almost identical.

Referring to the fuel created by NRL, Vice Adm. Cullom said, "It looks, smells, and acts just like petroleum fuel. It has all the right components."

The major difference is that the extraction process is nonpolluting and the net result for the planet is carbon-neutral. Although we'd all still be burning gas and spewing carbon into the air, we'd be pulling as much if not more carbon out of the ocean than we're putting back in. That's not the case with current hydrocarbons.

"I'm not getting fossil fuel out of the ground and putting more CO_2 in the air," said Dr. Willauer. "I'm actually using the CO_2 from the environment."

Again, whether we believe the climate scientists or not, we have to agree that increasing the carbon content in our atmosphere is not a good thing. Cities that do this on a consistent basis have the worst pollution on the planet. Do we really want to force our children and grandchildren to breathe a poisonous atmosphere? We can choose a better way, but not unless NRL gets the proper amount of attention and funding it needs.

Imagine a future where the U.S. oil and gas industry has gradually replaced their upstream operations with clean and green PetroConverters. Where our carbon footprint is neutral or even declining instead of skyrocketing toward oblivion. Where the U.S. economy is rocking and rolling and almost everyone has a great job and lots of money. Perhaps this is an optimist's pipe dream, but we'll never know unless we take a step in the right direction, and that first step comes with awareness. The second step requires action, and that won't happen unless someone comes forward and hands NRL a wad of cash to accelerate their research.

Perhaps that someone should be Chevron, ExxonMobile, or another energy firm. They may find that the upside far outweighs the downside. Some upstream jobs will be lost, of course, but the downstream benefits could easily eclipse the losses. Once there are enough PetroConverters operating at peak efficiency, the upstream costs should actually decrease exponentially as exploration and extraction costs disappear, along with lobbying environmentalists. There will no longer be a need to drill or frack or potentially harm Mother Earth. The public may begin viewing oil companies as planet-savers rather than destroyers, and they may even see them as the patriotic vanquishers of Putin's unbounded aggression.

THROTTLING PUTIN

We know that Putin's powers come from Russia's oil and gas exports. The EU is under his spell as they can't afford to risk having their energy spigots turned off. China has climbed into bed with Lord Sauron by inking a $400 billion gas deal, and our political antagonist is hell-bent on locking up the world's remaining oil and gas reserves in the Arctic. The U.S., with temporary help from Saudi Arabia, is trying to throttle one of Russia's main revenue sources and tank the ruble by depressing gas prices. As we've learned, they can't afford to play this game for long. What if the U.S. could *permanently* pull the energy rug out from under Russia's president while actually improving the U.S. economy?

It could take a decade to accomplish such a feat, but by moving in that direction, the U.S. and EU would no longer be left with limited options. By building dozens of PetroConverters along Europe's coastlines, EU leaders could pose a united front against Russian aggression. Over time, they could begin to achieve energy independence and thereby diminish the impact of Putin's threats to cut off supplies.

Most importantly, as we'll discuss in detail in another chapter, Petro-Converters could mitigate the economic damage Putin could do when he tries to move the world away from a petrodollar-backed economy to a petroruble one.

The above is one scenario of what could happen, but lack of awareness, funding, and political will may keep this from becoming a reality. In that event, we are likely headed toward skirmishes and eventually a full-scale resource war in the Arctic. According to a host of military and political experts, conflict is inevitable and will likely occur within the next few years, and it will happen whether we're prepared for it or not.

In that event, the U.S. Navy may be our best hope for survival.

The guided-missile cruiser USS Princeton (CG-59) and the aircraft carrier USS Nimitz (CVN-68) are underway in formation during the Great Green Fleet demonstration portion of the Rim of the Pacific 2012 exercise, July 18, 2012. Princeton and Nimitz took on a fifty-fifty blend of advanced biofuel and traditional petroleum-based fuel. (U.S. Navy photo by Petty Officer 2nd Class Eva-Marie Ramsaran/Released)

CHAPTER TEN

Prelude to War

Photograph courtesy of the U.S. Navy

T he U.S. Navy may indeed have the answer to stopping Putin and mitigating carbon emissions, and could perhaps help avert catastrophic global conflicts over Arctic resources, but unfortunately without the proper funding and interest by Western Elves, it could take another decade or more to become commercially feasible. In the meantime, global leaders are bickering over sea-lane passages and economic rights to precious natural Arctic resources, and preparing for imminent naval battles to defend their claims.

Human population growth peaked in 1963, but the number of people alive—consuming oil, gas, food, and water—has skyrocketed by more than two-thirds since then. Seven billion of us are devouring scarce resources, and within three decades we'll add another two billion mouths. Some experts are predicting severe resource scarcities along the way, exacerbated by crop failures and calamities caused by changing weather patterns. Many are prophesizing deadly confrontations by the end of the year 2020 over areas containing precious resources, such as oil, gas, and minerals, and the Arctic tops almost everyone's list for ground zero.

While hawks raise concerns over future Arctic conflicts, doves point to previous issues such as those governing Antarctic territorial disputes that were settled, at least temporarily, when a dozen countries signed an agreement in 1959. However, things were very different back then. The world's population wasn't skyrocketing out of control as much as it is today, and technologies did not yet exist that made it easier to extract resources. Furthermore, speculations regarding Antarctica's oil, gas, mineral, and food resources paled in comparison to those estimated for the Arctic region. In fact, such riches were not even discovered in Antarctica until many years after the agreement was signed, and some experts speculate that as global resources continue to diminish, nations that originally signed may try to get an annulment.

A 2012 U.S. Navy report titled *A Cooperative Strategy for 21st Century Seapower* states that "climate change is gradually opening up the waters of the Arctic, not only to new resource development, but also to new shipping routes that may reshape the global transport system. While these developments offer opportunities for growth, they are potential sources of competition and conflict for access and natural resources."

Rear Admiral Matthew Klunder, the navy's chief of naval research, met with leaders from U.S. and Canadian government agencies in December 2012 to talk about research efforts in the Arctic in light of recent climatic changes. Klunder stated, "Our Sailors and Marines need to have a full understanding of the dynamic Arctic environment, which will be critical to protecting and maintaining our national, economic and security interests."

The Office of Naval Research (ONR), Arctic Summit in December 2012 hosted a slew of important officials from the ONR, Defense Advanced

Research Projects Agency (DARPA), the Defense Research and Development Canada, the Departments of Energy and Interior, NASA, the National Oceanic and Atmospheric Administration (NOAA), the National Science Foundation, the Navy Task Force Climate Change, and more. A key goal of the summit was to discuss ways in which all these agencies could work together to address future concerns over Arctic oil, minerals, and other natural resource extraction; shipping; commercial fishing; tourism; and piracy.

"Popular perceptions of the Arctic as a distant, icy, cold place that has little relevance to those outside the region are being challenged," said Martin Jeffries, coeditor of the 2012 NOAA Arctic Report Card, Arctic science adviser and program officer for the Office of Naval Research and former research professor at the University of Alaska Fairbanks. "We are surely on the verge of seeing a new Arctic. And, since the Arctic is not isolated from the global environmental system—indeed it is an integral and vital part of that system—we can expect to see Arctic change have global environmental and socioeconomic consequences."

The former NATO supreme allied commander, retired Admiral James Stavridis, commented in a recent *Foreign Policy* article about potential Arctic security threats: "The risks are fairly well known," he said, mentioning the probability of confrontations due to more open sea routes and access to oil, gas, minerals, and food sources. Stavridis stated that he anticipates direct future Arctic conflicts and urged the U.S. to undertake a great deal of preparation to ensure adequate security in the region. Stavridis admonished that "there are issues that must be addressed in the High North if we are to avoid high tension."

The admiral pointed to the fact that the U.S. has only two operational icebreakers and one is on its last breath. Comparatively, Russia has two dozen and China is building several more. Given tight budgets and waning time frames, Stavridis stressed that the U.S. "should invest a reasonable amount in the sensors and technology to map and track the Arctic—satellites, reconnaissance flights, and undersea monitoring." Doing so could allow the Coast Guard to gain assistance from the navy and other Department of Defense organizations, and help them fulfill the charter they emphasized in a 2013 reported titled *The U.S. Coast Guard's Vision for Operating in the Arctic Region.*

On May 30, 2014, NATO Secretary General Anders Fogh Rasmussen signaled concerns over Putin's continued rush to exploit the Arctic. He intimated that NATO forces should plan for a potential response. Rasmussen commented that he found Putin's designs for Arctic domination as "quite remarkable." The general referred to a speech delivered by Putin when he said, "No doubt the Russians will focus more on the Arctic...NATO allies will have to address this issue." He went on to say, "The fact that new sea routes will be open increases the risk of more tension in the region. We should all be prepared to address that."

A group of retired U.S. generals and admirals stated in a 2014 report that the Pentagon has been caught off guard by how fast the ice is melting in the Arctic.

"Things are accelerating in the Arctic faster than we had looked at," said General Paul Kern, chairman of the Center for Naval Analyses (CNA) Corporation's military advisory board—the organization that created the report that cautions against security risks in the region. "The changes there appear to be much more radical than we envisaged."

The possibility that Arctic sea-lanes may be wide open within the next few decades has raised concerns about confrontations between Western countries and Russia and China. "As the Arctic becomes less of an ice-contaminated area it represents a lot of opportunities for Russia," said Kern. "We think things are accelerating in the Arctic faster than we had looked at seven years ago." This increases the potential to "spark conflict there."

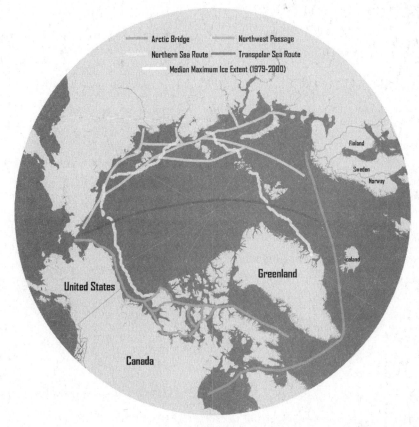

Arctic Bridge   Northwest Passage
Northern Sea Route   Transpolar Sea Route
Median Maximum Ice Extent (1979-2000)

Finland
Sweden
Norway
Iceland
Greenland
United States
Canada

Copyright © 1998–2015, Dr. Jean-Paul Rodrigue,
Dept. of Global Studies and Geography, Hofstra University, New York, USA

The United Nations' IPCC report also warns that as competition over Arctic resources escalates, so too could global conflict. The CNA report turns up the dial by upgrading Arctic risks from a "threat multiplier" to a "conflict catalyst." The former military leaders also point out the possibility of fighting in developing countries, motivated by a need to compete for water, food, and energy.

The report states: "In Africa, Asia, and the Middle East, we are already seeing how the impacts of extreme weather, such as prolonged drought and flooding—and resulting food shortages, desertification, population dislocation and mass migration, and sea level rise—are posing security challenges to these regions' governments. We see these trends growing and accelerating." The report further stated: "Populations will likely become disenfranchised and even more vulnerable to extremists and revolutionary influences."

One of the report's authors, Rear Adm. David Titley, former oceanographer of the navy, said, "For our national defense, we need to be making sure we are more resilient for the changes we have locked in. It is changing the battle space the Department of Defense operates in."

Leo Goff, a retired navy captain who also helped pen the report, commented that although Arctic energy exploration and shipping are on the rise, the U.S. military has done next to nothing to prepare for potential issues. "Right now there are plans and they don't have action behind them."

Several other officers who helped write the report agree that Arctic fights may be imminent. "As sea-pack ice goes away," said retired General Ronald Keys, former commander of the Air Combat Command, "and we have more navigable water, people will put down a marker and say, 'This belongs to us.'"

Several of the officers are worried that the Pentagon is not motivated to build new Arctic-capable ships or better train submariners to operate in the area, as verified by recent funding cuts for the navy's Arctic ICEX.

On May 6, 2014, Defense Secretary Chuck Hagel raised hairs on necks during a speech at the Chicago Council on Global Affairs. Speaking on the topic of the Arctic, he said, "We also must adjust our capabilities to meet new global realities, including environmental changes. Just today, the nation's top scientists released a national climate assessment that warns us in very stark terms that the effects of climate change are already becoming quite apparent.

"One area where we see this is the Arctic. The melting of gigantic ice caps presents possibilities for the opening of new sea-lanes and the exploration for natural resources, energy and commerce, also with the dangerous potential for conflict in the Arctic.

"The Defense Department is bolstering its engagement in the Arctic and looking at what capabilities we need to operate there in the future, as described in the DoD's first-ever Arctic strategy that I introduced at the Halifax International Security Forum last November."

Over 95% of Russia's natural gas and 60% of its oil reserves are in the Arctic. The Prirazlomnoye oil field in the Pechora Sea is expected to pump out 120,000 barrels of oil per day by 2020, and Gazprom, Russia's gas giant, sent its first oil-laden tanker from the area on May 1, 2014. Putin hailed the news as "the beginning of great and large-scale extraction of minerals and oil by our country in the Arctic." He also said that Russia's Arctic assertiveness would "positively influence Russia's future presence on the global energy markets and will strengthen both the whole economy and the energy sector."

On the other side of the icebergs, the Arctic covers 40% of Canada's land mass. Canadian regulators have scheduled hearings for late 2014 to discuss whether Imperial Oil should be allowed to dip their sticks into the Beaufort Sea and conduct seismic studies near Baffin Island. With environmentalists breathing down their necks, the Canadians increased their oil spill liability insurance by 300% to $1 billion in June 2012. Canadian Transportation Minister Lisa Raitt said that the precaution was necessary because "one oil spill or accident in the Arctic is going to be a visual you do not want."

Canadians have long expressed concerns over pollution, piracy, terrorism, and resource conflicts in the area, especially with the Northwest Passage—the Arctic sea route opposite the NSR—opening up to more traffic.

Typically peaceful Norway appears to share Canada's concerns over potential Arctic conflicts with Russia and other countries. Stephen Saideman, a professor at Carleton University in Ottawa and a leading expert on Canadian defense and foreign policy, met with Lieutenant General Morten Haga Lunde, who is in charge of Norway's military operational command headquarters. He also met with several Norwegian diplomats to discuss Russian Arctic aggression.

Saideman reported that the Norwegians are becoming more concerned about Putin's Artic strong-arming, especially against any nation that is perceived as a threat to Russia's Artic interests.

"Proximity breeds concern but not contempt," Saideman writes, referring to Norway's position on Arctic Russian advancements, especially in light of NATO's diminishing capabilities to defend common interests. "The Norwegians want NATO to look at ye olde plans and come up with some new ones, since the old ones were overcome by events in 1989–1991."

Reading between the lines, it's apparent that Norway wants NATO to be better prepared to fight a war against the Russians in the Arctic.

"The Norwegians would like to see more NATO activity up in the high north—more training, more doctrine, more exercises and the like—since it is a difficult 'battlespace,'" said Saideman.

China's Arctic endeavors are also a source of concern for Norway. In relation to China's mining and extraction deals with Iceland, Saideman said, "This would, of course, alarm anyone who read Tom Clancy's *Red Storm Rising*, since Iceland was pivotal to command of the North Atlantic."

Saideman concludes that the Norwegians "know how to punch above their weight."

When it comes to disputes with the Russians or Chinese over who owns what in the Arctic, they may have to. As evidence of their willingness to do so, Norway is spending billions on new *Aegis*-class cruisers, fifty-two American-built F-35 jet fighters, and modernization programs for six *Ula*-class submarines.

ARCTIC FISTFIGHTS

Several other Arctic Eight nations are also gearing up for fistfights in the Arctic. Canada's military has awarded a contractor $25 billion to build eight Arctic patrol ships, they've announced plans to buy armed Arctic drones, and they will soon replace four *Victoria*-class subs. Even peace-loving

Denmark is investing in new *Thetis*-class frigates, a special forces Sirius Arctic Patrol, and four diesel-electric submarines.

On March 18, 2014, former U.S. secretary of state Hillary Rodham Clinton, while warning about escalating tensions in Europe, spurred Canadian officials to form an alliance with the U.S. against Russia. In front of a packed house in Montreal, the potential next president of the United States slammed Vladimir Putin for his hostile moves against Ukraine, and warned Canadians that they might be next. She reminded the crowd that Russia has more coastline bordering Arctic waters than any other nation, and "they [the Russians] have been aggressively reopening military bases" in the area. She also reminded Canadians that Putin recently sent several Greenpeace activists to jail for peacefully protesting and frequently flies fighter jets over Canada and Alaska, thereby "testing our responses."

Clinton expressed concerns that increases in Arctic exploration, along with Canada's "huge coastline," could agitate the situation with Russia. In attendance were Premier Pauline Marois, the mayors of Quebec City and Montreal, and Federal Cabinet Ministers Denis Lebel and John Baird.

Clinton expressed concern about Russia's reopening of Cold War I-era military bases in the Arctic. "It's not only Ukraine and Georgia we're now keeping our eye on," she said. "It does threaten to militarize that pristine region that both Canada and the United States have interests in, to preserve the Arctic and help to develop it in a sensible manner."

Clinton summed up her address by stating, "There's a lot at stake here."

Many geopolitical experts concur with Clinton and also believe that it's not a matter of *whether* Arctic confrontations will occur, but *when*. These experts also predict that the world will soon reach a tipping point where uncontrolled leaps in population growth will make it impossible for countries to properly feed and house their masses without unparalleled increases in natural resources. There are simply too many mouths, too many cars, and too many stoves. Food, oil, gas, water, and other necessities will become scarce in many parts of the world, and governments may be forced to do whatever it takes to secure them. As an example, when pushed to the brink, what did Putin do to protect his Russian "family?"

When gas pipelines feeding Europe were threatened by Ukrainian government actions and plans, Putin ordered tens of thousands of troops to surround that country and eventually invade and annex the Crimea region. Certainly there is little doubt that he would defend Crimea with a great deal of firepower if the U.S. decided to send in troops to take back control. Imagine what he might be motivated to do should the U.S. or another country disagree with Russia's claims to the Peanut Hole or Lomonosov Ridge and send in drilling platforms to extract oil or gas in those territories? Or perhaps try to block Russian tankers from shipping gas by way of the NSR from the Arctic to the pipelines that feed European customers, or from the Peanut Hole to China by way of the Sea of Japan? Conversely, what if Putin decided to put up a blockade along the NSR to prevent the U.S. from bailing out Europe by shipping oil or gas from Alaska?

Some political experts are concerned that in the wake of recent events, any of the above or a dozen other scenarios could unfold in the Arctic. Recent comments made by Putin on March 28, 2014, while more than forty thousand troops readied for combat on the Ukrainian border, highlight the fact that Arctic domination is at the top of his priority list. While addressing senior officers in Moscow from the Defense Ministry, FSB, Interior Ministry, and Foreign Intelligence Service, Putin noted the importance of the Arctic in relation to the planned Vostok 2014 military exercises.

Said Putin, "This autumn, we will hold another strategic military exercise—Vostok 2014, which will give us the chance to put to the test the use of combined forces made up of personnel from different branches of the armed forces, and with forces from other security agencies taking part too. We also plan to continue developing our armed forces' different combat units, including in the Arctic region."

Later that same day, during a briefing session with permanent members of the Security Council, Putin discussed international agenda issues. Of particular interest was the topic of Russia's strategic position in the Arctic.

In late August 2014, NATO leaders called for emergency meetings after viewing evidence that Russian tanks and troops had crossed the border into Ukraine. The attack began with a massive Grad missile launch followed by artillery fire on targets in Donetsk. Russians ground troops then marched toward Veselo-Voznesenka, a border town in the Rostov Oblast region. Ukrainian border guards were quickly overrun before the Russians turned toward Novoazovsk with the assistance of pro-Russian insurgents.

Putin tried to turn the tables on public opinion by first denying the invasion, and then holding up a mirror by accusing Ukrainian forces of behaving like the Nazis in the brewing conflict. Russia's president accused Ukraine of being the villain by targeting civilians like the Germans did when they invaded Russia during World War II. He also claimed that Russians and Ukrainians "are practically one people" and referred to the disputed Ukrainian lands as Novorossiya, a tsarist name from a time when the region was ruled by Moscow.

A few sentences later, Putin verified that he has not taken his eye off the ball he's really trying to hit by saying, "Our interests are concentrated in the Arctic. And of course we should pay more attention to issues of development of the Arctic and the strengthening of our position."

As stated earlier, virtually all of the gas feeding Europe comes from the Arctic and travels through pipes inside or skirting Ukraine. For this reason, Russia has invested heavily over the past few years in Arctic infrastructure and military assets and will use them to protect their interests.

ARCTIC SUBMARINE BUILDUP

In July 2012, Putin attended a ceremony at Sevmash in Severodvinsk to celebrate the construction of the *Knyaz Vladimir*, the Russian Navy's fourth *Borei*-class ballistic missile submarine. Putin stepped to the podium and said, "By 2020 we will have eight submarines of the *Borei*-class. I am confident that the whole project will be implemented and that the *Knyaz Vladimir* and her sister vessels will be one of the symbols of the Russian Armed Forces."

The *Yuri Dolgoruky* was the first *Borei*-class sub, laid down in 1996. The second submarine of this class was completing sea trials in the Arctic even as the *Knyaz Vladimir* was starting construction at Russia's largest shipyard. During the *Knyaz Vladimir* ceremony, Putin chaired a state armaments program meeting where he said that Russia will reinforce its navy with fifty-one modern warships and twenty-four submarines. The investment for these new boy toys comes to more than $140 billion (U.S. dollars), which Putin said will be expended to realize the "potential of the sea-based nuclear force." He went on to say that Russia's navy has always been one of the main tools of "protecting national economic interests," which include a particular importance in such "resource-rich regions as the Arctic."

One month later, in August 2012, Russian Security Council Chief Nikolai Patrushev said that "authorities have drafted a list of key double-purpose sites in remote areas of the Arctic seas along the Northern Sea Route to enable the temporary stationing of Russian Navy warships and vessels operated by the Federal Security Service's Border Guard Department."

Putin's *Borei*-class missile subs were recently based on the Kola Peninsula at the Gadzhiyevo Naval Base. He also plans to position quite a few more attack submarines, now under construction, in Barents Sea ports near Norway. The nuclear-powered cruiser *Pyotr Veliky* has been patrolling along the NSR on a regular basis, and Russia's long-range bombers frequently buzz over the area to test responses from Norway by entering into that country's airspace.

As Russian forces amassed around Ukraine in March 2014, a substantial contingent also conducted the largest airdrop exercise since the Soviet era by dropping 350 paratroopers onto the New Siberia Islands. The soldiers donned special seven-layer suits and were graduates of an intense Arctic survival training program, similar to the one that members of SEAL Team Two—the only U.S. Naval Special Warfare Command team trained for Arctic operations—also endure.

On June 16, 2014, Alaska's Lt. Governor Mead Treadwell spoke at the 34th Annual U.S.-Russia Forum in Washington, D.C. Treadwell followed Sergey Kislyak, Russia's ambassador to the U.S. Treadwell stressed the need for cooperation with Russia, regardless of the unresolved issues brewing in Ukraine.

"My challenge to Russians is this: where we are neighbors, help bring our relations back to normal. Help us eliminate salmon by-catch in the North Pacific Ocean. Help us work together to prevent oil spills from all these ships coming through, and help us protect food security in the Arctic. Alaskans depend on this ocean for food and for jobs.

"My challenge to Americans is this: don't let Russia go it alone in the Arctic. A quarter of the world's oil and gas and one of the world's most important fisheries are located in the Arctic. Let's exercise leadership now, by developing our own energy and building ports and icebreakers, and not let just one country control shipping.

"In today's tough international climate, we can't forget we're neighbors," Treadwell added. "The Arctic situation demands cooperation and friendly competition. If we don't exercise stronger Arctic leadership, we will be sorry later."

Treadwell referenced a speech made by Russian President Vladimir Putin to his Security Council on April 22, 2014, wherein Putin called for an even stronger Russian military presence in the Arctic. The Russian president also predicted that Arctic shipping would expand from 1.5 million tons in 2013 to four million tons in 2015. In his speech, Putin strongly maintained that all ships crossing the NSR should be under Russian control.

Said Treadwell, "Russian control of Arctic shipping is likely to produce more of the same kind of disputes we've had in the Caspian region. To prevent that, U.S. icebreakers, U.S. Arctic ports, and a stronger U.S. Coast Guard presence will offer the world alternatives, healthy competition, instead of a monopoly."

In August 2014, a United States Naval Institute (USNI) news article outlined how confrontations between Russian and NATO submarines in the Arctic are on the rise as relations are spiraling downward over locked horns in Europe. The Russian media reported two skirmishes between their ASW forces and U.S. and Japanese submarines; apparent flashbacks to Cold War I bump-and-runs. They claimed that on August 7, Russian surface ships and an *Ilyushin Il*-38 patrol aircraft clashed with a U.S. *Virginia*-class attack submarine and vigorously chased it out of the Barents Sea. Some experts speculated that the fourteenth anniversary of the sinking of the Russian submarine *Kursk*, supposedly caused by the USS *Toledo* or USS *Memphis*, may have exacerbated the zeal displayed by Russian ASW forces.

Media outlet Russia Today, when reporting on the incident, fanned the flames by stating: "Such actions by the NATO undersea fleet have led to a number of navigation incidents in the Arctic." They continued with: "A collision with [the] U.S. nuclear submarine, *Toledo*, was one [of] the main explanations of the *Kursk* submarine tragedy in 2000."

The U.S. Navy denied any wrongdoing regarding the *Kursk*.

The Japanese navy helped shift the spotlight off the U.S. by claiming that Russian forces had perpetrated an incident in the La Perouse Strait, known to Japan as the Soya Strait. Apparently, a Japanese *Oyashio*-class diesel attack submarine had been harassed by the Russian Navy in the narrow passage between the northernmost Japanese island of Hokkaido and the Russian island of Sakhalin.

The La Perouse Strait has been an important defensive bastion for Japan since the early days of Cold War I. Back then, Japan was worried about the threat of a Soviet invasion of Hokkaido, launched from Sakhalin. Japanese submarines have taken to guarding the straight with their submarines ever since.

The Russians denied any wrongdoing by saying: "The Japanese submarine detected in the La Perouse Strait on Wednesday did not violate international law and did not cross the Russian state border." Meanwhile, Russian land forces conducted war games on the nearby southern Kuril Islands by amassing one thousand ground troops, five armed transport helicopters, and one hundred military vehicles. The southern Kurils contain four islands that were grabbed from Japan by the Soviet Union in the final days of World War II. Japan still claims ownership, and has tried to convince Russia to return the islands for decades, but their pleas have been ignored. Japanese authorities complained about the harassment of their submarine, and about the Russian exercises on the island, calling them "totally unacceptable."

Naval experts like Rear Adm. Kamensky fear that with the Bear once again flexing its muscles and flashing its fangs, the world might soon become embroiled in more than just a cold war. Despite assurances offered by well-wishing leaders that such an event won't happen, those of us who battled against the Russians in Cold War I never truly believed that the conflict came to end. Instead, we've always known that the cancer between by the U.S. and Russia simply went into remission for a few decades. Obviously it has flared up again and is perhaps even more malignant than ever. Those of us who survived near-death encounters with the Russians in Cold War I or II still struggle with nightmares to this day, and we pray our sons and daughters will not have to continue the war that we fought decades ago. If so, perhaps some of the events that occurred during Cold War I, and the lessons we learned back then, can help us understand what we may soon be up against, and what's needed to avoid defeat.

OWN THE ARCTIC, OWN THE WORLD

The country that maintains the most control over world's currency, and therefore the lion's share of international commerce, is at the top of the power mountain. Its leaders can collects fees when funds trade hands, have a strong say in trade terms and agreements, and shift the price of commodities up or down on a whim.

The United Kingdom once enjoyed this powerful position, but lost it after taking a beating in World War II. The U.S. picked up the ball and has led the pack ever since. Why is Putin highly motivated to steal the "economic crown" from the U.S.? Because the U.S. defeated Russia in Cold War I, and no other country poses a greater threat. The more the U.S. can be weakened economically, the more secure and safe Putin will feel.

When Putin signed a new military doctrine on December 26, 2014, NATO leaders raised two eyebrows. Some journalists cited this as a potential prelude to World War III. The doctrine reflected the Kremlin's concerns over perceived NATO aggression in the wake of fighting in Ukraine, and what they believe are U.S.-instigated efforts to pull the economic rug out from under Russia.

The doctrine stipulates that Russia can launch nuclear weapons against any country that "threatens the very existence" of Russia by using nuclear or other weapons of mass destruction against the country or its allies. For the first time, however, the doctrine authorizes the use of precision weapons "as part of strategic deterrent measures." These could include submarine-launched cruise missiles or guided bombs.

The doctrine cites NATO as the number one military threat to Russia in stating primary areas of concern, including: "a build-up of NATO military potential and its empowerment with global functions implemented in violation of international law, [and] the expansion of NATO's military infrastructure to the Russian borders."

NATO spokeswoman Oana Lungescu hurled a snowball back at Russia in saying that NATO posed no threat, and "in fact, it is Russia's actions, including currently in Ukraine, which are breaking international law and undermining European security."

Cleary Russia is poised for a fight, especially in the Arctic, and is setting the stage to use its large arsenal of weapons to bloody someone's nose.

NATO officials are likewise poised for imminent battles, with most officials expressing concerns that Russia is even more unpredictable now than during Cold War I. In early 2015, Adam Thomson, Britain's permanent resident to NATO, said: "NATO is strengthening its military posture in response, in particular, to the challenge that Russia's behavior represents."

ECONOMIC ARMAGEDDON

Lord Sauron's grand plan involves using his one Ring of Power—the profits derived from his energy exports—to subvert the petrodollar and knock the U.S. off its pedestal. The commodities that allow him to do this are oil and gas, and the greatest abundance of both can be found in the Arctic.

The U.S. has been in the economic driver's seat for decades, but now that lofty position is at risk. After Russia invaded Ukraine, and Obama levied a few sanctions, Putin countered by threatening to dump all U.S. treasuries. Veteran investor Jim Sinclair warned that if Russia started to accept payment for oil and gas in any currency other than the U.S. dollar, the petrodollar system could collapse. Why is this proposition so frightening?

President Nixon shifted the U.S. off of the gold standard on August 15, 1971. Nixon's actions turned George Washington's face into the symbol of the world's reserve currency. Saudi Arabia got on board and agreed that all oil and gas trades would be priced in U.S. greenbacks, and the rest of the world had little choice but to follow suit.

The good news? Dollars were no longer tied to gold. The bad? They were no longer tied to anything so the U.S. and most other governments could create money out of thin air. They just printed it. Money really did grow on trees, or at least came from them. Inflation ran rampant and the purchasing power of the dollar plunged. In fact, it has declined almost 80% since the early seventies.

To address this problem, Nixon invented the petrodollar. Instead of gold, black backed the green. Nixon flew Henry Kissinger to Saudi Arabia where the secretary of state cut a deal with the ruling House of Saud. The U.S. swore to protect the Saudi oil fields with military might, and even sell Saudi Arabia some weapons along the way. Old ones, of course. Protection from Israel and Iran was assured. In exchange, Kissinger asked for two things: One, all oil sales would be made exclusively using U.S. dollars. Two, oil profits made by the Saudis would be invested in U.S. Treasuries.

At the time, Saudi Arabia was a proverbial dichotomy. Most of the country was dirt-poor, infrastructure was dismal, its neighbors wanted to do them harm, and capitalizing on all that black gold required substantial investment. To the Saudis, the U.S. offer seemed like a nice deal. They signed up in 1974 and a year later the rest of OPEC tagged along.

Decades of oil prosperity followed and kept the U.S. at the top of the economic ladder. When the Soviet Union bit the dust in 1991, the resurrection of Russia came at a snail's pace. Then Putin entered stage right. He immediately saw the potential for his country to dominate the world's energy market. Thanks to his vision and leadership, oil and gas now account for 68% of Russia's exports. The Russians own almost 20% of the world's gas sales and around 12% of the oil market.

Putin's main competitors include the U.S. and the Middle East's three largest oil producers: Iraq, Iran, and Saudi Arabia. As mentioned earlier, Putin wants to stir up trouble in that region. The more unstable these countries are the better. Customers prefer to buy from a reliable source and conflict makes it harder for governments to invest in infrastructure and focus on production. Unfortunately, the past two U.S. presidents have ignored this obvious fact and played right into Putin's hands.

President Bush forced the invasion of Iraq. No doubt Vice President Dick Cheney convinced him that the U.S. could quickly and easily march in and take control of all those oil fields. That didn't happen and probably never will.

Then Obama entered the scene. He pulled all U.S. troops out of Iraq to garner votes and left the door open for ISIS terrorists to roam the land. He also found a multitude of ways to anger the Saudis. They had counted on the

U.S. to be a strategic partner after all these decades of sharing a bed, and were dismayed when Obama turned passive during the Egyptian protests in 2011. Then Mr. President pulled the rug on military aid to General Sisi, who needed U.S. help to battle the Muslim Brotherhood.

The ultimate betrayal, of course, was when Obama did an about-face on his promise to use force against Assad after the dictator launched chemical weapons on civilians in Syria. The Saudis also believe Obama was instrumental in gutting Iran's sanctions and essentially giving them carte blanche to build a nuclear weapon.

The Saudis have often complained that Obama's administration is clueless about Middle Eastern politics, and U.S. actions of late have been lamentable. Prince Turki went so far as to say: "The current charade of international control over Bashar's chemical arsenal would be funny if it were not so blatantly perfidious, and designed not only to give Mr. Obama an opportunity to back down [from military strikes], but also to help Assad to butcher his people."

Nixon courted the Saudis heavily and convinced them to back the petro-dollar. For over four decades that brilliant move has kept the U.S. on a GDP upswing and allowed its presidents to dictate quite a bit of world policy. Within the last decade, two presidents have managed to nearly unravel one of the most important relationships the U.S. has.

Most of Saudi Arabia's $750 billion in foreign exchange reserves is currently in U.S. dollars. How long will it remain that way? A member of the Saudi royal family was quoted as saying, "All options are on the table now, and for sure there will be some impact." If the Obama administration continues to disrespect and anger the Saudis, will Putin be successful at bending their ear? When he begins trading in rubles on his $400 billion gas deal with the Chinese in 2018, will that convince the Saudis to switch some of their $750 billion over to rubles?

When the price of oil dropped from $112 per barrel in June 2014 to $65 per barrel by late December, media analysts were quick to single out King

Abdullah bin Abdulaziz of Saudi Arabia as the mastermind behind the plot. They surmised that Abdulaziz's motivations were strictly to hurt three primary competitors for various different reasons: One, the U.S. because of its newfound fracking success. Two, Iran because of its nuclear ambitions and support of Syria's Bashar al-Assad. Three, Russia for its support of Bashar al-Assad. All of these assumptions are correct, but they only scratch the surface.

As we've discussed, the petrodollar remains in place to the extent that Saudi Arabia continues to sponsor it. The Saudis know that cutting oil prices in half will hurt his competitors, but it will also hurt all twelve-member countries of OPEC. Most OPEC countries need prices to be around $100 per barrel to balance their budgets. Not all of them have reserves as large as Saudi Arabia. Venezuela, a founding member of OPEC, is already on the ropes and further destabilizing by the minute. "There are parts of Venezuela where the state is already failed," said Adam Isacson, a senior associate at the Washington Office on Latin America. He said the situation there is so bad that "complete lawlessness" has occurred along the Venezuelan border and in "Caracas slums where you've had shootouts between pro-Chavez militias and police."

GEN-X SAUDIS

For now, lower gas prices feel good in the U.S., but this could soon turn into an economic quagmire. Experts have shown that the energy sector has accounted for most of the economic growth in the U.S. over the past several years, but due to Saudi oil price manipulations, tens of thousands are being laid off by large energy firms. If this continues, a terrifying scenario will transpire.

King Abdullah helped create the recent worldwide oil glut, but he died in January 2015. Salman bin Abdulaziz, Abdullah's half-brother, has taken control, which is a cause for concern. Salman is seventy-nine years old and has dementia. His reign will likely be brief. In line for the throne are the four sons of Abdullah, and none of them like President Obama or Hillary Clinton due to what they perceive as "lamentable" Middle Eastern policies implemented by both.

Not long after King Salman took over for his deceased brother, he appointed his assertive thirty-four-year-old son, Mohammad bin Salman, as defense minister and chief of the royal court. The younger Salman made sweeping changes to "middle management" bureaucracy within the ranks of the Saudi government. He canned senior princes, abolished a dozen unproductive committees, and created two new super-councils to oversee political and security affairs. Many of the newly appointed leaders are known to have Western leanings.

"I believe that this is the most important decision in the history of the Saudi state at its current stage," said Salman Aldossary, the editor of London-based Arabic newspaper *Asharq al-Awsat*.

In the short term, young Salman's changes appear to have benefitted the U.S. In the long run, especially after King Salman is removed from power, having younger minds in control could prove detrimental to the West. This is especially true if the current and future U.S. president and secretary of state continue to rub the Saudis the wrong way. You can only jab your friend in the eye so many times before he walks away and wants nothing more to do with you. That's when the bully on the playground takes your former friend under his wing and makes him a "best buddy." Then the bully gets your former friend to make your life a living hell.

Putin is likely hoping that such a scenario will occur in the near future, and is continuing to stir up conflict in the Middle East to keep such a possibility alive. If the U.S. remains "light gloved" toward Iran, which allows the mullahs to threaten the entire region, the next Gen-X king of Saudi Arabia may have no choice but to call the devil for help, and Lord Sauron will be happy to assist.

Measured on a "peace and harmony" scale, Obama's Middle Eastern policies have so far failed the litmus test. Since these policies were instituted, including the years Hillary Clinton was secretary of state, the Islamic State (ISIS) has doubled its foothold in Syria and Iraq. Jordan stepped into the fight after ISIS publicly executed one of its pilots, but they alone have little chance of victory against the Islamic State.

Unfortunately, unless the U.S. is willing to put boots on the ground, which the Obama administration will never do, Turkey is the only state large enough to take on ISIS. The Turks wanted Obama to punish Assad in Syria for using chemical weapons, but when the U.S. folded its hand, Turkey turned its back on the ISIS fight. For similar reasons, Saudi Arabia and other Arab countries also bowed out of the fight.

It appears that Obama may be more concerned with appeasing the Iranians than stopping ISIS or Putin, or keeping the Saudis from wrecking the U.S. economy. Perhaps there's a grand strategy to Obama's plan yet to be revealed, but until then, most geopolitical experts are labeling his actions as a "blind pursuit of détente with Tehran" that could destabilize the entire region.

Because of the continued loosening of economic sanctions by Obama, Iran may soon have a nuclear weapon. Perhaps several of them. No longer economically constrained, Iran has secured conventional domination over much of the Middle East. Formerly pro-American Arabs are worried and beginning to defect. After the fall of the Yemeni government, Iranian-backed Houthi rebels seized control. Despite Yemeni being mostly Sunni, the Houthi are puppets and the strings are dangled by Shiite Iranians. Their war cry is: "God is great! Death to America! Death to Israel!"

Without Yemen as a base, the U.S. drone war against al-Qaeda in the Arabian Peninsula will soon vanish. Syria is in even worse shape. Mullahs have come to Bashar al-Assad's aid with funds, weapons, and Iranian revolutionary guards. They have also convinced their Lebanese proxy, Hezbollah, to take up arms. In short, now flush with billions due to the removal of sanctions, Tehran has successfully exerted enough control in the region to further its war against Israel.

Meanwhile, Saudi Arabia is caught in the middle. To their west and north, Iran is bent on Shiite domination across Iraq, Syria, and Lebanon. To the east and south, Iran is in control of Yemen. How do the Saudis respond? The only way they can: by creating another oil glut. They know that Iran needs prices to be around $135 per barrel to stay within budget. Nuclear weapons aren't cheap.

Saudi Arabia is one of the most important countries in the world. In one afternoon, with the wave of a king's hand, they can control and manipulate large swaths of the world's economy. They can take entire countries to the brink of bankruptcy simply by pumping out enough oil to exceed demand.

Despite this sobering fact, the Obama administration has repeatedly ignored and even angered the Saudi regime. During her time as secretary of state, Hillary Clinton visited Saudi Arabia to discuss oil prices, but otherwise acquiesced to Obama's policies—most of which angered the Saudis.

If Clinton is elected president, will she repair relations with Saudi Arabia's new regime, or allow Putin to leverage the Saudi's discord with her to convince them to stop backing the petrodollar? If the latter occurs, the U.S. economic system will unravel almost overnight. Banks will fail, stocks will crash, home values will plunge, jobs will disappear, and millions of Americans will be left homeless and starving. Impossible? Not according to a vast number of geopolitical and economic experts.

THE PETRODOLLAR WAR

Recall that Saudi Arabia, at the behest of Nixon, agreed to stash large chunks of its oil profits in foreign reserves—primarily in the U.S., and they are backed by the U.S. dollar. We're talking about three-quarters of a trillion U.S. dollars. No doubt someone in Washington leveraged this fact to convince Abdulaziz, when he was alive, to temporarily create an oil glut to punish Putin for Ukraine. The Saudis voiced no objections as the glut also made it harder for Iran to move forward on its nuclear weapons program.

In October 2014, Venezuelan President Nicolas Maduro said, "What is the reason for the United States and some U.S. allies wanting to drive down the price of oil? To harm Russia."

The oil strategy employed by the U.S. and OPEC had a dramatic effect on Russia. When the price of oil tanked, one of Russia's primary sources of income fell off a cliff. When coupled with the economic sanctions against Russia, things got bad and investors dumped rubles and sent the Russian economy into a tailspin.

Moscow yanked the stick upward to pull out of the nosedive, but the ruble still plunged more than 25%, down to a new low of eighty per U.S. dollar by December 2014. It finally leveled out at around seventy-two, but earlier on that same day it had traded at fifty-eight. In response, Russia's central bank raised rates to 17%, the largest single day increase since the 1998 recession.

Inflation surged in Russia to a troubling 10% while the ruble plummeted by almost half during the latter six months of 2014. Elvira Nabiullina, Russia's Central Bank governor, pointed to declining oil prices—purposefully depressed by the U.S. and OPEC—as the primary culprit. Russia relies on oil revenue to fund more than half its state spending, and like most OPEC countries, needs oil prices to hover at around $100 per barrel to maintain a stable budget. If oil stays at below $60 per barrel for more than a few quarters, Russia's economy could begin to crumble.

OPEC Secretary General Abdalla Salem El-Badri said in December 2014 that the group could handle the price slump and would not decrease production. Oil Minister of the United Arab Emirates, Suhail bin Mohammed al-Mazroui, concurred by saying he believed there was no need to hold an emergency cartel meeting to discuss a price increase.

Furious, Putin wagged a finger at the U.S. while informing the world that Russia had plenty of reserves and could weather any storm, and warned of retribution if the screws were turned any tighter. He also reminded everyone that oil is not Russia's only resource, and they control a third of Europe's gas supply.

"Our economy will overcome the current situation. How much time will be needed for that? Under the most unfavorable circumstances I think it will take about two years," Putin said at a press conference on December 18, 2014. He used the occasion to throw spears at the West. Had Russia not annexed Crimea earlier that year, he lamented, the West would have found other reasons to target Russia, which he metaphorically described as "the bear."

"Sometimes I wonder, maybe the bear should just sit quietly, munch on berries and honey rather than chasing after piglets, maybe then, they would leave it alone? But no, they wouldn't, because they will always try to chain it up. And as soon as they chain it up, they will pull out its teeth and claws." By teeth and claws, Putin meant Russia's military might and ability to defend its claims to natural resources—especially those in the Arctic. The question must be asked: What might Lord Sauron do with the bear's teeth and claws if backed into an economic corner by the Western Elves? More importantly, what will he do if the U.S. and E.U. continue to push Ukraine toward a NATO alliance?

On December 23, 2014, the Ukraine Parliament, controlled by a pro-Western majority, voted 303 to 8 to cease the country's nonalignment policy and take a step toward the West. The odds are still against Ukraine actually joining NATO due to Russian opposition, but it appears the race is on. What if the opposition was diminished by a Russian economic crisis that lasted just long enough to woo Ukraine's Parliament? If the U.S. and E.U. are successful, they can win control over five of Putin's pipes and place troops and missiles on Russia's doorstep. This would be paramount to the Soviets installing nuclear missiles in Cuba. Are we headed toward a Ukrainian missile crisis? Perhaps, but it's more likely that Ukraine will stay neutral, which is at least a partial win for the West.

Some pundits are applauding the grand move made by the U.S. and the Saudis to gut Russia's ruble, but what hurts Putin will also eventually hurt the U.S. and Middle East. Saudi Arabia is ranked number three in the world for foreign exchange reserves, but other OPEC countries, like Venezuela, are not so rich. Russia is number four with almost $550 billion and the U.S. is number eighteen with less than $150 billion, so Russia can hold their breath almost four times longer. Eventually, the U.S. will have to "cry uncle" and convince OPEC to raise prices.

Recall that nearly all of the U.S. GDP growth is coming from the energy sector. Even though lower oil prices will have an economic benefit as transportation costs decline and bring down the price of staples and other items, it's only temporary. A glance at the financial section of the *Wall Street Journal* verifies a subsequent decline in energy sector profits and hence jobs and investments and eventually GDP.

In early 2015, a host of oil giants, including Baker Hughes, Halliburton, and Schlumberger, announced plans to lay off a combined total of seventeen thousand people. Dozens of other energy companies have taken massive stock hits and are poised to also trim their troops.

The U.S. can't allow Saudi Arabia to keep depressing oil prices forever and Saudi Arabia can't afford to push the entire world into an economic crisis or allow the eleven other OPEC members to starve. It's like the grocer who sells bread at a loss to lure away customers from a competitor but eventually has to end the "loss leader" before the red ink bleeds him to death. Despite the fact that the U.S. is now a quasi-competitor, Saudi Arabia will comply because oil represents 90% of their income and government sources estimate Saudi holdings in the U.S. exceed $500 billion. In this case, the fox can't afford to eat the hen.

Sooner rather than later, the Saudis will tire of being disrespected by Obama and forced to sacrifice profits just to let the U.S. remain in the economic driver's seat. Sooner rather than later, master-chess-player Putin will find a way to leverage his gas sales, which are impervious to OPEC meddling, to bolster Russia's GDP. Sooner rather than later, the Saudis may abandon their sponsorship of the U.S. dollar and open the door for Putin to move the world over to the petroruble. When that day comes, it will come with much wailing and gnashing of teeth from Wall Street to London.

The U.S. may have won the first Cold War, and maintained a draw in the second, and may win the first battle in the dollar against the ruble, but it's highly probable that Russia and China could eventually win Cold War III. In doing so, they could become the top dogs on planet Earth, and a large majority of U.S. and European citizens could be licking their boots for decades to come.

THE ECONOMIC TORNADO

Is there another perfect storm brewing? Is the convergence of unrest in the Middle East, Putin's meddling in Syria, Iran's nuclear ambitions, and Obama's failures in the Middle East about to go Chernobyl? When we throw in the massive debt the Obama administration has amassed since 2009, do we have the makings of an economic tornado? Do all these factors set up Putin as the orchestrator of a change from the petrodollar as the he world's economic standard to the petroruble? If so, there is one key ingredient that needs bolstering.

Everyone knows Russia's current petro supplies are dwindling and the ruble is not stable. Convincing leaders and financial institutions to make a massive shift requires collateral and trust. Gold is good, which is why Putin is gobbling up tons of it, but energy is what makes the world go around in today's economy. Putin must demonstrate that he has long-term sufficient supplies of oil and gas, along with a robust infrastructure to extract and deliver it, to prove that Russia has plenty of "energy collateral." He needs to increase his gas profits—which he will do with the China and Japan deals—and lower Russia's reliance on oil profits. He also needs to help shift Saudi Arabia's loyalties away from the U.S. and at least get them to stop gutting oil prices. Only then can he move the world toward a petroruble standard.

Lord Sauron needs his three rings: the Lomonosov Ridge, the Peanut Hole, and the NSR. The first two all but guarantee trillions of tons of oil and gas, and the latter ensures he has control of the real estate needed to extract and ship his spoils while charging others for the same privilege. Once these rings are firmly in place, perhaps as early as 2018, he can energize his One Ring and use it to pull the petro rug on the U.S. dollar, and the loss of the petrodollar standard may one day prove to be far more devastating to human life in the U.S. than any terrorist act extent.

Should that tragedy come to pass, the U.S. economy will tank, perhaps even overnight. Russia and China are obviously working toward this end. In late 2010, Putin and Chinese Premier Wen Jiabao agreed to settle trades in rubles and renminbi (yuan) for many of their transactions. "China will firmly follow the path of peaceful development and support the renaissance of Russia as a great power," Wen Jiabao said. This agreement, the first of its kind, is a direct assault on the petrodollar and on the U.S. as the world's economic leader.

Emboldened by Putin's brash move to dump the dollar, China convinced Japan to begin dealing in yuan in 2012. The two countries don't even like each other. This marked the first time in over forty years that China swapped yuan for anything other than U.S. dollars. The Bank of Japan bought 65 billion yuan ($10 billion). It's a small amount in the grand scheme of things, but definitely a shot heard around the world.

That shot was followed by a cannon boom in September 2013 when China said it would begin accepting yuan instead of the U.S. dollar to buy or sell crude oil.

Other countries, especially those upset with the U.S. for a host of reasons, may look to Russia and China for inspiration to wiggle free from their dependence on the dollar. The U.S.-led sanctions against Russia for invading Ukraine may wind up pouring fuel on this fire. Fuming over the sanctions, Putin instructed the Russian Central Bank to implement Project Double Eagle in March 2014. Now, all energy trade partners can deal in gold instead of U.S. dollars. Russia has been stockpiling gold reserves, and is convincing other countries who are tied to the petrodollar to commit mutiny.

"Some hotheaded decision makers have already forgotten that the global economic crisis of 2008, which is still taking its toll on the world, started with a collapse of certain credit institutions in the United States, Great Britain, and other countries," said Valentina Matviyenko, the speaker of Russia's upper parliament house. "This is why we believe that any hostile financial actions [toward Russia] are a double-edged sword and even the slightest error will send the boomerang back to the aborigines."

Definitely fighting words.

THE COSTLY CONSEQUENCES

What happens to the U.S. when Putin shifts the world to the petrodollar? The best case scenario is a slow fade into oblivion, but Putin will probably push for a more rapid unwinding, in which case the breakup will happen within a few short years. In the worst (and most likely) scenario, interest rates will skyrocket. The rate on the thirty-year Treasury bond could once again hit 15%, which is where it was in the 1970s. Existing bond prices could be chopped by more than half.

The Federal Reserve will have little choice but to cut down more trees and print more worthless dollars to buy the bonds sold by foreigners, but the eventual effect will be a further devaluation of the dollar. If we thought the U.S. bank meltdown in 2008 was bad, we'll long for those days again when interest rates cause a huge gap between prior loan rates and current loan rates so wide that it pushes a large number of banks toward insolvency.

The Fed will print even more money. Interest rates will climb higher, maybe up to 20%. Main Street America and small businesses will pay through the nose for loans to stay afloat, if they're lucky enough to get an approval. Then the dominoes in financial markets will topple. Banks, hedge funds, stock brokerages, insurance companies, and others will see their derivative investments unravel. Simply put, all these institutions have investment values based on other investments that derive their value from various assets. As those assets, such as real estate for example, rapidly lose their value, everything "on top" will lose its value. Remember when gas prices went through the roof? If you owned a gas-guzzling car, you couldn't sell it to your brother for more than a few bucks. That's what will happen to the assets owned by these firms.

When that occurs, the fallout will cause massive panic attacks and perhaps even suicides. Stockbrokers may once again jump from buildings like they did in 1932. At that point, President Hillary Clinton—or whoever is unlucky enough to get elected—will be forced to require the U.S. to default on its foreign debt. That means countries like China will stop getting interest payments. When the Chinese start blockading sea-lanes with their new and formidable warships to force the U.S. to pay, things will get ugly fast.

At that point, Hillary's advisors will "suggest" that it's time for a measure of last resort: the U.S. government must raid the savings accounts of almost every American. I say almost because we know that congresspersons, senators, union bosses, and campaign donors will remain untouched. Those registered with the political party opposed to the president will probably be first in line. If we think this is impossible because it's illegal, we have a short memory span. Recall that the IRS went after conservatives with unbridled passion prior to the 2012 election. Your IRA, 401K, or whatever you have will be cleaned out to pay for your government's inability to win an economic war, and it won't be their fault. It will be *your* fault. After all, you elected the president and legislators. If you failed to consider whether the persons you elected could compete against the likes of Putin, you have only yourself to blame.

You might be hopeful that your favorite political candidate will tip the scales in your favor for immigration reform, the environment, gay rights, education, medical insurance, retirement benefits, gun control, social security, or whatever you're passionate about. All of these issues are important and worthy of attention, but pale in comparison to the most important concern: the global economic war. If the next president and his or her team are clueless about global business and foreign affairs, or are too weak to stand strong against Putin and other world leaders, they will be eaten for lunch and the U.S. and European economies will pay the price.

To fund popular entitlements and pet projects demanded by campaign contributors, the U.S. government borrows almost half of what it spends. That's like you and I having to use credit cards to pay for half of everything we buy on a monthly basis just because we don't have the guts to force all the people living off of us to move out and get jobs.

When the above proverbial stuff hits the fan after Putin destroys the petrodollar, middle-class America will be in shock. A trip to Costco today is enjoyable for most of us, but within a few years, it could become a nightmare. Commodities like milk, eggs, flour, hamburger, fruit, vegetables, snacks, and even coffee will become luxury items. Starbucks and Taco Bell and McDonald's will see massive layoffs as people stay home and reuse coffee grounds and eat the cheapest noodles they can find. Pink slips and foreclosure notices will be commonplace.

© Olivierl | Dreamstime.com - Real Estate Foreclosure Notice and House Key Photo

The hardest hit will be the ones who have incomes tied to unions and the government. Instead of negotiating affordable salaries and retirement packages, most union bosses have twisted the arms of politicians to allow for unsustainable benefit packages. Government employees, teachers, auto workers, electricians, and scores of others will be laid off and forced into soup kitchens as organizations and whole cities file for bankruptcy. Blue-collar workers will be on the street first, but even bellwether technology companies will start axing engineers as their customers freeze spending. Then the riots and looting will start.

People living in gated communities will soon realize that gates are worthless against starving mobs with guns. Martial law will be enforced, with the National Guard patrolling neighborhoods in trucks and even tanks. As the U.S. continues to default on its loans to foreign nations, those countries will retaliate with sanctions, blockades, and eventually even shots fired. The two nations most likely to start shooting to force payments are China and Russia. They have already become economically connected at the hip, and will be motivated to assist each other in the collection of debts. After all, if China can't pay Russia for $400 billion in gas because the U.S. isn't paying China, how motivated will Putin be to fire warning shots across the bow of American tankers?

Perhaps the above scenario seems improbable or even impossible to most of us. How could our respective governments allow such a thing to happen? How could it possibly get that bad? It can't, right?

That's what they said in 1932.

As we've read in the last several chapters, "they" are already allowing it to happen by making bad chess moves. Again, it is not up to "them" to avoid a future filled with poverty, it is up to us. If we continue to elect leaders who do not know how to lead, and who do not have the strength, business acumen, chess-playing skills, and courage to stand up to Putin and his ilk, we will sow what we reap. And what we reap will be an economic war followed by a fighting war—most likely over Arctic resources—that may leave the U.S. and its European allies devastated and defeated unless immediate actions are taken to avoid the inevitable.

CHAPTER ELEVEN

Cold War I

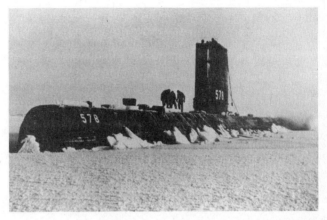

USS Skate (SSN-578) surfaced at North Pole.

Photo courtesy U.S. Navy

Should world events drive us toward a shooting war or even small skirmishes in the Arctic, who will fight these battles? As we have learned, icebreakers are in short supply and are not well armed. There are few ice-hardened warships that can operate in all areas in the High North, and they obviously can't hide under the ice. That leaves submarines and other submersibles as the front-line defenders of U.S. and NATO interests, and they may soon be pitted against formidable assets from Russia and China. How will they fare?

United States and NATO forces have been learning how to fight against enemies in the Arctic since World War II. While battling Germany, U.S. submariners noted that Arctic conditions prevented their sonar systems from working normally under the ice. This made it nearly impossible to detect German U-boats operating in the Gulf of Saint Lawrence.

To solve this problem, the U.S. Navy enlisted Dr. Waldo K. Lyon to lend his expertise in underwater and Arctic sciences to the Navy Radio and Sound Lab in 1941. Lyon and his team dove into the task and designed new sonar systems for Arctic operations. They eventually tested the equipment aboard the USS *Boarfish* (SS-327) while coordinating the boat's under-ice dives. Excellent initial results led to an initiative destined to impact the navy's ability to dominate underwater polar warfare.

After World War II, Lyon recalled: "When Admiral Byrd took the expedition to Antarctica, I got a letter asking if there was any research I wanted to do in conjunction with the expedition. I said yes, try a submarine in the cold water down there." That recommendation eventually led to the creation of the Arctic Submarine Lab (ASL), which was first housed in a converted World War II mortar emplacement at Battery Whistler in San Diego, California. Lyon became head of the Submarine Studies Branch in 1947, and helped create a special pool at Battery Whistler to test equipment for deep submergence vehicles, such as the bathyscaphe *Trieste*. Lyon's team equipped the pool to grow its own sea ice so they could study the physical properties of a frigid environment, but they soon reached a knowledge barrier, overcome only by sending men into harm's way.

In the fall of 1947, nineteen-year-old Harry Hall knew something wasn't quite right aboard the diesel submarine USS *Queenfish* (SS-393). Having just completed an overhaul in Pearl Harbor, Hawaii, rumors started spreading. Hall's buddy, engineman Joe Prince, whispered that he'd seen the sub's CO, Commander Ralph Lockwood, stride across the brow after returning from a briefing with the mucky-mucks at Command Submarine Force U.S. Pacific Fleet (COMSUBPAC). Prince said the CO had a worried look on his face. Hours later, Hall and Prince were heaving lines onto the pier. The *Queenfish* rounded Oahu, turned north, and cranked the diesels up to flank speed. Over the course of the next few days, the temperature dropped so low that Hall said he felt like he had two navels.

The sub went deep and slowed to one-third speed. Hall sauntered into the control room and stole a glance at the navigation table. His eyes lit up when he saw the plot line running past Little Diomede. Once known as Krusenstern Island, the tiny ocean speck housed around one hundred people and sat smack dab in the middle of the Bering Strait between Alaska and Siberia. Big Diomede lay a few miles to the west, and although the population was larger, they were all Russian. The nav line ended several miles west of the island, well inside Soviet territorial waters.

Hall shivered, and not just from the cold. They had left Hawaii sans anything warm. No foul-weather jackets, gloves, wool undies, or thick socks. Hall and his mates had taken to layering up on khakis to keep from freezing in the Arctic waters. "Blue nose" *Balao*-class diesel boats were notorious for having less than desirable heating systems.

A day later, Hall finally found out why the *Queenfish* had been cordially compelled to wander into Ivan's backyard. Apparently, COMSUBPAC had been asked by some guy named Waldo Lyon at the Arctic Submarine Lab to take temperature and density readings at various depths in the Bering Strait. Explanations as to why they needed these were not offered. Then again, they never were, at least not to the common crew.

"Somebody smarter than me decided they wanted to take all these ocean readings in the Arctic," Hall said. "But somebody dumber than me forget to consider how we'd accomplish that."

The *Queenfish* had left port in such haste that no one had thought to bring aboard any instruments suitable for taking the readings. As the sub's auxiliary electrician, Hall pondered the dilemma for several hours before coming up with a plan.

"I jury-rigged a hydrometer," Hall said. "Diesel boats run on batteries, and part of my job was to maintain the 'cans' so they didn't die, explode, or kill us all with poison gas."

Doing so required instruments and diligence. Batteries were filled with triple-distilled water and inspections were made frequently to check for hydrogen buildup—which could cause an explosion—or salt—which could create deadly chlorine gas. Hall "borrowed" a battery-checking hydrometer, ripped it apart, and removed the lead shot so the instrument could be used with saltwater. Resembling Grandma's turkey baster, the meter consisted of a glass tube bottomed by a red rubber bulb.

"It worked just fine," said Hall. "We were able to take readings at different depths and strata variations to see how the Arctic might affect sonar beams."

Hall later learned that Lyon and company needed the information to help save lives. Submarine skippers are trained to hide under thermal layers, which can reflect enemy active sonar pings. ASL needed to know how Arctic waters might affect various strata so they could recommend different tactics in relation to passive and active sonar. Gathering the data took Hall and the *Queenfish* crew two days to complete. While they were down, the sub started rolling from side to side. Officer of the Deck, Lieutenant A. E. May, ordered the diving officer to descend to two hundred feet. The rolling didn't stop. May called Commander Lockwood to the conn.

"Lt. May was worried," Hall recalled. "He said there must be a huge storm above us 'cause we were getting batted about at two hundred feet. We were starting to run out of air and some of us were getting dizzy from the CO_2 buildup. We also needed to fill the cans."

Even with the boat's batteries (cans) near depletion and the air almost unbreathable, Cdr. Lockwood chose to stay down another day and go slow to conserve the batteries. He didn't want to risk trying to surface in a bad storm.

"If you come up in the middle of a huge wave," Hall said, "you might capsize the sub. With our heavy ballast on top versus underneath, the weight could send us to the bottom. The captain was also worried about surfacing underneath a Soviet ship. In a bad storm, our sonar jockeys wouldn't hear them until it was too late."

After three days down, Lockwood had no choice. Sub commanders are chosen for their ability to make life-or-death decisions. When faced with disaster to the right or left, they must have the guts and intelligence required to select the lesser of two deads. Lockwood decided to surface.

"I was in the control room when it happened," Hall said. "The diving officer gave the order to surface and we angled up at the bow."

Freezing and wheezing, dizzy and scared, Hall stood near the gyro compass in the conn. His eyes shifted downward, and he noticed that the glass cover on the compass housing had been removed for repairs. Knowing that the gyro contained mercury, and concerned that a jolt might spill the metallic liquid onto to the deck, Hall craned his neck to see where the cover had gone. He spotted the metal plate on the port side.

The diving officer yelled a report: "One hundred feet, ten degree up bubble."

Standing near the number one periscope, Lockwood acknowledged the update. The boat shuddered and rolled while the helmsmen struggled to maintain control. Grabbing onto the overhead piping, Hall tried to pull himself toward the compass cover. He didn't make it far.

"Sixty feet, ten degree up bubble."

The sub lurched as the bow sliced toward the surface. Hall's stomach fluttered. His feet and legs shot upward. Centrifugal force flung him toward the starboard side of the boat. Someone screamed. A khaki-clad officer slammed against a three thousand-pound air line with a dull thud. Hall whacked his head on a two hundred-pound air manifold. The sub rolled further to starboard. Hall bit his lip. His temples throbbed. He saw a half-dozen sailors and officers pinned against the starboard bulkhead. The diving officer, chief of the watch, and helmsman remained strapped in their seats, but were powerless against the wrath of Mother Nature.

Panic welled up inside Hall's throat. He knew the sub was close to a thirty-degree angle. If they rolled much further to starboard, they'd capsize. If that happened, they'd all drown near the Siberian border.

The sub continued to roll. At about forty degrees over, mercury flew out of the open gyro compass and splattered about the control room. A large glob smacked Hall on the cheek and shoved its way into his nose. The smell reminded him of a morgue. Men nearby swatted at the silver orbs that rolled across their faces and uniforms.

The boat rolled even more. Hall figured they were close to forty-five degrees. Through clinched teeth, Lockwood barked out an order. The diving officer forced a strained reply. The boat whined and groaned. Hall muttered a silent prayer. He wanted to live to see twenty.

Thirty seconds passed, then another.

"That was the longest minute of my life," Hall said. "I really thought it was my last."

Mother Nature and God ruled otherwise. The USS *Queenfish* finally pulled out of her death spiral and crashed into the trough of a massive wave.

"We were out of the fire," Hall said, "but back into the frying pan."

Tossed about in a bad storm, absent a working compass, unable to dive again due to low batteries, the *Queenfish* flailed about for days on the surface. Lost and alone, still in Soviet waters, they were far from safe.

"We wanted to get spotted," Hall said, "but not by the enemy."

Praying for a miracle, Hall worked with the crew to gather up the spilled mercury. "We used every silver coin and object we could find to pick up the globs. We looked like a bunch of kids in science class."

Several nervous days later, a U.S. plane homed in on the *Queenfish*'s radio signal and helped the crew find their way back to Alaskan waters. The navigator managed to use star fixes to get them home to Hawaii.

"That was my first time in the Arctic," Hall said. "And I'm glad it was also my last."

Hall ended his enlistment shortly after that mission. His buddy, Joe Prince, tried to talk him into going into the reserves, but Hall had experienced enough excitement to last him a lifetime.

"I decided on a career as far away from the Arctic Ocean as possible," Hall said.

Despite the near-catastrophe suffered by the *Queenfish*, Waldo Lyon and his team at ASL were ecstatic. The readings brought back by Hall and crew proved invaluable in understanding more about Arctic conditions. Hungry for more data, Lyon established a field station at Cape Prince of Wales, Alaska, in 1951.

Over the next few years, researchers at ASL measured brine content and ice elasticity to provide submarine designers with data to create boats that could surface through thick ice cover. Cold rooms and calibration facilities were used to study ways to eliminate icing on snorkel head valves—a problem that could prevent diesel submarines from sucking in enough air to run their engines and charge batteries. All this research led to the first submerged transpolar voyage by the nuclear submarine, USS *Nautilus* (SSN-571), followed by dozens of additional under-ice scientific excursions to further Arctic operations.

When the Soviets launched the Sputnik spacecraft in October 1957, President Dwight D. Eisenhower was humiliated. Other free countries started questioning their alliances with the U.S., and the military wondered if they faced a technologically superior enemy. To address these concerns, Captain William Anderson and the crew of the *Nautilus* were ordered to complete a dangerous voyage to the North Pole, traversing under the polar ice cap for the first time in history.

The public heard about some of this, but never knew what really happened under the polar ice cap in 1958. What we now know after the release of heretofore classified information and logs, and after retired submariners have divulged their stories, is that the *Nautilus* conducted two top secret missions in the Arctic known as Operation Sunshine I and II.

The *Nautilus* made the first trek to the geographic North Pole by crossing underneath the ice in August 1958. Navigating accurately beneath a shear wall of frost was no easy task. The boat's gyrocompass didn't function well above eighty-five degrees north longitude, and Anderson's crew referred to the risky excursion as "longitude roulette." In fact, Anderson almost blew a hole in the ice with a torpedo to allow the boat to surface so he could gain an accurate bearing. The *Nautilus* passed near the Russian coastline on her second voyage to the Arctic near Alaska, flaunting her reactor in the face of the Soviets, who had yet to deploy their first nuclear submarine.

Mike Olsen, as a twenty-year-old quartermaster aboard the USS *Seawolf* (SSN-575), departed for North Atlantic waters in August 1958. After fifty-five years of not telling anyone about this top secret mission, including his wife, Mike revealed what happened during this journey. "We tracked and recorded Soviet submarines as they left the base in the Kola Inlet," said Mike. "We were operating deep inside Russian territorial waters and were prepared to fire on a moment's notice. The *Seawolf* logged the longest recorded time under the ocean on that SpecOp while we were in Arctic waters. When we got back, they gave us a bunch of lectures about never telling anyone what we did...ever. But after fifty-five years, I figured it was time."

In July 1962, following in the footsteps of the *Nautilus*, the USS *Skate* (SSN-578) logged the first surfacing through Arctic ice when she popped up at the North Pole. The risky maneuver, if done incorrectly, could have damaged systems or caused severe flooding. The *Skate*, in similar fashion to the *Nautilus*, faced a number of near-fatal scenarios while operating in northern regions. The crew quickly learned that, due to abundant freshwater runoff, unique salinity gradients, massive surface ice, and a host of other challenging conditions, submerged things operate differently in the Arctic. Sonar systems, torpedoes, communication gear, and navigation equipment transported to this northern "Bermuda Triangle" often become problem children when temperatures drop below zero and ice enters the equation. These revelations spurred hundreds of subsequent jaunts by submariners during biannual U.S. Navy Ice Exercises (ICEX).

"Thanks to Waldo Lyon and other pioneers, U.S. submarines have been coming to the Arctic to train for decades," said Jeff Gossett of ASL. "Without ICEX, fast attack submariners operating up here don't stand a chance against the elements or the enemy."

As we'll see in the next chapter, despite being armed with Arctic knowledge, training, and systems, you can still be outflanked by a clever enemy.

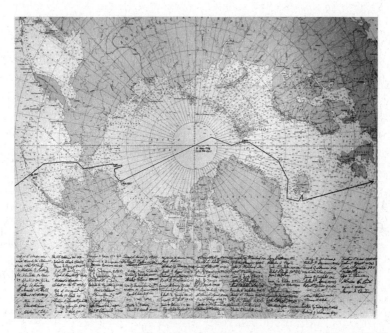

Operation Sunshine map courtesy of the U.S. Navy

CHAPTER TWELVE

Ice Hazards

North Pole 1986, courtesy of the U.S. Navy

I n 1962, the Arctic remained one of the most dangerous places on earth to operate a submarine. To help solve this problem, the USS *Skate* and USS *Seadragon* (SSN-584) made the first rendezvous at the North Pole. In 1969, the USS *Whale* (SSN-638) surfaced at the North Pole, sixty years to the day after Admiral Robert Peary planted the first flag there. The USS *Pargo* (SSN-650) and USS *Skate* completed joint ICEX operations in 1969, and despite the fact that more than a dozen submarines had crisscrossed the Arctic over the previous two decades, the navy had yet to conduct any surveys or complete bottom contour or shelf maps. This lack of knowledge created a high risk to boats operating in the area, and was an embarrassment to the U.S. government.

The year 1970 was a difficult one for America. Vietnam protestors lined streets and Russia kept escalating tensions with aggressive political and military moves. The U.S. Navy suspected that the Soviets were building new ballistic missile submarines with greater launch ranges so they could hide under the Arctic ice until it was time to lob missiles at America. For U.S. submariners, the difficulty of finding and sinking those subs was already a tough task; now it would be even harder. To help mitigate this problem, the navy tapped Captain Fred McLaren, CO of the second USS *Queenfish* (SSN-651), to skirt the Siberian coastline, navigate around hazardous sea ice, and complete an extensive survey. Shifting ice floes, deep ice keels extending down to one hundred feet or more, and tumultuous sea conditions made this mission one of the most dangerous conducted during Cold War I.

The *Queenfish*'s first jaunt retraced much of the 1958 *Nautilus* track, starting in the Bering Strait near Big Diomede where the first *Queenfish* had almost met her demise in 1947. The second excursion began 240 nautical miles past the North Pole down to the Laptev Sea to complete a detailed survey of the Siberian shelf. The crew endured several close calls as the sub dodged enormous icebergs, scraped its hull across massive ice keels, and more than once almost collided with the bottom.

The *Queenfish* inched across three seas at less than seven knots and covered 3,100 miles in under a month. What ice warriors fear the most in the Arctic is getting wedged into an "ice garage" in shallow water—stuck in between deep ice keels with no way out. Backing a three hundred-foot-long by sixty-foot-wide submarine out of an ice garage using a single propeller is nearly impossible. But that's exactly what Capt. McClaren and his crew had to do while surveying a Siberian shelf. When they reversed the prop, it threw the stern down and to port. Going forward was not an option. Only through perseverance and blind luck did McClaren and his crew finally maneuver out of harm's way by backing up and going forward—in similar fashion to dislodging a large truck from a mudhole.

Many similar incidents occurred in Arctic waters in years to come. The USS *Haddo* (SSN-604) was a boat I served on during Cold War I. In 1976, the

Haddo was on station in Arctic waters. The officer of the deck, Lieutenant Junior Grade Ladeau Tomlin, was in the control room peering out the number two periscope. Tomlin was a Naval Academy graduate and a fine officer, but even his ultrafast instincts could not help him avoid a large iceberg before it slammed into the periscope. The collision caused serious flooding and some injuries that required the *Haddo* to limp into Adak, Alaska, whereupon the navy flew out a replacement periscope. After dissecting what happened, Tomlin later learned that the boat's navigation systems started to act up in the freezing ocean and sent them off course. They ventured too near a collection of icebergs and floating ice floes. This incident and many others underscore why training and tactics to improve Arctic navigation is critical to the survival of submarines operating in that region.

ICE WARRIORS

Howard Reece is an expert at surviving in the Arctic. He's an ice pilot involved with the U.S. Navy's ICEX operations, conducted every few years in the Arctic. He notes that subs use ring laser gyroscope navigation (RLGN) systems to find their way around under the ice. These generally work well, he says, but they can sometimes "walk out" over time due to a number of reasons. When they do so in open waters, navigators simply come to periscope depth and get a "fix" via stellar observance, or use bottom contour maps to verify locations. Neither of these tactics work well in the Arctic. For the U.S. Navy, there are only two *Seawolf*-class subs left in the fleet that can safely crack through ice that's around three-feet thick, and even then it's dangerous and can give away the boat's position. As for bottom contours, they simply don't exist for most areas in the Arctic.

"The U.S. only has one icebreaker and she's a research vessel built for medium duty," Reece said. "It would take years for several icebreakers to create bottom contour maps. That's why at ICEX we train sub navigators how to use new techniques to operate safely under the ice."

During the 1970s, to further help submarines like the *Haddo* and *Queen-fish* avoid ice mishaps, Dr. Waldo Lyon and researcher Art Roshon invented a new under-ice sonar for Arctic operations by inverting a Fathometer and placing it atop a submarine, whereas before the normal location was underneath the boat. This paved the way for the first winter cruise by a *Sturgeon*-class submarine.

When the Soviets launched the *Delta III* ballistic missile sub in 1976, the U.S. military raised a worried eyebrow. This formidable platform could now launch up to sixteen nuclear missiles, with up to seven warheads each, at targets almost five thousand miles away. The Russians knew about the Arctic's unique acoustic conditions and were well aware that our hunter/killer attack submarines had a tough time locating them under the ice. So that's where they hid back then, and continue to hide to this day. In the event of a launch order, Russian ballistic missile submarines, like the new *Borei* class, can let loose Armageddon by surfacing through the ice cap and firing their missiles in rapid succession.

To deal with this threat, ongoing research at ASL during Cold War I, aided by ICEX operations, pushed forward Arctic testing, training, and advancements for submarine systems and tactics. Without such developments, finding and tracking the Soviet's new ballistic missile submarines under the ice would have been far more difficult, if not impossible. But even aided by advanced sonar and other systems, U.S. submarines continued to smack into their Russian counterparts, and some of these collisions brought crews to within an inch of death.

CHAPTER THIRTEEN

Dead Men Tapping

Photograph of a Russian Oscar class sub courtesy of the U.S. Navy

On the evening of August 10, 2000, a cool Arctic wind whipped across the Litsa Fjord and hurled droplets of saltwater onto the back of an odd-shaped beast. Russian sailors scurried about the deck of the *Oscar-* class submarine, clearing lines, stowing gear, and securing hatches. Tugboats pulled alongside and guided the vessel into the channel.

From high up in the sail, forty-five-year-old Captain Gennady Lyachin released the tugs and scanned the fjord. Navigation lights winked through the damp fog. He ordered turns for six knots. Steam from the sub's twin reactors turned two massive propellers that struggled to overcome inertia. Finally, the sub lurched forward and a dark blue wake formed across her bow. The topside crew bid farewell to the tugs and scurried below. Once into the channel, Lyachin requested course 020, toward the Barents Sea, and a speed increase to all ahead standard.

Smooth and quiet, the submarine *Kursk* sped through the channel and passed by the mouth of the bay. Dry tundra lined both sides of the kilometer-wide fjord. Lyachin scanned the horizon, ordered the deck crew below, and shimmied down the bridge ladder. A michman (warrant officer) slammed the hatch shut and slid to the deck. Beads of water dripped from his cap.

In the rigged-for-red central command post (CCP), bent over the navigation table, Senior Lieutenant Sergey Tylik studied a chart. Lyachin asked for an update on the ocean depth. Tylik confirmed they had enough room beneath the keel to dive, and Lyachin ordered the ship to periscope depth.

A michman opened the ballast tank vents. More than twenty men in the CCP felt their ears pop with the pressure change as the fifteen-thousand-ton sub angled downward and disappeared beneath a ring of foam. Lyachin gave the order to make turns for twenty-eight knots, unaware that the command had brought his crew one step closer to death.

Sixty miles north of the Kola Peninsula, hiding beneath a thermal layer, the USS *Memphis* accelerated toward the sound of a Russian submarine exiting the fjord. Commander Mark Breor brought the *Los-Angeles*-class attack sub to periscope depth. He grabbed the orange wheel surrounding scope number two and yanked to the left. Hydraulics hissed as the chrome cylinder shot up from the well. The sonar shack reported a contact in the area making turns for twenty-eight knots on two propellers. He designated the master contact as a probable *Oscar*-class submarine. Breor acknowledged the report, positioned his face against the scope's rubber eyepiece, and rotated the scope left, then right. The night sky revealed no lights save for the stars, now abundantly scattered across a clear sky.

A loud beep from the WLR-10 Electronic Surveillance Measures (ESM) system warned Breor of distant Russian radar sweeps. Sensors mounted atop the periscope had detected the beams "painting the scope." Breor took one last sweep, scanned his eyes across the calm summer sea, and cranked the orange wheel to the right. The scope slid back into its cubbyhole.

Tall and fit, Commander Breor was often compared to General Patton by his crew of 130 men. Although some found him intimidating, most considered him worthy of respect and claimed they'd follow him all the way to a watery grave. While "on station" in foreign waters, often before what submariners referred to as a Holy Stone or "spy and pry" mission, Breor frequently grabbed the 1MC communications microphone and preceded his commands with: "Attention, prowlers!" The seasoned commander showed no fear in the face of danger and never shied away from close encounters with foreign vessels. Sneaking in behind fifteen thousand tons of steel required nerves of the same, and in this department, Breor was overqualified. Evidence of the skipper's hard-driving leadership could be seen in the wardroom where proudly displayed were awards won by the *Memphis*.

While on Special Operations (SpecOps) in Russian waters, orders from COMSUBPAC to the *Memphis* often included collecting PHOTINT, or photo intelligence, in the form of photos and footage captured while peering at Russian exercises through a periscope. Also ACINT, or acoustic intelligence, by sniffing up a Ruskie's tail and recording every hiccup and pop. Finally, SIGINT, for signal intelligence. Highly trained Russian-speaking espionage "spooks" sat behind closed doors and listened to radio transmissions while communications technicians locked onto radar and other transmission signals for analysis. Accomplishing all these duties while on a SpecOp usually required sneaking into foreign harbors, which necessitated oversized gonads on the part of the skipper.

As Breor inched closer to his prey, he was certainly aware that this SpecOp represented a rare opportunity to observe a once-in-a-decade naval exercise that included several weapons tests. If Breor hoped to achieve another stripe on his sleeve, this might be a gold star moment like none he'd had before. But grabbing the brass ring meant he'd have to lean a lot further off the horse and stick his nose way up Ivan's ass.

Now on station, more than fifty kilometers from port, Captain Lyachin issued orders to line up the *Kursk* for a missile shot. The meaty smell of fresh-baked piroshki drifted from the compartment four galley and filtered into the CCP. Stomachs growled. Lyachin turned toward twenty-two-year-old Senior Lieutenant Alexei Ivanov-Pavlov and told him to prepare for Battle Readiness Two. The new head of torpedo control repeated the command and briskly stepped through the hatch into the forward compartment.

Inside the torpedo room, located near the bow of the *Kursk*, Pavlov and his team hurried to ready a Granit missile. Appropriately called "Shipwreck" by NATO, the missile stood at attention in a side-mounted tube. When finished with the Granit, Pavlov inspected the racks that housed a load of "Fat Girl" torpedoes. The weapon's nickname had been inspired by its odd, bulging shape. Designated as a Type 65–76, the thirty-six-foot-long cylinder was heavy and difficult to handle. The *Guinness World Records* book would not argue that Fat Girls, in a weight class equivalent to an eighteen-wheel truck, were the largest torpedoes ever made.

Russian submariners had little doubt that this formidable weapon was feared by NATO, and for good reason. Each came loaded with enough TNT to split a warship in half. If enemies shivered at the sight of a Fat Girl, they weren't alone. Russian Navy torpedomen also felt threatened by the unstable phallic symbol. The Russians had opted to use a volatile hydrogen peroxide (HTP) fuel versus the safer combination of liquid fuel and compressed air oxidization. Designers touted faster speed and a lack of rubles as the main reasons for selecting HTP as the propellant. American experts refused to consider the less expensive HTP as an option, stating that "you get what you pay for."

The 85% hydrogen peroxide solution in Fat Girls had a bad reputation of eating through rubber gaskets and valves and working its way into the torpedo's sealed casing. HTP was also chain reactive and easily agitated by almost anything found in a torpedo room, up to and including the metal sides of a torpedo tube. Fat Girls needed frequent ventilation and inspection to ensure they didn't "go Chernobyl." Glass tubes positioned near the weapons kept a constant vigil and triggered alarms in the event of a threshold breach. Should that occur, ocean water sprayed down on the casing to cool off the bitch before she could have a hot flash. If all else failed, torpedomen were trained to eject the weapon within six hours or risk being ripped apart by an explosion.

Launched on April 3, 1976, the USS *Memphis* had seen better years. New *Virginia*-class submarines were destined to replace *Los Angeles*-class boats as the next generation of starting quarterbacks. Still, Commander Breor knew his weathered girl could hold her own. Aided by a TB-29 passive towed array and ARCI-capable BQQ-5 sonar, the *Memphis* could "hear" almost as well as any teenager in the fleet. ARCI stood for Acoustic Rapid Commercial Off-the-shelf Insertion, which replaced the expensive "hardwired" systems of the past with easily upgraded components and software. During the '90s, the *Memphis* had also undergone a few knee and elbow replacements, which included the addition of a new towed array, a fiber optics databus, hull friction noise reduction, a glass-reinforced plastic turtleback behind the sail to support a Dry Deck Shelter (DDS), and fifty-eight new test gear equipment racks.

The latter two upgrades turned the *Memphis* into one of the navy's premier spy boats. The DDS housed Swimmer Delivery Vehicles (SDVs) to support Navy SEAL insertion missions, and also allowed for saturation diving excursions under the codename Ivy Bells. The fifty-eight racks contained the latest espionage listening and analysis systems also to support Ivy Bells—considered by submariners and divers as the most daring and dangerous missions in the navy.

Breor, like most submariners, had heard about Cold War I-Ivy Bells jaunts where boats like the USS *Parche* (SSN-683)—the most decorated naval vessel in history—snuck deep into enemy harbors, descended seven hundred feet down to the seabed, and deployed saturation divers breathing a helium/oxygen mixture. The divers trudged across the sand in complete darkness and wrapped induction "jumper cables" around Soviet communication lines connecting naval bases. The cables were used to wiretap conversations. Russian-speaking spooks listened to and recorded trans-missions while supersmart communications experts captured, filtered, and analyzed the signals. Ivy Bells missions were so dangerous that each one required prior presidential approval. More than once, hundreds of men had come within a hairline of not returning to home port.

For Breor, an Ivy Bells mission was not part of his plan of the day. A Holy Stone operation *was* on the docket, and not just an ordinary one. As he eased his sub into position, less than a dozen nautical miles away from a Russian *Oscar* submarine, a hush came over the crew. Rigged for all quiet meant a cessation of unnecessary noise, including nonessential fans, loud talking, and activities like movies in the crew's mess. Heaven forbid that a machinist mate should drop a wrench.

Breor reduced speed to three knots and sonar rolled out the long towed array from the stern dispenser. "Waterfall" displays in the sonar shack regis-tered everything heard by the towed array and BQG-5D wide aperture array in cascading effect, with dark lines representing noise flanked by white areas of silence. Sonar petty officers cupped hands around headphones and strained to hear the swoosh of the *Oscar*'s twin blades. A tiptoeing crew, infused with a heavy dose of anticipation, exchanged excited whispers. This is what "bubbleheads" lived for, worked for, trained for, and spent three months underwater to accomplish.

This was their chance to sneak up on Ivan, steal his secrets, return home alive, and never tell a soul.

With twenty tons of TNT strapped between his legs, Captain Lyachin aimed his bow toward the target and positioned his vessel to fire a volley. The clock in the CCP read 0845. For the experienced captain, this war game was old hat. He'd graduated from the Submarine Navigation Higher Naval School in Leningrad (now Saint Petersburg) in 1977 and served as the weapons officer on the *Juliett*-class diesel submarine K-58. His competence led to a stint as the captain 3rd rank executive officer on the K-77, also a *Juliett*. He received his first command in 1988 on another

Juliett, the K-304, and remained onboard until after the fall of the Soviet Union in 1991. The Russian Navy promoted Lyachin to captain 1st rank in 1996 and gave him the keys to the K-141, a Project 949A *Oscar*-class named after the Russian city of Kursk. Now, four years later, he and his crew of 117 operated at the peak of efficiency as best allowed by budget cuts and personnel turnover.

Lyachin brought the *Kursk* to periscope depth and zigzagged toward the missile launch zone. He turned over the CCP to a junior officer and marched into the radio room. Earlier chatter on the radio, received from First Submarine Flotilla Commander Vice Admiral Oleg Burtsev, now aboard the *Pyotr Veliky Kirov*-class battle cruiser, had validated Lyachin's orders. The captain keyed the radio mic. He verified the *Kursk*'s exercise code of *Vintik*, which translated into English as Little Screw. Lyachin's boss responded. Admiral Burtsev confirmed a "T-time" of noon on that bright Saturday to launch the first practice missile. He also reminded Lyachin to follow the command table and rendezvous with the control ship, maintain communications, and use the proper exercise signals.

Lyachin returned to the CCP and ordered the watch officer to bring the *Kursk* to a depth of fifty-five meters. He called into the "acoustic" sonar shack and asked for an update on the target's bearing and speed. Using this information, he made a quick calculation in his head and maneuvered his craft into firing position. Calling back into acoustic, he told them to "prepare first measurement."

Acoustic replied with a bearing update.

Lyachin responded with "Acoustic . . . zero. Regimen . . . one minute."

Following proper procedures, having heard their captain start the ball rolling with the word "zero," Acoustic started feeding bearings every minute to the weapons attack crew, which included the navigator, electronics officer, and fire control team. Michmen assigned to the fire control team entered the range data into the digital weapons systems using measurements called *cabeltovs*. Ten *cabeltovs* equaled one nautical mile of distance to the target. In the torpedo room, sailors verified readiness of the Granit cruise missile.

Acoustic reported that the target, a dilapidated craft that had exhausted its last breath during the first Cold War, was now two thousand *cabeltovs* away. Lyachin raised his right arm. In one quick move, he lowered his arm and said, "Fire!"

At precisely 1240 Moscow time, the *Kursk* shuddered as the Granit screamed from its tube. The missile flew upward, broached the surface, lit off its rocket engine, and sped away. Traveling at more than two times the speed of sound, the seven-ton, thirty-three-feet-long projectile streaked across a blue sky. A yellow-orange trail marked the path of the assassin, now en route to a kill.

Within minutes, radio bursts from the *Pyotr Veliky* validated a direct hit. Cheers erupted in the *Kursk*'s CCP. Lyachin held his smile. They had one more missile to fire. Executing the same moves as in the first dance, Lyachin lined up for shot number two. He brought his arm down again, only this time, nothing happened. The fire control team reported a problem with the second Granit. Lyachin informed his superiors of the failure using the sub's underwater hydrophone system.

At 1400, the *Kursk* returned to periscope depth and contacted the *Pyotr Veliky* on the radio. Vice Admiral Burtsev dismissed the second shot bad news and congratulated Lyachin and his crew for a successful first launch. Lyachin had little time to revel as he needed to prepare for the next phase of the exercise. It was now time to conduct the test launch of a highly volatile Fat Girl.

Aboard the *Memphis*, Commander Breor slapped up the handles on the number two scope and lowered it into the well. The *Memphis* had participated in ICEX the year before, and the training and tactics learned by his crew came in handy while sneaking up on the *Kursk* in quiet Arctic waters. From only a few nautical miles away, using digital photo and video cameras inside the Type 18 periscope, Breor had captured some excellent shots and footage of the *Kursk* launching a Shipwreck missile. He had anticipated another firing, but the *Oscar* did not comply. If a malfunction had prevented the Russian Navy from executing a second launch, it wasn't untypical, and Breor had witnessed many such mishaps over the years.

He'd taken command of the *Memphis* two years earlier after a stint as a senior submarine school instructor. Books and simulators are never a match for the real thing, and most submariners long for another dose of adrenaline, even if they won't admit it. One of the best locations on the map to find a good thrill ride is in the Barents Sea. The depth in that area averages only 750 feet, about twice the length of the *Memphis*. A miscalculation here can end a career, if not a life. Although Breor had so far avoided a collision with an adversary, he knew there had been eleven recorded submarine smacks since 1967, including eight in northern waters. Several had been serious.

If Breor believed the rumors, the accident between the USS *Drum* and the Soviet K-324 *Victor III* definitely topped the list. The *Drum* had apparently been spying on the K-324 submarine deep inside Vladivostok harbor in 1981, and accidentally surfaced underneath the *Victor III*. The *Drum* crunched her sail, suffered severe flooding, and almost got tagged by the business end of a torpedo. The Soviets chased the *Drum* for three days, pinging with active sonar, dropping depth charges, and shooting Fat Girls. If not for the hand of fate, the *Drum*'s crew would now be on eternal patrol at the bottom of the Sea of Japan.

Breor, like any good submarine skipper, was highly motivated to ensure that his submarine never slammed into another vessel, and his crew never had to endure seventy-two hours of living hell.

Fifty-five meters beneath the Barents Sea, gliding through cold Arctic waters, the *Kursk*'s crew completed preparations for another battle. Captain Lyachin's original orders had called for the launch of a smaller USET-80 torpedo, but he received approval from command to launch one of the Fat Girls instead. Torpedo Chief Murat Baigarin had earlier expressed concerns that the weapon's oxidizer tank was starting to "sweat." The HTP bubble-sensor monitor had twitched, causing Baigarin to do likewise.

Baigarin entrusted the job of making the Fat Girl go away to Senior Michman Abdulkadir Ildarov. Experienced, easygoing, and over four decades old, Ildarov had shoved more than a few Fat Girls into the water. Operating slowly, so as not to anger the "bitch in heat," Ildarov and his team of torpedomen took almost twice the normal time to load the torpedo into one of the 650-mm tubes.

Better to go slow than risk the wrath of a Fat Girl. Especially a pissed off one.

At 1005, Acoustic reported bearings to four contacts. Lyachin acknowledged and slowed the *Kursk* to six knots. Acoustic confirmed that the turns on one contact classified the vessel as a fishing trawler. Another was a battle cruiser. The two additional contacts were classified as escort warships. Lyachin knew that the battle cruiser was the *Pyotr Veliky*, but in keeping with the rules of the game, he treated this contact like a hostile American ship.

Ninety minutes remained before the *Kursk* was scheduled to fire the Fat Girl. During that time, two other subs participating in the exercise had the privilege of firing first. Lyachin called down to the torpedo room and received assurances that the Fat Girl's fever was still mild. He also verified that if the temperature increased, Baigarin and Ildarov would not hesitate to jettison the weapon.

Thirty minutes later, Lyachin turned the *Kursk* northwest onto course 320 to line up on his target: another derelict destined for a watery grave. In less than one hour, he'd give the command to fire.

The *Memphis* was not alone in these Arctic waters. Breor knew that the USS *Topeka* (SSN-754) and HMS *Splendid* were also on station, not far away. No doubt they had been monitoring the other Russian submarines involved, and had snuck in close enough to observe two earlier practice torpedo shots. Now it was Breor's turn.

Sonar had just reported that the *Kursk* opened an outer torpedo tube door. Breor wasted no time in ordering his boat to close the gap. If they were about to fire a Fat Girl, or even better, a rocket-propelled Shkval torpedo, he wanted to be near enough to record every nuance of the event. At the risk of being heard, but motivated by scant time before the *Kursk* fired, Breor increased speed.

Sonar maintained a constant stream of reports from the shack. The tinted voice of a petty officer piped in every few seconds with bearing, range, and speed information. In the control room, Breor peered over the shoulder of another petty officer. A color monitor on a MK117 fire control system panel displayed the *Memphis*'s relative position to the *Kursk*, indicated by a small triangle inching its way toward the target. Breor had no intention of firing at the *Oscar*, but he knew there were digital recorders in the sonar shack that were collecting every noise the Ruskies made. Still, he wasn't quite close enough to grab the important launch sounds, but he soon would be.

The digital numbers on the clock in the CCP aboard the *Kursk* changed to 1112. The *Oscar* sub was now thirty miles distant from the *Pyotr Veliky*. From the torpedo room, Pavlov reported an uneventful loading of the Fat Girl into tube number four. Lyachin resumed Battle Readiness Two and requested a bearing update from Acoustic. They provided one.

As before, Lyachin replied with "Acoustic... zero. Regimen ... one minute."

Members of the weapons attack crew sat up straight on their benches. The fire control team entered *cabeltov* range and other data into the fire control computers. Lyachin ordered a course and speed change. Within the next few minutes, he would finally be rid of the worrisome Fat Girl, and, if all went well, he'd receive another pat on the back from his boss.

An agitated voice from the *Memphis*'s sonar shack reported a sudden course and speed change by the *Kursk*. Procedures called for Breor to slow and assess the situation, but the *Memphis* was still too distant to pick up the distinct sounds desired during the torpedo firing, which could be valuable to Naval Security Group analysts. After the superspy upgrades had been installed, the *Memphis* had been assigned to the ultrasecret Submarine

Development Squadron Twelve, and DevRon was always hungry for juicy recordings. Breor's mission would be more than successful if he delivered one. Also, he was competing with the USS *Topeka*, not far away and monitoring the event to ensure that at least one American submarine came away with a good recording.

A sonar petty officer called into the conn. With an excited voice, he reported that the *Kursk* had changed course again and was now headed right at the *Memphis*. Breor had seconds to react. He ordered a deep dive, hard right turn, and an increase in speed to avoid the impending collision. The Diving Officer quickly relayed the order. The helmsman and planesman struggled to obey. Their hands gripped two half-circle "steering wheels;" one cranked to the right and the other pushed downward. The boat angled toward the bottom. A coffee cup crashed to the deck. The sound of shattered porcelain was no more than a whisper compared to the earsplitting clap that followed.

Lyachin instinctively shot his head upward at the deafening sound of something metal scraping across his submarine's deck. The crunch came from the forward section, just above the torpedo room. The *Kursk* shook violently. Those standing in the CCP, including Lyachin, were thrown against piping. He steadied himself near a periscope. Years of training kicked in. He ordered all ahead flank, hard right rudder, and a steep dive. Thirty seconds passed. He did not hear any further smacks. He keyed the ship-wide comm system and asked for a damage report. All but one compartment reported no major damage.

No report came from the torpedo room.

Less than a minute after he had witnessed the mysterious crunching noise, and after the sub's rocking had jostled him about, Pavlov heard a strange hiss. He turned toward the torpedo tube housing the angry Fat Girl. Within seconds, the low hiss crescendoed into a loud whine. Pavlov turned and looked at the watertight door leading into the second compartment, now open to alleviate the pressure buildup that always accompanied a torpedo firing. With the Fat Girl screaming in his ear, he knew he should shut that watertight hatch.

He also knew he was about to die.

Around him, Pavlov heard the sounds of panic. Baigarin and Ildarov raced to eject the errant weapon from its tube. Pavlov was seasoned enough to know they'd never make it in time.

He was right.

Two minutes and fifteen seconds after the collision, the torpedo tube housing the Fat Girl erupted with the roar of a canon. The eight-hundred-pound breech door blew off its hinges, flew into the air, and whisked a sailor off the deck. The door slammed against the aft bulkhead. Blood oozed from around the edges. Shattered pieces of the Fat Girl sailed about the torpedo room like shrapnel from a grenade, slicing through flesh and bone. Killed by the shock wave, Baigarin and Ildarov dropped to the deck. Intense heat from the fire ignited by the mingling of the Fat Girl's kerosene and HTP engulfed Pavlov and most of his shipmates. As the flames sucked the air from his lungs, perhaps Pavlov's last thoughts were of his home, his family, and the life he would never see again.

If Commander Breor had any hope of gaining another stripe on his sleeve, that possibility had likely just vanished. But the skipper of the *Memphis* had no time to ponder this while issuing orders, assessing the situation, and racing to get the hell out of the area. Certainly the collision had been heard by nearby Russian warships, and without a doubt they were motivated to seek an explanation.

Breor called into the sonar shack. A first class sonarman reported hearing popping ballast tanks, secondary explosions, and whining propellers. The noises were descending toward the bottom. Breor recognized the sounds of a dying submarine. He could not feel anything but shock and dismay. The strong smell of navy coffee in the shack served as a morbid reminder that he was still alive, and the crew of the *Kursk* might not be so lucky.

A few miles away, a quartermaster aboard the USS *Topeka* heard and felt the gunshot sound of the explosion. "The *Topeka* was close enough to fire upon the *Kursk* but was running ultra quiet and trailing," he said, "close enough to be shaken . . . so strong that my equipment was knocked off the plot. The CO actually came running into control in his skivvies."

To the northwest, almost two hundred nautical miles distant, sonar operators on the USNS *Loyal* intercepted the *Kursk*'s death throes on the ship's towed array. West of the incident, secret NATO SOSUS hydrophones picked up the explosion, preceded by the crunch sound of the collision. Operators were puzzled by the two stylus jumps on the recording plots. A similar seismograph scribble showed up at a site in Norway, registering the main event as a possible earthquake with a Richter scale rating of more than two.

A sailor aboard the *Topeka* reported that the *Memphis* was "leaving the area" shortly after the collision and so concluded that this sub could not have been involved in the incident. If his report was accurate, why did the *Memphis* not reverse course after the collision? Even if they weren't involved, certainly their sonar operators would have heard the explosion. If the *Topeka* was close enough to be rattled, how could the CO of the *Memphis* be certain that his partner sub hadn't been damaged? Why would he continue to hightail it out of the area instead of returning to assess the damage and offer assistance?

A U.S. NAVY COVER-UP?

The rest of the *Kursk* story is generally well known. Damaged by the explosion, the *Kursk* rocketed to the ocean floor and skidded to a stop in the sand and silt. Twenty-four survivors aboard the Russian submarine tapped out an SOS against the inside of the hull, but the Russian navy was ill-equipped to rescue them. When the U.S. and other NATO countries offered the help and equipment needed, Vladimir Putin turned them down. Days passed, and by the time Putin finally accepted outside assistance, it was too late. The entire crew of the *Kursk* had perished.

Russian experts, after reviewing all the information obtained, convicted the USS *Memphis* of killing their *Oscar*-class submarine. The U.S. pleaded innocence (just as they had done in the incident involving the USS *Drum* and the *Victor III* submarine) despite the fact that seismic data revealed a collision scraping sound followed by an explosion more than two minutes later.

The Soviets offered additional evidence of U.S. guilt in the incident. Their aircraft had tracked the USS *Memphis* to a port in Norway where the Norwegians confirmed that the sub pulled in for repairs—then later changed the reason to "load more food and water." The Russians pointed out that no U.S. nuclear submarine had or ever would consider pulling into Norway to load up on more food, and that submarines are capable of creating their own water.

Later, the Russians claimed they had found a piece of a *Los Angeles*- class sub near the wreck of the *Kursk*, further implicating the USS *Memphis* or perhaps the *Topeka*.

The U.S. Navy continued to deny, deny, and deny.

THE USS DRUM INCIDENT

I was not in the Barents Sea when the *Kursk* went down, so I can't state with impunity that I know what happened. Circumstantial evidence certainly builds a strong case against the *Memphis* as the possible culprit, but it's not conclusive. It is quite possible that a Russian Fat Girl torpedo simply exploded on its own with no help from a collision.

Other authors have written excellent books about the *Kursk*'s demise, and all take the position that an American submarine was not involved. But none of these authors served aboard a U.S. attack submarine or survived a collision with a Russian sub. I did.

In my book, *Red November*, I detail an incident that was covered up for more than thirty years. We were on a spy mission deep inside Vladivostok harbor, trying to obtain photographs of a Soviet *Victor III* submarine while it was on the surface, not more than a mile offshore. We accidently collided with the *Victor* and severely damaged both vessels. With cold ocean water raining down inside our boat, we ran at flank speed through the Sea of Japan while Soviet ships and submarines depth-charged us and fired torpedoes at us. Only by luck did we make it out alive.

The U.S. Navy and government officials vehemently denied that my boat, the USS *Drum*, was anywhere near the *Victor III* we hit. I know intimately how an accidental collision can occur, how submarines operate while on station, what they will do after a collision, and most importantly, to what length the U.S. government will go to cover up the truth. To this day, the U.S. Navy has never admitted to the collision between the *Drum* and the Soviet K-324, even after the printed story appeared in my book.

In the end, whether the USS *Memphis* was truly guilty or not is immaterial. The fact that Vladimir Putin *believed* that a U.S. submarine sank one of his vessels and killed all 118 sailors and officers aboard is *very* material as it reignited tensions and mistrust between the U.S. and Russia. Given that Putin's father was a submariner, certainly young Vlad had developed an affinity for those who served the Russian Navy under the waves. That said, why did he wait so long to accept outside help? Submarine officers and experts I spoke with about this incident believe it's due to several reasons: One, Putin had probably been advised by his navy that secret information could fall into foreign hands if they were given access to the sub. Two, Putin is driven by a high degree of pride, and accepting outside help is akin to admitting that his navy is not good enough. Three, if there had been a collision, witnesses might have revealed this truth to the outside world before the Russians could debrief them. Why was the latter scenario not in Russia's best interests?

Perhaps intimating that a collision had occurred was actually better than having eyewitnesses validate one. The former allowed Putin a negotiating tool with the U.S., while the latter could have triggered an international war. Putin's staff contained several war hawks who may have tried to force such an outcome. Shortly after the collision, Russia's GRU Chief, Army General Valentin Korabelnikov, had supposedly commented that "The U.S. . . . sunk the ship, there will be a war!"

Perhaps the next time the U.S. has an encounter with a Russian vessel in Arctic waters, the hawks will get their way and the outcome may not be so benign. If so, submarines on both sides of the fence will bear the brunt of any conflicts, and the success or failure of the U.S. Navy's Ice Exercises may help determine which side comes out on top.

CHAPTER FOURTEEN

Technical Tweets

Author photo of Raytheon's Deep Siren communications system

The U.S. Navy completed an ICEX camp in March 2014. U.S. Senator Angus King, an Independent from Maine, visited the camp and rode aboard the USS *New Mexico* (SSN-779), a *Virginia*-class submarine. While there, he expressed that he'd gained valuable insights about the Arctic—a region of the world he believes is increasing rapidly in strategic importance. Given the recent heat between the U.S. and Russia, coupled with Putin's assertive moves to control resources in this area, the excursion appeared timely and important.

King said, "There's no substitute for seeing something with your own eyes. It was tremendously informative for me." He also commented about seeing the effects of sea ice abatement firsthand.

"It's almost as if we're discovering a new ocean that just wasn't there before," King said. He went on to quote from the U.S. Navy Arctic Roadmap

2014–2030, which warns that average Arctic temperatures are rising at almost twice the rate of other world areas.

King was joined aboard the *New Mexico* by Chief of Naval Operations, Admiral Jonathan Greenert, who commented on the strategic importance of the Arctic.

"The fact is," King said, "the Arctic is melting, which means largely unchartered and unclaimed waterways will be open to new avenues of commerce and exploration." That increases its importance to the United States, he said.

While discussing the fact that receding ice is spurring more oil and gas exploration and commercial sea traffic, King said, "We need to be pragmatic in facing the realities of the present day."

Indeed we do. Should a conflict arise in Arctic waters, for all the reasons discussed previously, U.S. and NATO submarines will become the quarterbacks in the game. To win the day, they will need to focus on three Ts: training, technology and thunder. The latter refers to things that go boom, like torpedoes and missiles, which we'll cover in a later chapter. We talked about training in relation to ICEX, so now let's go behind the scenes to learn more about Twitter technology for submarines.

When I visited the ICEX camp in March 2011, not even five months had passed since the Chinese launched a ballistic missile off the coast of California. Upon mentioning this to the officers and crew aboard the *Connecticut*, and to ASL/APL personnel in the command hut, I noticed visible signs of concern. Years earlier the submarine navy had taken a hard blow to the gut when the Russians planted that flag at the North Pole. Now they were on the ropes again after a swift jab to the jaw from the Chinese, and were working hard on new technologies to trump the competition.

The Achilles' heel of nuclear submarines has always been their inability to communicate with command while running deep and fast. They must slow down and come shallow to string out a very low frequency (VLF) radio wire, which can undermine stealth. In the Arctic, this operation carries far more risk. In order for a VLF wire to work, a CO needs to get close enough to the surface to ensure the cable actually touches the bottom side of the ice pack. Crews need to maintain exact depth in relation to a moving ice floe while avoiding upcoming ice keels that could smash into the sail and cause flooding. There is no other way for a submarine to effectively communicate with the outside world while operating under Arctic ice.

Raytheon wants to solve this problem with their new Deep Siren communications system, which is essentially sophisticated software code residing on a laptop computer. The system allows for one- and two-way communications with submarines via sonar buoys dropped into the water. Short coded messages can be sent through the buoys and received by submarines via their sonar systems. The signals are translated by a Deep Siren setup on the boat, and the truncated sentences resemble mobile phone texting, but between navy officers instead of teenagers. The mind conspires to figure out what those texts might contain. Something like: "XO beats CO w/pr of jacks. Crew pays $. No pizza tonite."

Operators can choose between three text levels, with Level One offering only basic coded messages but fast transmission times. Level Two, which was used at ICEX 2011, provides for a selection of words that can form short sentences; and Level Three is essentially free text, but takes much longer to send, thus undermining stealth. Subs can respond either via tones sent from sonar systems, which could expose their location, or via buoys launched from trash disposal units that are programmed to send messages once they're far enough away from the boat.

Jeff Gossett explained that while Deep Siren certainly helps with Arctic communications, hard ice cover limits the effectiveness of this system. "In their current state," he explained, "the buoys need to be launched in open ocean areas as they can't transmit through the ice." Gossett then smiled and said, "Maybe Raytheon could solve this by designing ninja laser buoys that can burn holes in the ice pack."

Curious about this newfangled way to text with subs, I convinced Gossett to let me go inside the secret command hut at ICEX 2011 and take a look. I had to wait until classified operations had ended, and they had covered up anything compromising, but what I did get to see was worth the wait. Gossett demonstrated the one-way system and actually sent a message to the two participating subs, the USS *New Hampshire* and the USS *Connecticut*.

Gossett creaked open the door to the hut. Inside sat a dozen headset-wearing operators mesmerized by blinking monitors. A large display on one wall charted the course of both the *Connecticut* and *New Hampshire*, now hundreds of feet below us, as the boats played simulated games of cat and mouse. Gosset explained how operators used the gear, tracked and communicated with the subs, and monitored weapons tests where the two boats fired dummy torpedoes at each other.

"How do you retrieve the spent torpedoes?" I asked.

"We carve holes in the ice, send in divers, and pull them out," Gossett said.

Having served as a navy diver during Cold War I, I shivered at the thought.

Once a U.S. attack submarine has received orders from command—perhaps via Deep Siren—to hunt down enemy vessels in Arctic waters, they may need some help from a bunch of smart kids. We learned previously that submariners rely on acoustic layers that develop when warmer ocean water mixes with colder water. These layers form at various depths and act like invisible barriers to deflect sonar beams, like those emitted from active "pinging" sonar systems on ships, planes, or in buoys. Ships and subs have long played games of cat and mouse where the underwater mouse tries to find a layer to hide under while the surface cat pings away and tries to find them. When this game is played out in Arctic waters, rules that operators relied on in other geographical areas don't always apply.

What might happen if a sonar system or torpedo was "fooled" by anomalies under the polar ice cap, like Doppler shifts caused by long keels? Could a submarine or weapon run into a wall of ice? Might the crew fail to detect an enemy vessel until it was too late? One government think tank believes it has an answer to this problem, and has enlisted dozens of middle schoolers to help them refine their tactics.

UNDERWATER ROBOCOPS

Founded in 1958 and headquartered in Arlington County, Virginia, the U.S. Defense Advanced Research Projects Agency (DARPA) is another DoD think tank responsible for the development of new military technologies. Lately they've been working on mini-robot sub trackers and underwater satellites to find and prosecute enemy submarines in open oceans, and especially in Arctic waters.

Ultraquiet diesel-electric and mini-submarines are a growing threat for several key reasons. Nations, drug lords, or terrorists can design and build them at a lower cost than nuclear submarines, so they can develop more of them. This makes it harder for stretched-thin anti-submarine warfare forces to keep up. Also, when running on battery power—which they can do now for much longer than in the past—they are near-silent. This again translates to greater difficulty for ASW ships and planes. Traditional diesel boats have difficulty operating under the ice, in that they need to surface every few days to snorkel and recharge batteries. Newer nonnuclear air-in-dependent propulsion (AIP) submarines employing fuel cells, closed-cycle diesel engines, or the like, are even quieter than nuclear subs and can stay submerged much longer than standard diesel "smoke boats." As we recall from our earlier discussions, since Arctic waters have less background acoustics than other areas, a less noisy AIP could pose big problems for U.S. nuclear subs that need to hunt them down.

One of the quietest AIPs is Russia's new *Amur*-1650 class submarine. This boat can stay submerged for almost a month, which is nearly ten times longer than World War II diesel subs, and it can carry a slew of modern torpedoes and long-range cruise missiles. That's why foreign customers are clamoring at Russia's door.

"Of the nine countries that are planning to modernize or develop their submarine fleets," said Anatoly Isaikin, director of Rosoboronexport, Russia's state-run arms dealer, "three have already chosen the Amur-1650 project."

Isaikin has not yet divulged which countries have selected the 1650, but the Indian Navy has publicly announced a tender to buy six submarines at a cost of almost $12 billion. While the U.S. does not anticipate future conflicts with India, there is no way to predict where other 1650s may end up, and several other countries have competitive designs including the *Scorpene* from France, the Type 214 from Germany, and the S-80 from Spain.

How does the U.S. plan to deal with the influx of these new super-silent predators? DARPA's new Distributed Agile Submarine Hunting (DASH) program just might be the game changer the U.S. Navy has been praying for to detect and go after AIPs like the 1650, especially in quiet Arctic waters. Not too unlike a series of satellites orbiting the planet, DASH deploys small "subullites" loaded with the latest sonar systems endowed with long-range "Spock" ears. These versatile underwater satellites are unmanned, silent, and mobile.

Where satellites glance downward, DASH subullites look upward and outward from deep ocean locales and listen for the swish of submarine propellers, whether powered by a diesel engine or nuclear one. In littoral waters or harbors, or in shallower areas like the Bering Sea, DASH systems glance downward using cutting-edge non-acoustic sensing abilities. To help with this aspect of the project, DARPA awarded a contract to Cortana Corporation to head up the Shallow Water Agile Submarine Hunting (SWASH) program. SWASH teams are working on lightweight, small, low-powered submarine surveillance techniques that experts are calling the "next generation" beyond traditional sonar systems. Other firms with a piece of the action include SRC, Inc. and Applied Physical Sciences Corp.

The outcome of the DASH program, DARPA hopes, is the development of revolutionary new equipment that can address a multitude of navy challenges including long-range detection, accurate classification, and most importantly, efficient tracking. To solve the latter problem, DARPA is also creating an army of robocops. Once the DASH system has detected and identified a submerged vehicle of interest, a small "X-ship" robot will be deployed to run after the target like a trained underwater hunting dog.

A fleet of mini-sub surveillance vehicles, dubbed ACTUV for Anti-Submarine Warfare Continuous Trail Unmanned Vessels, will track a target and stay on its tail indefinitely, all without the need for manned intervention. Cold War I is long over, but the practice of sneaking into harbors or tailing foreign submarines is still very much alive. As we learned earlier, collisions still occur, and only a few are reported by the news. ACTUV robots could lower the need for these "up close and personal" Holy Stone missions and lower the risks often faced by submariners. They could also make it much easier to find and trail submerged pirates, terrorists, and smugglers.

To accomplish their missions effectively, ACTUV robots will need to be injected with a dash of artificial intelligence. They must independently make smart decisions on the fly to stay on the trail of an enemy submarine, across thousands of miles of ocean, and for weeks or even months at a time. They'll need to interact with manned submarines or support units, transmit information and updates, take remote direction when needed, and avoid collisions—far beyond the capability of a pool-cleaning robot. To help them gain the knowledge and tactics necessary to accomplish all of the above, DARPA recently enlisted a bunch of thirteen-year-olds.

Using a new internet resource called crowd sourcing, which invites multitudes to provide feedback on innovative ideas, DARPA created a web presence and posted an open invitation to computer game enthusiasts with the challenge: "Can you best an enemy submarine commander so he can't escape into the ocean depths?" Gamers brave enough to try—many of them not yet in high school—downloaded the DARPA ACTUV tactics simulator called *Dangerous Waters*. By using the simulator, programmed with real-world evasion tactics that enemy vessels employ, gamers tracked enemy subs, tested tactics and systems, and provided feedback to DARPA. Game enthusiasts earned points for successfully completing missions and using effective techniques, with top scorers recognized on web leader boards.

DARPA is analyzing the tracking and tactics used by dozens of top gamers and plans to update ACTUV robot programming with the best of the best. Putin beware. Your submarines will soon be sniffed out by unmanned DASH drones, chased by intelligent ACTUV robots, and outsmarted via tactics created by a bunch of eighth-graders.

Photo of a Distributed Agile Submarine Hunting (DASH) system courtesy of DARPA

BRAINS OVER BRAWN

When a shooting war does occur in the Arctic, a key deciding factor in who becomes the victor may well come down to intelligence technologies. The more intelligent players will find ways to get the upper hand, of course, but I'm actually referring to the spying kind of intelligence. During Cold War I, we had several types, and some required submarine crews to risk all to obtain key morsels of it for the National Security Agency (NSA).

Acoustic Intelligence, which we called ACINT, has to do with capturing sounds coming from various platforms. I wrote about this extensively in my book, *Red November*, and will share some of that information here. Capturing ACINT required submarine captains to maneuver their subs to a close position behind—sometime within mere yards—a Soviet submarine or ship. Sonar operators then listened intently with hands cupped over headphones. They used recording devices and computers to catalog distinct sounds that were unique to a particular class of vessel, or even the exact vessel itself. A nick in a screw, a "singing" propeller shaft, or humming engine noise could become a fingerprint or noise signature that identified a particular sub or surface ship, right down to the hull number.

As part of a Holy Stone mission, we might spend hours, days, or even weeks trailing closely behind a Soviet nuclear missile or attack submarine. We trailed and listened to every noise made by our prey while high-speed reel-to-reel recorders captured the information for subsequent input into data banks. This "up close and personal" aspect sometimes led to collisions or near collisions while shadowing the Soviets, especially during a Crazy Ivan maneuver.

I soon learned just what that phrase meant, and would come to reason that we called it Crazy Ivan not so much in reference to the shadowed, but perhaps to those of us in the shadow. The baffle area on most submarines spans a sixty-degree arc directly behind the screw. A submarine's sonar is usually mounted in the bow, which creates a "blind spot" in the baffle area. This is where U.S. submarines might be found...in Ivan's shadow. We could play there during Cold War I due to our superior sound suppression technology that made it hard for Ivan to hear us. That's not necessarily the case anymore.

When U.S. boats cleared baffles, they slowed to one-third, turned ninety degrees to port or starboard, listened for any signs of unwanted visitors, then resumed their previous course. When Ivan cleared baffles, he made a 180-degree turn along his previous track, ran in the opposite direction for a while to ensure nothing suspicious lurked in the shadows, then made another thrilling 180-degree turn to resume his original course. The "thrilling" part related to speed. Unlike Americans, Soviets did not always slow down to clear baffles.

Hearing "Crazy Ivan!" from the sonar shack caused serious nail-biting in the control room. The cry meant that better than five thousand tons of Russian submarine had turned back in your direction, and if she didn't smack you, she might hear you. Either one of those scenarios could end your life. So, I reasoned, perhaps it was not just Ivan who deserved to be called crazy.

PHOTINT involves capturing photographic intelligence, generally through the periscope via cameras. In my book, *Red November*, I wrote about the serious collision I was involved in while conducting a spy mission aboard the USS *Drum*. ACINT and PHOTINT Special Operations, or SpecOps as we called them, were very dangerous, but they paled in comparison to what submariners and many in the intelligence community hailed as the most daring, dangerous, and definitely the most decorated missions of Cold War I: SIGINT.

As mentioned earlier, signal intelligence operations required sneaking deep inside Soviet or other harbors, or getting quite close to various vessels, and capturing the signals they emanated. These might come from spinning radar, fire control, or other masts jutting from ships, subs, or land-based installations. We also captured signals from another source, and these missions were not only the coup de grace of SIGINT, they carried far more risk than any other.

To accomplish these daring jaunts, U.S. Navy Divers and Navy SEALs spent weeks inside tiny compression chambers mounted atop submarines positioned a few miles off the Russian coast in the Sea of Okhotsk and the Barents Sea. Using sled-like skids mounted to the bottom of the hull, special boats like the USS *Parche* descended to the ocean floor some seven hundred feet down. Navy Divers, breathing a mix of helium and oxygen and outfitted in bulky deep-diving suits, trudged across the mud to "wiretap" Soviet communication cables.

During one such operation, the USS *Seawolf* got stuck in the sand during a massive storm. Four days passed and the crew was certain they'd never survive. Only luck and skill on the part of the crew allowed them to dislodge and limp home.

Ivy Bells missions were some of the most fruitful of the first Cold War. A treasure trove of information was collected and proved so valuable that many experts believe it may have helped shorten the duration of the war. While most might think that such missions are long since over, those who are currently serving aboard submarines know this is definitely not the case.

As mentioned earlier, while describing the guts of the USS *Connecticut*, I discussed the multi-mission platform (MMP) aboard this class of submarine. This area contains a hyperbaric chamber to allow saturation divers, breathing the helium-oxygen mixture required to go down to as deep as one thousand feet, to undertake clandestine Ivy Bells missions. The MMP also houses the required electronic systems needed to capture and record the signals found inside communication cables. A splicing chamber supports fiber-optic cable tapping and racks of special signal processing gear that technical "T-Branch" communications experts use to pull apart and analyze various signals obtained. As noted earlier, the USS *Jimmy Carter* is loaded with more of this type of gear than most subs, which is why it's often referred to as "Washington's premier spy platform."

The victor of various battles that may ensue in the Arctic will likely rely on SIGINT, perhaps gathered during Ivy Bells missions, to gain an edge over the enemy. The sub crews best trained and experienced in this type of operation will have a distinct advantage. Given that the U.S. has more experience and technical know-how in this area, the check mark for this category goes to that side, but if Russia beefs up its budget and training in this area in the near future, that advantage could evaporate. Regardless, advanced intelligence will do little to help a U.S. submarine captain avoid one of their worst nightmares: a rocket-propelled torpedo that's three times faster than most cars on a freeway.

CHAPTER FIFTEEN

Thunder Down Under

Shkval torpedo photograph courtesy of the U.S. Navy

Russia's newest submarines, including the *Borei* class, most likely carry supercavitating Shkval rocket torpedoes capable of hitting speeds up to two hundred knots underwater. The Soviet Research Institute NII-24 started working on this design back in the 1960s in an effort to create a new weapon that could take out nuclear submarines. The NII-24 merged in 1969 with the GSKB-47 to create the Research Institute of Applied Hydromechanics in Kiev, Ukraine. Out of that merger came the first Shkval.

A decade passed before the first rocket became operational, which sent a shudder down the spine of almost every submariner in the U.S. fleet. If a Soviet sub fired one of these things at you, there might not be enough time to run away. Also, if you fired a torpedo at them and they shot a Shkval back in your direction, you'd be forced to evade and cut the guidance wire on your MK-48 before it exploded. Game over with no hope of retribution.

Dubbed the VA-111, the Shkval is one of the fastest torpedoes in the world. How does it achieve its mind-boggling speed under the ocean? That was the question I asked Chuck Brickell, one of the directors at the Advanced Research Laboratory (ARL) located on the Pennsylvania State University campus in University Park. The spry seventy-two-year-old former submarine commander took me on a tour of the lab and showed me their famous water tunnel, where the latest torpedo designs have been tested since the lab's inception over sixty years ago.

To some, ARL could easily be called the eighth wonder of the world. Originally launched by the U.S. Navy in 1945, this technology "think tank" is operated by Penn State and is one of the world's best-kept secrets. ARL has been at the forefront of numerous technological advancements for underwater systems including breakthroughs in torpedo, sonar, propulsion, navigation, and other technology disciplines. Today, the lab is involved in a number of secret projects including supercavitating weapons, Advanced SEAL Delivery Systems for clandestine operations, underwater "jet engine" propulsion systems, *Star Wars* laser weapons, *Star Trek*-like command centers featuring holographic systems, and more.

During the first Cold War and beyond, submerged frontline heroes barely made it home alive due to technological limitations and problems. ARL is committed to solving these real-world issues with inventions that demonstrate how American ingenuity is still very much alive and well. While standing in a back room at the lab, Chuck explained to me how supercavitation allows the Shkval torpedo to run faster than a track star.

"The torpedo is really a rocket," Chuck said. "It flies inside a giant gas bubble created by an outward deflection of water that wraps around the nose cone. The expansion of gas that creates the bubble comes from the rocket engine. That bubble actually keeps water from contacting the surface of the torpedo, which reduces drag and increases speed."

Proof that force fields actually do exist.

Shkvals are launched from 533-mm torpedo tubes at fifty knots—around the top-end speed for a MK-48 torpedo. Within seconds, the liquid-fuel rocket ignites and propels the cylinder to two hundred knots, although Chuck said he thought the Russians had newer versions that could hit three hundred knots. Propellant tanks on the Shkval contain 1.5 tons of H_2O_2 and five hundred kilograms of kerosene. When the two are combined, ignition happens. Initial Soviet designs called for nuclear warheads, but that was later changed to conventional explosives. Still, if one of these babies explodes near your boat, you're dead either way.

The rocket uses four fins that skim the inner surface of the supercavitation "force field" to control the direction in the water. To make a course correction, a fin on the inside is extended while a fin on the opposite side is retracted. For whip-fast turns, there's a push plate on the nose that controls the cavitating bubble shape, which in turn modifies the direction.

Sensing that I was captivated by information about the Shkval, Chuck flashed me a coy smile and said, "If you think that baby is fast, take a look at this one."

He turned and placed a hand on a long, sleek cylinder sitting on a shelf. "This is the new German Barracuda supercavitating torpedo. Guess how fast she goes?"

I shrugged. "Wicked fast?"

"Somewhere between five hundred and eight hundred knots," Chuck said with a wink.

I dropped my jaw.

Chuck chuckled. "The Germans couldn't get it to work right, so they sent it us."

Built by Germany's Diehl BGT Defence and Atlas Elektronik, the once top-secret Barracuda features remote guidance and advanced maneuverability that can even home in on and take out a Shkval. German designers boasted that the technology was ten years ahead of Russia and the U.S., but eventually ate crow and shipped the rocket off to ARL for troubleshooting.

Chuck wouldn't divulge any details, but he hinted that the U.S. was working on something even more advanced than the Barracuda. Although I can't verify this fact, I've heard rumors that ARL and NUWC have been designing rocket torpedoes that can exceed one thousand knots underwater. That's something like two miles in 1.2 minutes. The odds of dodging such a projectile are somewhere between nil and piss-poor.

Should a U.S. submarine go up against a Russian or Chinese submarine carrying Shkval torpedoes, they'd better hope that the rumors of a faster U.S. torpedo are actually true. In the pages to follow, we'll discover how U.S. Navy officers rely on the training they receive during realistic "war games" where they battle against Shkval-firing Russian subs to provide them with the knowledge and skills they need to survive an attack in a real shooting war.

CHAPTER SIXTEEN

War Games

U.S. Navy photo

I n late August 2014, even though EU officials had repeatedly stated that energy should not be used as a weapon to solve the crisis in Ukraine, EU Energy Commissioner Günther Oettinger said, "If they [the Russians] don't try for peace in the east of Ukraine . . . If they don't decisively try to do something to prevent escalation, then there is no reason for us to help promote the growth of their industry and develop new resources for gas and oil and therefore to put this equipment on the list of sanctions."

Oettinger was referring to specialized equipment, systems, and software needed by Russia to exploit the gas and oil reserves buried in the Arctic's Peanut Hole and Lomonosov Ridge. "The Russians see offshore oil and gas in the Arctic, for example, as a good potential for the future," Oettinger said. "But this can only be developed by hardware and software from the West, by drills and . . . equipment that their industry cannot supply."

Oettinger surmised that should the West stop supporting Russia's ambitious Arctic oil and gas developments, they could throw a hard punch at gas giants Gazprom and Novatek—which is the main developer involved in the Arctic Yamal Peninsula LNG extraction project. That project is located in a remote Arctic region that necessitates specialized technologies provided by Western Elves. Novatek is hoping to export almost seventeen million tonnes of LNG a year, the absence of which could result in a blow to the Russian economy.

One of Novatek's Western partners is France's Total. Obviously they'd prefer not to be hampered by sanctions levied on Russia. "We are closely monitoring the situation and the sanctions imposed on our partner Novatek," said a spokesperson at Total. "We are analyzing the possible impacts on our ongoing projects in Russia to maintain the current planning."

Despite all the rhetoric and posturing in front of the cameras, Oettinger later said, "I've always argued in favor of the fact that energy supplies from Russia—oil, gas, uranium, etc.—should not be included on lists of sanctions."

Nevertheless, analysts remarked that sanctions on energy technology could include fracking technology and bans on advisory firms and future financing for Russian energy projects.

"Most major Russian gas projects are working closely with several European banks and consultancies," said an advisory source. "So if we get targeted, that would at least delay Russia's biggest projects in terms of due diligence and project finance completion. And delays cost a lot of money in this business."

Some EU officials expressed concerns that the bans could lead to a severe recession just as the European economy is getting back on its feet. Even so, what choice will the EU have if Putin continues his aggression unabated? Will concerned EU leaders point to the months leading up to World War II when Winston Churchill warned the world about Hitler's unabated invasions, and England's prime minister, Neville Chamberlain, did nothing to stop the Nazi advance?

If OPEC and the West continue to back Russia against the economic wall by encouraging OPEC to glut oil and sink the ruble, how might Putin respond to such a threat? Recall his passion to protect his Russkii people from harm; his strong, controlling nature; and his relatively short fuse. After spending tens of millions over more than a decade to send submarines and expeditions to the Arctic to gather evidence to present to the UN CLCS voting members, and after finally securing the rights to the Peanut Hole and perhaps the Lomonosov Ridge, he's now denied the technology, equipment, and systems he needs to exploit all that bounty? The wrath displayed by Lord Sauron might pale in comparison to the anger that will flush Putin's face with red.

Will he then call out the dogs and position his ships and subs in the Peanut Hole and NSR to cut off traffic as a way to force the EU to cooperate? Will he deal a double blow by allowing his new energy ally, China, to traverse the NSR but block any European or U.S. ships? Will he cut off gas supplies to Europe as a way to tighten the noose and freeze the EU into pulling their sanctions? Will the U.S. respond by shipping oil and gas from Alaska through the NSR to European ports? Will Putin fight back by blocking those tankers from traversing the NSR? Will all of these escalations cause a global conflict on a scale not seen since World War II? Will U.S. and NATO forces wind up fighting Russian and Chinese navies at the same time?

Even without Chinese help, Russia has plenty of reserves to weather the ruble crisis, and has invested heavily over the past decade to build a rather formidable navy. The Russians have made substantial improvements in their submarine fleet, and the first Project 885 *Yasen-* class nuclear attack submarine, the *Severodvinsk* (K-329), recently hit the streets with improved weapons, better sonar, sound-quieting technology, and more. Let's not forget about the eight new *Borei*-class ballistic missile subs that Putin praised in his July 2014 speech.

Lieutenant Commander Tom Spahn, USNR, expressed his opinion on the matter in a June 2013 article on Russian submarine forces in the Naval Institute's *Proceedings*. "Although Moscow has made no attempt to conceal the fact that it plans to accelerate submarine operations, the audacity of some recent patrols exemplifies a troubling trend.

"In late 2012, an *Akula* [attack submarine] allegedly remained undetected for several weeks while conducting operations in the Gulf of Mexico. Later that same year, a *Sierra II*-class guided-missile submarine crept within a mere two hundred miles of the Eastern Seaboard of the United States. In the Mediterranean, Russian submarines have similarly increased operations, likely including participation in a massive naval exercise off the coast of Syria in January 2013."

At the Naval Submarine League's annual symposium in October 2014, CNO Greenert said, "Not as many people know what the Russians are up to. I can't go into detail, obviously, but they spend a lot of money." He went on to say, "They've probed in the Alaska area in [our] DIZ if you will. We responded and they acted professionally in all regards. So far so good in that regard but I would call them [busier] in their operations."

What happens when it becomes far too busy and not so good?

PLAYING FOR KEEPS

Burning questions about what the U.S. should do if things turn hostile with the Russians and/or Chinese may seem a bit over the top, but they are frequently asked by U.S. Navy admirals, captains, and commanders when creating realistic "war games." These "games" allow the U.S. fleet to conduct exercises and prepare for various confrontations at sea. When they're ready to conduct these exercises, they turn to the experts at the navy's Tactical Training Group in San Diego, CA, which is supported by various civilian consultants. Many of these consultants are retired naval officers who once commanded ships, squadrons, and battle groups during Cold War I and II. Let's go behind the scenes to see how these experts might roll up their sleeves alongside active naval officers to conduct an actual war game with ships, planes, subs, and Navy SEALs in the Arctic.

Aside from offering various training classes, such as the Tomahawk (cruise missile) Tactical Commander Course, the Tactical Training Group Pacific (TTGP) in San Diego, CA, is responsible for ensuring that the U.S. Navy's Pacific Ocean battle groups are properly trained for scenarios just the like the ones described above. Training scenarios are initiated from the top by an admiral, such as the commander of Task Force 54 (submarines), 7th Fleet commander, or the commander of Destroyer Squadron One (Pacific). The commanders outline the scenario they want, and typically provide minute details such as which class of ships, subs, and support craft they want; and the supply vessels, aircraft, and even Special Warfare units like Navy SEAL teams. They even detail the order of battle for the opposing forces.

TTGP then creates a detailed war game plan to include patrol patterns, weapons envelopes, reporting parameters, enemy assets and weapons, protocols, and so forth. To accomplish all of this, they usually employ several contracted war gaming specialists (CWGS), most of which are retired military with direct experience in the areas needed, such as a former CO of an attack submarine.

My inside source is a CWGS. He requested anonymity, so we'll call him Henry. "Everything is color coded," said Henry. "The bad guys are red, the good guys blue, and others are yellow, black, etc. The secondary bad country is usually purple."

"So no fuchsia pink?" I asked.

Henry smiled. "Very funny, but no, we take these war games seriously."

Henry explained that the initiator, such as 7th Fleet, dictates the parameters of the war game. TTGP and their CWGS team schedules a series of planning meetings where all of the parameters and details are mapped out, including the intricate timeline for every asset or "player" in the game.

"Let's say our initiator wanted to simulate taking on Russia in the NSR because they tried to block shipments of oil and gas from the U.S. to Europe," Henry said. "We would create a war game with Russia as the red player and the U.S. as blue."

"What if China was also involved?" I asked.

"They would be purple, and other NATO countries would be black and green and yellow."

"So no pink?"

"No pink."

The training timeline starts with timestamp 0000, or they might use local times and start at 0600 or 1600, etc., military time. Games progress toward a terminal objective, which might be to punch a hole in a Russian and Chinese blockade while limiting casualties. The game might begin with intelligence, surveillance, and recon (ISR) to locate the red bad guys. Once located, or when red makes a move, blue reacts based on the outlined protocols—which simulate real warfare. Let's say an Exxon-Mobil tanker is transiting the NSR and is blocked by the *Admiral Nakhimov*, a Russian Navy *Kirov*-class nuclear-powered missile cruiser that was recently hardened for Arctic operations. The *Kirov* fires a warning shot across the bow of the tanker, and the tanker radios the U.S. Navy for help. All these moves are predetermined on a timeline via mission essential scenario lists (MESL).

"The red guys just made a move," said Henry, "so now the blue guys need to respond."

Protocols dictate what those next moves might be, such as send surface ships, submarines, aircraft, or all the above to the area asap. Each of these assets, and what they do, is governed by a timeline and warfare syndicates, or warfare commanders for each group, and each is designated by a timeline letter. For example, submarines with SubRon 3 are governed by the X-ray (X) timeline and their protocols dictate that if the red bad guys do something in particular, they will deploy to specific coordinates in the NSR starting at time 00:45. Under the Zulu (Z) timeline, certain destroyers with DESRON 1 will deploy to specific coordinates at time 00:50. Air resources, under timeline Romeo (R) will fly toward the U.S. tanker to provide air cover, and so on. Names for various work areas for the CWGS team members include: Zulu—sea combat commander; Whiskey—air defense commander; Romeo—AREC (air resources commander); X-ray—undersea warfare commander; Quebec—electronic/information warfare commander; India—intelligence; Bravo—theater warfare commander; and Alpha—the fleet commander, aka the Big Guy.

During the planning meetings, all the attendees review each move made by units under their command and correct inaccuracies, such as a sub getting on station at 02:00 when they would have to hit an impossible seventy-five knots to get there in time. All of the actions much match real-world capabilities, and all the moves are mapped against each other in the Integrated Timeline meetings. Not only does the overall game have an objective, but each day in the timeline also has an objective.

"Every asset has a control area, or a patrol box, if you will," said Henry. "We map all this out, such as the X-ray subs will be patrolling here and the electronic warfare guys will be there. Every box or area is also given a name, something like Jack Murphy Stadium or Margaritaville or Jack Daniels. We're very creative when it comes to our names."

"But no pink Pandora's box?"

"Afraid not."

Once the action begins, war gamers use secure, online chat rooms to communicate with each other and with the actual vessels, aircraft, or units participating just like they do in the fleet using actual radio transmissions. Details that are transmitted might include the time period, vessel name, latitude and longitude, positioning, intelligence discovered, intentions, next communication period, and so on. Although real submarines are not a part of these war games, real-world communications are simulated with finite detail and actual fleet-formatted message trafficking. Previously, to talk with a sub, gamers needed to simulate having the boat come shallow to string out a very low frequency (VLF) radio wire. As mentioned earlier, this has been the Achilles' heel of submarines. Now, these platforms can use advanced communication systems like Raytheon's Deep Siren (underwater Twitter), which can be used in the games.

The wargaming software system (WSS) employed for these simulations is called the Joint Semi-Automated Forces (JSAF) system. This is a government-owned and developed simulation system now widely used in experimentation and real-world training. Government entities using the JSAF system include the Navy Warfare Development Command (NWDC), the Joint Forces Command, and the U.S. Marine Corps Deployable Virtual Training Environment (USMC DVTE) program. The JSAF system was developed as a component of the DARPA Synthetic Theater of War (STOW) Advanced Concept Technology Demonstration (ACTD). Obviously, the military loves their acronyms.

Where does all this simulation take place? Each ship, warplane, or entity participating, with the exception of submarines, is equipped with onboard systems that connect to the JSAF system. For example, all P-3, P-8, F-18s, MH-60R/S and other aircraft all have simulators integrated into their systems.

"Some of these simulators are so sophisticated that you can't tell it's not reality," said Henry. "It's almost like being in *The Matrix*."

Contractors like Henry program all asset parameters and capabilities into the JSAF system prior to the game start. Each asset can be set up to act in various ways depending upon the program. For example, a ship might be programmed to maintain a certain course and speed unless a triggering event occurs, in which case it will be instructed to change course and speed or head toward a certain location and fire Tomahawk missiles, if that's what the protocol dictates.

Examples of a triggering event might be an enemy aircraft that has approached within a thirty-mile radius, or a U.S. warship that has detected enemy radar signals. What each "entity" can radiate or use for detection is governed by Emissions Control (EMCON) protocols. For example, EMCON Alpha might prescribe that everything is radiated, whereas EMCON Delta might require that everything is off to avoid detection.

"The simulation area where the war games are conducted resembles a NASA mission control room in Houston," Henry said. "You have a room full of war gamers in dozens of modules or cubicles that are interfacing with the JSAF system using PCs with monitors. Standing in the middle is a retired navy admiral with a headset that acts like a NASA spaceflight director, giving everyone directions in accordance with the timeline. It's actually pretty cool to watch."

Sometimes all those wargamers "crosstalk," and occasionally they even interject some humor.

"During the verification and validation phase of one game," Henry recalls, "before we commenced the actual war game, I simulated an Iranian warship communicating with a U.S. Navy destroyer. There were some junior officers on the bridge of the destroyer who'd never done a war game before, so I faked an Iranian accent during an information bridge-to-bridge communication. A question the Iranians like to ask is, 'How many men are aboard your ship?' or 'What is your next port of call?' They do this to trick crews into giving them intel, so I asked a few of these clever questions. One of the junior officers bit and gave me some intel, so I let him know he'd messed up by saying, 'U.S. Navy warship, this is Iranian naval vessel, how many men, goats, and whores on your ship?' The gamers in the room didn't stop laughing for ten minutes."

Any war games Henry's team conducts that involve Arctic operations would also likely include scenarios to deploy the ultrasecret U.S. Navy SEAL Team Two. Nearly everyone has heard of SEAL Team Six, but few have heard about Team Two, which is considered by many operators to be one of the most grueling and demanding teams in the Special Warfare community. These guys are based in Little Creek, Virginia, and are led by a navy commander (O-5). They have eight operational platoons predominately concentrated in Stuttgart, Germany, under Naval Special Warfare Unit Two. NSWU-2 maintains operational control of two forward-deployed SEAL platoons and a Special Boat Unit detachment.

SEAL TEAM TWO

Team Two is the only team trained in Arctic warfare capability. Team Two was formed back in the mid-sixties under Lieutenant John F. Callahan. At that time, they were comprised almost entirely of former Underwater Demolition Team-21 members, and started with only ten officers and fifty enlisted men.

One member of Team Two recalls leaving his family farm in the Midwest after dropping out of high school. He joined the navy at the young age of seventeen, and after a stint as an enlisted man, he volunteered for SEAL training during Cold War I. He served for a time with SEAL Team One but then decided to transfer to Team Two. He'd heard they did all the Arctic training and thought the challenge of mountain and ice warfare in the world's coldest and most demanding climates might be exciting. Some guys just can't get enough.

Cold weather and Arctic missions are some of the most demanding and dangerous in the world. Imagine zipping up your dry suit, locking out of a nuclear submarine in freezing waters, loading up your zodiac rubber boat, and enduring biting cold winds while paddling for more than thirty miles to shore. Once on land, you trade your suit and fins for dry gear and a pair of cross-country skis, then head toward an ice ridge some twenty klicks away. To stay undetected, you must travel at night and hide inside ice caves. No fires are allowed.

At the kill zone, near the edge of a ridge, you spot three small boats in the water, nuzzled against a sheer wall of ice. While keeping your hands steady in twenty-below weather, you assemble your sniper rifle and chamber a round. You must shake off the numb and keep your hands rock steady while you line up the scope and pull the trigger to take out the Tangos near the boats.

Now comes the hard part. You glance up. A tall mountain looms in the distance. You need to ski another twenty klicks, traverse the mountain, and rendezvous with your extraction unit in time. To make things a bit more challenging, a huge blizzard has just descended on the area and reduced visibility to near zero.

SEAL Team Two training for these types of scenarios is conducted in Alaska, Montana, Norway, Korea, Canada, Britain, and other frosty locales. The Team Two Mountain & Arctic Warfare Platoon workup includes several months of specialized preparation including cold weather amphibious operations, weeklong ski patrols, winter survival, and avalanche training.

Cold weather equipment must be versatile and durable to withstand the cruel effects of the Arctic elements. Team Two operators pack a first line, second line, and third line of gear. They are trained to create body heat from exertion in subzero environments and prevent heat loss from radiation, conduction, convection evaporation, and expiration. What they wear, and how they wear it, can mean the difference between life and death. Layering is key. SEALs add clothing when at rest, and "layer down" when on the move.

Diving in Arctic regions is not for the faint of heart and requires the right gear and strong stamina. Dry suits are a must, and special adaptations of the Dräger LAR V allow divers to operate underwater without producing bubbles. Breathing time for a Dräger canister is diminished exponentially as the water temperature drops. The Mark Six mixed-gas rig is often used for submarine-launched swimmer delivery vehicle (SDV) missions. In some cases, divers might wear specials suits that include warm-water jets, similar to the ones used by saturation divers during the first Cold War to conduct Ivy Bells missions.

Should terrorists, pirates, or hostile nations decide to use the Arctic as a means to infiltrate America via the Alaskan shoreline, or take out oil rigs in the Beaufort Sea, or board Norwegian tankers traversing the NSR, it's quite possible that operators in SEAL Team Two will hear their pagers beep. When that day comes, which could be sooner than navy officials have previously imagined, submariners must be trained to maneuver past dangerous ice keels, quietly sneak into insertion points, hold their boat steady in rough seas while deploying SEAL teams, and rendezvous at precise locations for extraction.

SEALs need to be trained and ready to lock out of submarines, ride zodiacs or kayaks across freezing oceans, survive thirty-below conditions for days, complete arduous missions, and return safely to an awaiting sub. It's not an easy life, but any Team Two operator will tell you that's it's one of the most rewarding on the planet. Every war game they play is virtually no different than the real thing, and death is just one wrong move away.

U.S. Navy photograph of SEAL Team Two in the Arctic

CHAPTER SEVENTEEN

Conclusion

I n February 1938, Adolph Hitler coerced the Austrian government into accepting *Anschluss*—essentially a forced union between Germany and Austria. Many within the Austrian government sought help from Great Britain to oppose Germany's aggression, but none was offered. Instead, Great Britain's Prime Minister, Arthur Neville Chamberlain, remained committed to a nonaggressive appeasement foreign policy and later signed the Munich Agreement, thereby conceding the German-populated Sudetenland region of Czechoslovakia to Germany.

Although Winston Churchill warned that Hitler could not be trusted or appeased, and would respond only by force being met by force, the Brits had no appetite for another war. After all, they'd suffered through a miserable one only a few decades earlier during World War I. Popular opinion continued to back Chamberlain's do-nothing posture until September

3, 1939—the day Hitler rolled tanks into Poland. Left with no choice, the United Kingdom declared war on Germany and catapulted Europe into World War II. Chamberlain resigned the following year, and Winston Churchill stepped to the podium to take his place.

Hillary Rodham Clinton compared Vladimir Putin to Hitler after the Russian president invaded Crimea in March 2014. "Now if this sounds familiar," Clinton said, "it's what Hitler did back in the '30s." On the surface this may appear true, but Hitler made no attempt to hide his ultimate goal: the complete domination of Europe, and perhaps the entire world. Putin, on the other hand, appears less interested in global conquest than in guaranteeing the survival of his Russkii family. To attain this goal, he wants to shift the world from the petrodollar to the petroruble. This will weaken the U.S. and Europe and mitigate potential threats from the West. Putin will then be in a better position to secure his supply lines including the gas pipes that run through Ukraine and other parts of Europe. He has already taken the first few steps toward this end, including the annexation of Crimea.

Aside from teaming with OPEC to lower gas prices and devalue the Russian ruble, which can only be a temporary measure, the free world responded tepidly. Admirals and generals have warned about Putin's Arctic exploits but those admonishments have fallen on deaf ears. Should the U.S. and EU continue to mimic Chamberlain by maintaining an appeasement policy? Or should they recall Churchill's advice to fight fire with fire? Perhaps we can "help" the U.S. and EU decide on the best course of action by employing the Scenario Planning Analysis model originally developed during Cold War I by Herman Kahn for the RAND Corporation.

Back then, Kahn gained notoriety for using the model to assist the U.S. government in making key decisions regarding nuclear war strategies. Kahn later formed the Hudson Institute to refine the model, which was adopted by commercial firms like global petroleum company Royal Dutch Shell in the 1970s.

In essence, the model dictates that enlightened minds should convene and brainstorm factors and forces affecting their organization (or the world as a whole). The object is to narrow the field down to only two critical uncertainties that require action from a list developed by the group. For example, a high versus low probability that Russia will continue its aggression and resource dominance versus a high versus low probability that NATO will need to take military action to halt the aggression. Items regarded as certain *and* important are disregarded as the actions required are essentially clear in these cases and need no deliberation (or so it is assumed by the model). Team members are asked to vote on each item to rank the level of uncertainty and importance (perhaps up to five points for each item). The top two items are given life on a chart in horizontal and vertical axes, respectively.

Once the chart has been created, we have four quadrants wherein we list four scenario actions or decisions we should explore. The group is then faced with four strategic directions:

1. All In: This assumes that one of the four strategies hits the nail on the head and will most likely unfold as foreseen. In other words, the group was clairvoyant and can start charging $20 for fortune-telling sessions. Betting the farm, as one would assume, is the highest risk strategy.

2. Core: This places more emphasis on one of the scenarios over the other three but includes contingency plans for the other outcomes. More resources and efforts are devoted to the chosen scenario, but backup plans are in place if the bet is wrong.

3. Hedge Bets: Here we are placing an equal emphasis on all four quadrants as we believe any of the scenarios are possible. In other words, anything can happen so we'll hope for the best and plan for the worst. The downside is the high cost.

4. Robust: This is similar to bet hedging where we believe any outcome is feasible, but instead of betting on all four, we vote on one and go

in that direction. Corporate firms, such as Royal Dutch Shell, often use this approach as it allows for a certain amount of bias based on opinions and other factors, and mitigates the cost.

Having used the Scenario Planning Analysis model with leading technology company clients in my consulting career, I decided to apply this approach to the brewing situation in the Arctic, primarily in relation to decisions facing the United States. I didn't have a committee in the room, so I contacted various experts and asked them to offer brainstorming ideas and vote on likely scenarios. From their input, I created a chart where the horizontal "importance" axis represents confrontations, issues, and battles over resources and routes (as in shipping lanes). The vertical "uncertainty" axis is represented by climate changes, resource/route exposure, and resource constraints. This provided four quadrants, with the upper-right (high conflict, high change) scenario stated as: "U.S. aggressively invests in Arctic military preparation." The upper left and lower right are both "moderately invests" and the lower left is "does not invest."

The experts I contacted unanimously agreed that the most likely scenario was the upper right as it appeared probable that continued sea ice abatement would drive more resource exposure in the Arctic, along with resource constraints in other areas due to adverse weather patterns. Also, Putin would likely continue his aggressive posture to dominate Arctic resources, which feed his oil and gas pipes and keep his coffers full. Given these probabilities, a greater importance needs to be placed on potential Arctic confrontations and battles, as well as issues such as ecological damage and territorial security threats.

Unfortunately, just the opposite is happening, which indicates that the U.S. believes in a lower-left quadrant "all in" high-risk scenario represented by low climate changes or impact, and a low probability of confrontations or issues. But what if they're wrong?

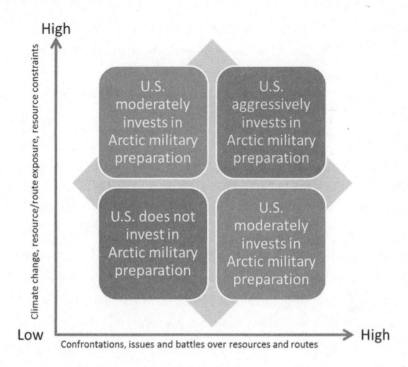

LEFT OUT OF THE COLD

President Obama's administration routinely promises to project more power abroad and ensure "freedom of the seas," but the U.S. is not equipped to effectively patrol the Arctic waters that border Alaska, an area now considered by most experts to be a top priority. Conversely, other Arctic Eight countries are leaving the U.S. out of the cold. Russia, Norway, Canada, China, and several other nations are focusing a great deal of attention and resources on the Arctic, but the U.S. is not. We know that Russia already has twenty-five operational icebreakers, and seven are nuclear-powered. Canada is currently building new icebreakers and Arctic patrol ships under a navy and coast guard modernization program. Even China, with no bordering lands, has more icebreakers than the U.S., including the world's largest.

The U.S. Coast Guard has only three Arctic-capable icebreakers at their disposal, but two are now approaching forty years of age and are often not sea worthy. In fact, as of the writing of this book, two were not fully operational. The *Polar Sea* is about to be scrapped. The *Polar Star* is the only heavy-duty icebreaker, and that ship is undergoing an extensive overhaul at Vigor Industrial shipyard in Seattle. That leaves the *Healy*, a medium-duty icebreaker, as the lone wolf on an ice pack filled with hungry predators.

The Coast Guard has called for at least six more heavy-duty and four medium icebreakers to meet its mission requirements, but so far the request has not been approved. The U.S. Navy is even worse off. At the conclusion of the 2011 Fleet Arctic Operations Game, several admirals conceded that the navy could not adequately maintain reasonable Arctic operations and would need to call upon the Coast Guard for help. One can only feel pity for the crew of the *Healy*.

At least one senator and congressperson also feel sympathy for the *Healy* and its crew. U.S. Senator Maria Cantwell, and U.S. Representative Rick Larsen, teamed up in 2012 to push for a Coast Guard authorization bill that increases funding for icebreakers. The bill also halts the scrapping of the icebreaker *Polar Sea* in order to buy time to build new ships, which will cost $1 billion each and take ten years to complete.

For the submarine navy, which will bear the brunt of any Arctic naval battles, budget cuts have forced the ICEX training program to practically gut its curriculum. This could severely lower the U.S. Navy's ability to stay ahead, both technically and tactically, in northern regions. Also, there are only about a half dozen qualified ice pilots, and for ICEX, the navy always assigns two per sub. If the U.S. became embroiled in a skirmish or war, the navy could effectively man only three submarines with ice pilots. Moreover, only a handful of subs and crews are currently Arctic-trained, and only a few submarines can crack through thick ice.

Despite desperate pleas from the navy and Coast Guard, Obama's 2013 fiscal year budget only included enough funding to build one more icebreaker, but even that requisition was on the chopping block by 2015. Dollars for ICEX and Arctic-capable submarines is practically nonexistent, and with even more military cuts looming, the navy does not have the ability to properly invest in Arctic military preparation. But ignoring this last great expanse of unexplored beauty and wealth could place the U.S. at a great disadvantage to other nations, especially Russia, and perhaps even push the country—and therefore much of the free world—toward the depths of economic despair. How can we prevent this? Unless we act quickly and decisively, we may not be able to.

THE FINAL QUESTION

Some two hundred miles north of Alaska on the USS *Connecticut*, four hundred feet beneath the ice, I asked Commander Varney one final question: "What message do you have for the American taxpayers who are footing the bill for ICEX, and for continued submarine operations in the Arctic?"

Varney leaned forward, focused his eyes, and said, "Most Americans don't realize how important our sea-lanes are to the global economy. And with new Arctic routes opening up, keeping them safe is more important than ever. In order for products to reach our shores, most need to arrive by merchant ships. For those ships to get here safely, our seas need to be free and clear. Submarines like the USS *Connecticut* are one of the best means we have of ensuring that they are. Why are we so concerned about new Russian and Chinese submarines? Because they can impact our ability to keep our sea-lanes secure, especially up here in northern waters. And that can have a dramatic effect on all of our livelihoods."

For a nation consumed with consuming, perhaps that's the best motivation for all of us to petition our government leaders to increase funding and focus on Arctic naval operations. Putin has already grabbed the first Elven ring—the Peanut Hole—with its treasure trove of natural resources. He will likely secure the other two rings—the massive deposits of oil and gas in the Lomonosov Ridge, and complete military dominance of the NSR—a route that now hosts hundreds of merchant ships each year.

Lord Sauron will continue to negotiate lucrative deals with China and Japan, and keep most of Europe under his thumb. In the not-too-distant future, after weathering the temporary oil glut and ruble devaluation, he will capture all three of the Elvin rings he needs to keep his economic energy One Ring of Power fully charged. He will then move forward with his plan to force the world away from the petrodollar currency standard and adopt the petroruble in its place. In doing so, according to a host of financial experts, the U.S. economy will likely collapse. If so, within the next decade, many U.S. and European citizens could lose their jobs and homes and become statistics in bread lines. The impact could be far worse than anything seen in world history, including the Great Depression.

OUR LAST SLIVER OF HOPE

"It is now three minutes to midnight," said Kennette Benedict, the executive director of the Bulletin of the Atomic Scientists in Washington, D.C. "The probability of global catastrophe is very high. This is about the end of civilization as we know it."

Benedict was referring to the infamous Doomsday Clock, maintained by the Bulletin since 1947. Three minutes marks the closet to midnight the clock's hands have moved since 1984—during the height of the first Cold War. It's only moved to two minutes once, in 1953, on the day scientists tested the first hydrogen bomb.

Weather pattern changes and potential global conflicts previously moved the symbolic clock from six to five minutes to midnight in 2012.

"Human influence on the climate system is clear," Richard Somerville of the Bulletin said at a conference in early 2015. "Each of the last three decades has been successively warmer than any preceding on record."

Other Bulletin scientists underscored Somerville's stern warnings by stating: "In 2015, unchecked climate change, global nuclear weapons modernizations, and outsized nuclear weapons arsenals pose extraordinary and undeniable threats to the continued existence of humanity. World leaders have failed to act with the speed or on the scale required to protect citizens from potential catastrophe. These failures of political leadership endanger every person on Earth."

We don't have to sit on our hands until the Doomsday Clock strikes midnight. We have a choice. If we, as citizens of the free world, encourage our respective governments to take action—especially in the U.S.—and invest heavily in technologies like the NRL PetroConverter to keep Putin from getting his "MacGuffin," we might have a chance to move our clock hands back a minute. What it will take are leaders with vision.

Leaders like former U.S. vice president Al Gore.

In the early nineties, several popular comedians jumped on the bandwagon to tell jokes about how Al Gore had been credited with "inventing the Internet." We all laughed. Turns out the jokesters may have delivered more truth than humor.

Packet switching networks sprang to life in the late 1960s. One in particular, called ARPANET, spurred the development of protocols to allow separate networks to communicate with each other. Vinton Cerf, often referred to as the "father of the Internet," worked for DARPA in the early seventies and was involved in the development of a protocol that techies now call TCP/IP—basically a way to let data (like e-mails) ride on top of telephone lines, then radio waves, and finally fiber-optic cables. This breakthrough led to what we know today as the Internet.

Cerf and his buddies created a private Internet of sorts to share information and files for defense purposes. The Defense Department endorsed it to allow information to be safeguarded in the event of a natural or manmade disaster. The technology and capability invented by Cerf and other collaborators was nothing short of revolutionary, but it was like an airplane lacking the fuel to fly.

Senator Al Gore entered the picture in 1986. He met with Cerf and learned about this interesting invention that had yet to be named. Gore's eyes grew wide. He excitedly suggested they set up meetings with key commercial contacts to see where this invention could be used. Cerf was skeptical. He did not see any useful applications outside government and educational information sharing and collaboration. Gore was insistent. He set up the commercial meetings and later helped push through a bill called the High-Performance Computing Act of 1991, aka the "Gore Bill."

This monumental bill laid the foundation for commercial businesses to have access to what had previously been a DoD "technological toy." The rest, of course, is history, but the economic impact is often misunderstood or ignored. In June 2011, President Obama told the world that ATMs had essentially destroyed all the bank teller jobs. He has also intimated that a large number of blue-collar jobs had been lost to the progressions of technology. This is true, but the overall net job and GDP upsides far outweigh the downsides. Unfortunately, many in the media often pontificate the shortsighted view that innovation is a job killer, but the facts say otherwise.

Due to the invention and proliferation of the Internet, the U.S. economy boomed for decades. Experts calculate that the windfall to the U.S. GDP was around $100 trillion, meaning the Internet accounted for that much *extra* cash, along with hundreds of thousands of *extra* jobs that would not have existed without the now-famous World Wide Web.

Technology giant Hewlett-Packard employs 324,000 people. Microsoft increased its payroll from 61,000 in 2005 to 128,000 in 2014. Google now employs 77,000 and the list goes on. Why is this important? Because the end game *must* be about jobs.

THE COMING JOBS WAR

Jim Clifton is the CEO of Gallup, as in Gallup Polls. His company is well known for conducting tens of thousands of interviews each year to determine what the world is thinking...and what every human on the planet wants. In his excellent book titled *The Coming Jobs War*, Clifton reveals a startling fact that took more than six years to discover. His firm interviewed hundreds of thousands of people in 150 countries to complete a "massively comprehensive poll of the world." The goal was to determine the answer to a simple yet profound question: What do you want more than anything else in the world?

If you're thinking it's love, spirituality, altruism, or to be filthy rich, you're not correct. The answer Clifton and his team at Gallup uncovered is that the entire world, above all else, just wants a good job.

"That is as simple and as straightforward an explanation of the data as I can give," Clifton writes. "Whether you and I were walking down the street in Khartoum, Cairo, Berlin, Lima, Los Angeles, Baghdad, or Istanbul, we would discover that the single most dominant thought on most people's minds is about having a good job."

A good job is defined as sufficient hours and income to support a family and enjoy life.

Armed with this knowledge, Clifton admonishes world leaders to place job creation at the top of their list, above all other goals because "good jobs are becoming the new currency for all world leaders." To ignore this critical endeavor places cities and entire countries at risk. Imagine what would happen to the U.S. if it went the way of Detroit. How many citizens would be happy, fulfilled, at peace, able to worship or donate, have health insurance, or be free? Without good jobs and income, all else quickly falls apart. When you're consumed daily by the stress and worry of not being able to feed or house your family, happiness is a word with little meaning.

Psychologist A. H. Maslow understood this dynamic when he created his "hierarchy of needs" chart, which places basic needs like food and water on the bottom of the pyramid and self-actualization at the top. Employment is listed on the second rung, only one level above using the bathroom.

How does having a good job relate to Putin, the weather, and NRL's PetroConverter? Due to innovations like the Internet, the U.S. has been in the global economic driver's seat for decades, and was able to maintain its status as the leader of the free world. Using its economic might, the U.S. could often dictate world policy—such as reducing nuclear warheads or banning the use of bioweapons or outlawing genocide. With U.S. GDP crawling along at a snail's pace since 2008, foreign policy dictation has become far more difficult as witnessed by recent events in Syria, Iran, and Ukraine.

If Lord Sauron captures his three rings, and continues to partner with China, the combined GDP of those nations could soon eclipse that of the U.S., which would place the free world at great risk of having global policies set by others with vastly different agendas. They could convert the world's currency standard to petrorubles or petroyuan and devastate the U.S. and European economies. In short, they'd own all the marbles and everyone else would be left holding the bag.

What kind of world do we want to live in? One where freedom and common rights are maintained and defended? Or one where individuals are tortured and beheaded for their beliefs? One where everyone of working age has a "good job," or where tens of millions of children are left starving in the streets? These scenarios sound harsh, and to some even impossible, but those who lived through World War II know otherwise.

Survivors of the bombings in London recount the fear they shared as the bombs fell from German warplanes. They did not know if one day in the near future they would be tortured or burned alive by the Nazis. Veterans of that terrible war speak about the heroes on the battlefield who gave their all to prevent that outcome, but they also give thanks to the countless heroes back home who helped win that war economically. For without the war bonds, the taxes, the hard work, and the sacrifices made by millions of civilians in Allied countries, World War II might have been lost.

As Clifton explains in his book, we are once again fighting a world war. Only this time we're not fighting with bullets, tanks, planes, bombs, and missiles. We are instead in the midst of a global economic and resource war, where battlefields are oil fields and our most formidable weapon is innovation.

To lead the charge and win this war, we need another Al Gore—a leader who will step forward and help pave the way for innovations like NRL's

PetroConverter. Imagine what might happen if something like this transformed the world and lined the pockets of NATO countries with hundreds of trillions of dollars. Could something like the PetroConverter also put a dagger into the heart of Putin's plans to dominate world resources? Can we reinvent our world to ensure that our great-grandchildren are not burned or drowned to death by climactic changes?

Perhaps we can.

Let's imagine a new world together, and then put down our television remotes and do something to make that vision a reality.

RESOURCES

To watch a video on YouTube filmed by the author during the 2011 ICEX Arctic expedition aboard the USS Connecticut visit: https://www.youtube.com/watch?v=143waLURQgE

"Aker Unveils New Concept, the Arctic Drillship," *World Maritime News*, April 23, 2014, http://worldmaritimenews.com/.

Allen, Jared, "Sakhalin Offshore Oil and Gas Reserves—Sea of Okhotsk—Russia," *ArcticEcon* (blog), December 3, 2012, https://arcticecon.wordpress.com/2011/12/03/sakhalin-offshore-oil-and-gas-reserves-sea-of-okhotsk-russia/.

Ames, Paul, "Putin Takes NATO Back to the Future," *Global Post*, April 2, 2014, http://www.globalpost.com/.

Andelman, David A., "New Saudi King Muscles Up to Help USA: Column," *USA Today*, Febrary 8, 2015, http://www.usatoday.com/.

Anderson, Alun. *After the Ice: Life, Death, and Geopolitics in the New Arctic*. New York: HarperCollins, 2009.

Anderson, Captain William R., and Don Keith. *The Ice Diaries: The True Story of One Mankind's Greatest Adventures*. Nashville: Thomas Nelson, 2008.

Anderson, Jared, "Energy Quote of the Day 'The E.U. Cannot Have its Cake and Eat it, Too,'" *The Energy Collective*, May 4, 2012, http://theenergycollective.com/.

Anderson, Terry L., "Adaptation Key to Dealing with Climate Change: Column," *USA Today*, June 4, 2014, http://www.usatoday.com/.

Aris, Ben, "New Gas and Oil Pipelines in Europe and Asia Could Take the Politics Out of Transportation," *Rossiykaya Gazeta* (Russia), March 3, 2010, http://www.telegraph.co.uk/.

"Armoured vehicles break into Ukraine base in Crimea, shots fired," *Express Tribune*, March 22, 2104, http://tribune.com.pk/.

Aron, Leon, "Putin's Petro State Approaching Empty," *American Enterprise Institute*, June 5, 2013, http://www.american.com/.

Bacon, John, "NATO: Russian Buildup Threatens Ukraine's Neighbor," *USA Today*, March 23, 2013, http://www.usatoday.com/.

Bailey, Samuel, "File Nordstream.png," *Wikipedia*, s.v., last modified November 15, 2009, http://en.wikipedia.org/wiki/File:Nordstream.png.

Bazzi, Mohamad, "Saudi Arabia is Playing Chicken with Its Oil," *Reuters*, December 15, 2014, http://blogs.reuters.com/.

BBB, "U.S. Think Tanks Weigh In on Arctic Oil and Gas Development," *Arctic Mapping and the Law of the Sea* (blog), April 18m 2014, http://arctic-healy-baker-2008.blogspot.com/2014/04/1-us-think-tanks-weigh-in-on-arctic-oil.html.

Beehner, Lionel, "Putin Just the Nemesis We Need, Column" *USA Today*, March 25, 2014, http://www.usatoday.com/.

Bender, Jeremy and Michael B. Kelley, "Militaries Know that the Arctic is Melting—Here's How They're Taking Advantage," *Business Insider*, June, 3, 2014, http://www.businessinsider.com/.

Benko, Ralph, "Forty Years Ago Today Nixon Took Us Off the Gold Standard," *Fox News*, August 15, 2011, http://www.foxnews.com/.

Bennett, Asa, "UK to Start Buying Gas From Russia Despite Threats of Sanctions Over Crimea," *The Huffington Post UK*, March 25, 2014, http://www.huffingtonpost.co.uk/.

Bennett, Mia, "China-Russia Gas Deal Win for Arctic," *The Maritime Executive*, April 7, 2014, http://www.maritime-executive.com/.

Bennett, Mia, "Extractive Frontiers—The Arctic and Central Asia," *Alaska Dispatch News*," April 23, 2014, http://www.alaskadispatch.com/.

Benson, Jeff W., "Opinion: A New Era in Anti-Submarine Warfare," *USNI News*, August 27, 2015, http://news.usni.org/.

Birke, Sarah, "Syria: How ISIS Serves the Interests of the Assad Regime," *War in Context*, December 28, 2013, http://warincontext.org/.

Blair, Laurence, "Arctic Cold War Is Heating Up," *The Moscow Times*, April 23, 2014, http://www.themoscowtimes.com/.

Blake, Matthew, "Russia Wins Oil Rich Territory as Big as Switzerland Without Any Violence as it Is Handed 'Ali Baba's cave' of Natural Resources in Arctic," *Daily Mail*, May 12, 2014, http://www.dailymail.co.uk/.

Bluitt, Rebecca, "Cold, Cold War: Putin Talks Tough Over US Arctic Rivalry," *ABC News*, December 5, 2013, http://abcnews.go.com/.

Borenstein, Seth, "Arctic Losing Snow and Ice, Absorbing More Heat, Federal Report Says," *The Huffington Post Green*, February 16, 2015, http://www.huffingtonpost.com/.

Brady, James S., "Press Briefing by Secretary Jay Carney, National Security Advisor Susan Rice, and Deputy National Security Advisor for Strategic Communications Ben Rhodes," March 21, 2014, http://www.whitehouse.gov/.

Buckell, Tobias S. *Arctic Rising.* New York: Tom Doherty Associates, LLC, 2012.

Byers, Michael. *Who Owns the Arctic?: Understanding Sovereignty Disputes in the North.* Vancouver: Douglas & McIntyre, 2010.

Casey, Michael, "Natural Gas Exports Set to Take Off as Energy Department Approves Two New Projects," *Fortune*, September 10, 2014, http://fortune.com/.

Chase, Steven, "Turf War with Russia Looms Over Ottowa's Claim to Arctic Seabed," *The Globe and Mail*, December 5, 2013, http://www.theglobeandmail.com/.

Chasmar, Jessica, "Vladimir Putin Wants to Reclaim Finland for Russia, Former Advisor Says," *The Washington Times*, March 31, 2014, http://www.washingtontimes.com/.

Cheadle, Bruce, "Canada Makes Territorial Claim for North Pole Despite Not Mapping Area Yet," *Maclean's*, December 9, 2013, http://www.macleans.ca/.

"China's Future," *The Economist*, accessed February 18, 2014, http://www.economist.com/news/essays/21609649-china-becomes-again-worlds-largest-economy-it-wants-respect-it-enjoyed-centuries-past-it-does-not.

Chevron, "How Energy Can Supercharge the U.S. Economy," April 2014, http://www.chevron.com/.

"Chinese Army Think-Tank Says Arctic Energy Would Help Economy," *Reuters*, June 18 2014, http://in.reuters.com/.

Clifton, Jim. *The Coming Jobs War*. New York: Gallup Press, 2013.

Collins, Jennifer, "Obama Says West Is United Against Russia," *USA Today*, March 26, 2014, http://www.usatoday.com/.

Coyle, James J., "South Stream Advancing," *Eurasian Energy Analysis* (blog), June 13, 2012, http://eurasianenergyanalysis.blogspot.com/2012/06/south-stream-advancing.html.

"Crimea Base Invaded as US Rallies Support against Sanctions for Putin," *The Australian*, March 23, 2014, http://www.theaustralian.com.au/.

Critchlow, Andrew, "Sea Change for Commodities as Arctic Melt Transforms Trade Routes," *The Telegraph*, March 30, 2014, http://www.telegraph.co.uk/.

Dallaire, Romeo and Erica Simpson, "Freezing Out the Nukes," *Chatham Daily News*, May 3, 2014, http://www.chathamdailynews.ca/.

Daly, John, "Why Hasn't the US Place Sanctions on Gazprom?" *ValueWalk*, May 6, 2014, http://www.valuewalk.com/.

Dodds, Klaus, "Geopolotics of Ice," *Globalgeopolitics Weblog* (blog), accessed February 18, 2015, http://globalgeopolitics.wordpress.com/tag/gazprom/.

Doyle, Alister, "Norway Bets on Global Warming to Thaw Arctic Ice for Oil and Gas Drive," *Scientific American*, May 13, 2014, http://www.scientificamerican.com/.

Durden, Tyler, "Gazprom Chairman Sold All His Shares Just Before Russia Invaded Crimea," *Zero Hedge*, March 14, 2014, http://www.zerohedge.com/.

Durden, Tyler, "Two Russian Warships Enter Black Sea Through Bosphorous; Another Docks in Cuba," *Zero Hedge*, February 27, 2014, http://www.zerohedge.com/.

"East Asia Arctic Relations: Boundary, Security and International Politics," *CIGI*, accessed February 18, 2015, http://www.cigionline.org/series/east-asia-arctic-relations-boundary-security-and-international-politics.

Economy, Elizabeth C., "Beijing's Arctic Play: Just the Tip of the Iceberg," *The Diplomat*, April 5, 2014, http://thediplomat.com/.

Eftimiades, Nicholas. *Chinese Intelligence Operations*. Annapolis: Naval Institute Press, 2011.

Scientific American, Eds. *Storm Warnings: Climate Change and Extreme Weather*. Scientific American, 2012.

Ehrenfeld, Rachel, "Saudi Interest in America," *The Washington Times*, January 15, 2006, http://www.washingtontimes.com/.

Elder, Miriam, "Behind the Russia-Ukraine Gas Conflict," *Bloomberg Business*, January 3, 2009, http://www.businessweek.com/.

Emergency Prevention Preparedness and Response, "Ministerial Direction," The Arctic Council, http://www.arctic-council.org/eppr/reports/ministerial-direction/.

Emmerson, Charles. *The Future History of the Arctic*. New York: PublicAffairs, 2010.

Engelking, Carl, "U.S. Wants to Fuel Ships Using Seawater," *Discover*, April 8, 2014, http://blogs.discovermagazine.com/.

Erickson, Erick, "Barack Obama Thinks an ATM Ate Your Job," *RedState*, June 15, 2011, http://www.redstate.com/.

Fairhall, David. *Cold Front: Conflict Ahead in Arctic Waters*. Berkeley: Counterpoint, 2010.

Fields, Joseph III, "A Different Route for Export of Alaska's Natural Gas," *Daily News-Miner*, April 13, 2014, http://www.newsminer.com/.

Flynn, Ramsey, *Cry from the Deep: The Sinking of the* Kursk. New York: HarperCollins, 2011.

"Forget Russia Dumping US Treasuries . . . Here's the Real Economic Threat," *WashingtonsBlog* (blog), March 21, 2014, http://www.washingtonsblog.com/2014/03/forget-treasuries-russias-real-leverage-u-s.html.

Freedman, David H, "America Is Burning: The Fight Against Wildfires Gets Real," *Mens Journal*, August 2014, http://www.mensjournal.com/.

Friedman, Uri, "Where the U.S. and Russia Could Square Off Next," *The Atlantic*, March 28, 2014, http://www.theatlantic.com/.

Garamone, Jim, "Hagel Gets Assurances About Russian Troups on Ukraine Border," *DoD News*, March 20, 2014, http://www.defense.gov/news/.

"Gazprom Cuts Supplies to Belarus," *The Moscow Times*, June 7, 1998, http://www.themoscowtimes.com/.

"Gazprom Doesn't Want 'Gas Crisis'—CEO," *RT*, March 13, 2014, http://rt.com/.

Gazprom, "Kirinskoye field," accessed February 18, 2015, http://www.gazprom.com/about/production/projects/deposits/sakhalin3/kirinskoye/.

Gazprom Neft, "JSC Gazprom to Start Fourth Shale Oil Exploration Project," March 18, 2014, http://www.gazprom-neft.com/press-center/news/1100132/.

Gazprom Neft, "Russia's Gazprom Neft, Novatek Agree 50/50 Ownership of SeverEnergia," April 2, 2014, http://www.oilandgaseurasia.com/en/news/russia%E2%80%99s-gazprom-neft-novatek-agree-5050-ownership-severenergia.

Gazprom, "Nord Stream," accessed February 18, 2015, http://www.gazprom.com/about/production/projects/pipelines/nord-stream/.

"Gazprom Proposes to Develop Crimea's Oil and Gas," *RT*, March 18, 2014, http://rt.com/.

Gazprom, "Saipem to Lay First Line of South Stream Offshore Gas Pipeline," March 14, 2014, http://www.gazprom.com/press/news/2014/march/article186360/.

"Gazprom Urges Ukraine to Fill Gas Storage for Stable Flows to Europe," *Sputnik International*, April 3, 2014, http://voiceofrussia.com/.

Gent, Edd, "Ice-proof Arctic Rig Starts Pumping Oil," *Engineering and Technology Magazine*, December 20, 2013, http://eandt.theiet.org/news/2013/dec/gazprom-rig.cfm.

"Germany accuses Russia of trying to break apart Europe," *Japan Times*, March 22, 2014, http://www.japantimes.co.jp/.

Gifford, Rob. *China Road: A Journey into the Future of a Rising Power*. New York: Random House, 2007.

Gloystein, Henning and Oleg Vukmanovic, "Britain to Import Russian Gas Under 2012 Deal as Tensions Mount," *Reuters*, March 21, 2014, http://www.reuters.com/.

Goldenberg, Suzanne, "Climate Change Poses Growing Threat of Conflict in the Arctic, Report Finds," *The Guardian*, May 14, 2014, http://www.theguardian.com/.

Graeber, Donald, "South Stream Good for Europe, Gazprom Says," *UPI*, March 25, 2014, http://www.upi.com/.

Gregory, Paul Roderick, "Putin's Brazen Demand In Return for Him NOT Invading Ukraine," *Forbes*, March 30, 2014, http://www.forbes.com/.

Gumuchian, Marie-Louise and Phillip Taylor, "NATO Concerned Over Russian Army Buildup on Ukraine Border," *CNN News*, March 23, 2014, http://www.cnn.com/.

Henley, John, "Is Europe's Gas Supply Threatened by the Ukraine Crisis?" *The Guardian*, March 3, 2014, http://www.theguardian.com/.

Herszenhorn, David M., "Signs of Momentum Shifting to Protestors in Ukraine," *New York Times*, December 14, 2013, http://www.nytimes.com/.

Herszenhorn, David M., "Ukraine Vote Takes Nation a Step Closer to NATO," *New York Times*, December 23, 2014, http://www.nytimes.com/.

Hess, Alexander E.M., and Thomas C. Frohlich, "Seven States Running Out of Water," *USA Today*, June 1, 2014, http://www.usatoday.com/.

Hill, Fiona, "The Real Reason Putin Supports Assad," *Brookings*, March 25, 2013, http://www.brookings.edu/.

Howard, Roger. *Arctic Gold Rush: The New Race for Tomorrow's Natural Resources.* New York: Continuum, 2009.

Huebert, Rob, "How Russia's Move into Crimea Upended Canada's Arctic Stragegy," *The Globe and Mail*, April 2, 2014, http://www.theglobeandmail.com/.

Hunziker, Robert and Jack, "The Melting Arctic and Revolutions to Come," *Ecologist*, April 26, 2014, http://www.theecologist.org/.

International Energy Agency, "How to Ensure Energy Supplies Underground Can Be Tapped in the Future," June 6, 2013, http://www.iea.org/.

Katusa, Marin. *The Colder War: How the Global Energy Trade Slipped from America's Grasp.* Hoboken: Wiley, 2014.

Kharlamov, Illya, "The Arctic Ceases to be a 'Province,'" *The Voice of Russia*, November 6, 2013, http://voiceofrussia.com/.

Kilmentyev, Michael, "Putin Wants Greater Russian Presence in Arctic," *The Moscow Times*, April 23, 2014, http://www.themoscowtimes.com/.

Kirchick, James, "Putin Warned of Fascism in Ukraine, But a Look Across Europe Suggests He's to Blame," *Tablet*, April 4, 2014, http://www.tabletmag.com/jewish-news-and-politics/168504/kirchick-putin-ukraine.

Koch, Wendy, "Climate Changes Visible by Zip Code with New Online Tools," *USA Today*, April 20, 2014, http://usat.ly/1lp0nNP.

Koningstein, Ross and David Fork, "What It Would Really Take to Reverse Climate Change," *IEEE Spectrum*, November 18, 2014, http://spectrum.ieee.org/.

Koranyi, Balazs and Gwladys Fouche, "Exxon Oil Rig Enters Unchartered Waters of Russian Political Storm," *Fox Business*, July 21, 2014, http://www.foxbusiness.com/.

Koranyi, Balazs, "Crunch Year Ahead for Norway's Arctic Oil Adventure," *Reuters*, April 1, 2014, http://www.reuters.com/.

Kraska, James. *Arctic Security in an Age of Climate Change.* Cambridge: Cambridge University Press, 2013.

LaGrone, Sam, "CNO Greenert: Russian Navy 'Very Busy in the Undersea Domain,'" *USNI News*, November 4, 2014, http://news.usni.org/.

Laruelle, Marlene. *Russia's Arctic Strategies and the Future of the Far North.* London: Routledge, 2014.

Leary, William M., and John H. Nicholson. *Under Ice: Waldo Lyon and the Development of the Arctic Submarine*. College Station: Texas A&M University Press, 1999.

Levine, Steve, "Russia's Invasion of Crimea Has Caused it to Lose the Latest Battle in the Pipeline Wars," *Quartz*, March 25, 2014, http://qz.com/.

Loehrke, Janet, "Massive Wildfire Only 16% Contained," *USA Today*, July 22, 2014, http://www.usatoday.com/.

"Lomonosov Ridge Could Bring Russia 5 bln Tons of Extra Fuel," *Sputnik International*, October 1, 2007, http://en.ria.ru/.

Main, Douglas, "Arctic Temperatures Highest in at Least 44,000 Years," *The Australian Climate Sceptics* (blog), April 21, 2014, http://theclimatescepticsparty.blogspot.com/2014/04/arctic-temperatures-highest-on-44000.html.

Maverick, Tim, "After China, Will Putin Go for a Russian-Japan Gas Deal?" *EconMatters*, June 19, 2014, http://www.econmatters.com/.

Mayeda, Andrew and Greg Quinn, "Canada Approves Cnooc, Petron Bids for Nexen, Progress Energy," *Bloomberg Business*, December 9, 2012, http://www.bloomberg.com/.

Maynes, Charles, "Putin Is Popular in Russia, But So Is American Culture," *PRI*, April 2, 2014, http://www.pri.org/.

McCoy, Kathleen, "Hometown U: New Transportation Routes in the Arctic," *Alaska Dispatch News*, March 29, 2014, http://www.adn.com/.

McDermott, Deborah, "King Finds Insight into Submarines, Climate Change on Arctic Trip," *Seacoast*, March 29, 2014, http://www.seacoastonline.com/.

McGwin, Kevin, "Arming the Arctic Front," *The Arctic Journal*, April 23, 2014, http://arcticjournal.com/.

McKew, Molly M. and Gregory A. Maniatas, "Putin Has Ambitions Far Beyond the Former Soviet Union," *The Washington Post*, March 31, 2014, http://www.washingtonpost.com/.

McLaren, Alfred S., and William R. Anderson. *Unknown Waters: A First-Hand Account of the Historic Under-ice Survey of the Siberian Continental Shelf by USS Queenfish (SSN-651)*. Tuscaloosa: University of Alabama Press, 2009.

McNamara, Jennifer and Jerrold Post, "Putin the Great: Struggling to Hold On to a Crumbling Empire," *The World Post*, April 1, 2014, http://www.huffingtonpost.com/.

Medvedev, Yevgeny, "Arctic Too Important to Ignore—Russian Expert," *Russia & India Report*, November 25, 2013, http://in.rbth.com/.

"Melting Pot of Riches," *Business Day Live*, May 4, 2014, http://www.bdlive.co.za/.

Miranovsky, Anatoly, "It was US and UK that sank Russia's Kursk Submarine," *Pravda.ru*, May 18, 2012, http://english.pravda.ru/.

Mizokami, Kyle, "Russia Playing Politics with Alleged Submarine Confrontation," *USNI News*, August 26, 2014, http://news.usni.org/.

Moore, Robert. *A Time to Die: The Untold Story of the Kursk Tragedy.* New York: Three Rivers Press, 2007.

Mortimer, Edward, "Designing and Effective European Arctic Strategy," *ISN* (blog), April 18, 2014, http://isnblog.ethz.ch/international-relations/designing-an-effective-european-arctic-strategy.

Moss, Trefor, "Frosty Relations: Militarizing the Arctic," *World Policy Blog*, April 22, 2014, http://www.worldpolicy.org/.

"Mystery Missile Launch Seen off Calif. Coast," *CBS News*, November 9, 2010, http://www.cbsnews.com/.

Neuhauser, Alan, "U.S. Takes Int'l Approach to Arctic, Offshore Energy," *U.S. News and World Report*, April 21, 2014, http://www.usnews.com/.

Nilsen, Thomas, "Putin Orders Arctic Army Development," *Barents Observer*, March 28, 2014, http://barentsobserver.com/.

"No Benefit to Develop Arctic Shipping: US Report," *CBS News*, April 27, 2014, http://www.cbc.ca/.

Northam, Jackie, "Can Europe Wean Itself Off Russia Gas?" *WBUR News*, March 21, 2014, http://www.wbur.org/.

Novosti, Ria, "UN Declares the Sea of Okhotsk Enclave Part of Russia," *Sign of the Times*, March 15, 2014, http://www.sott.net/.

Organization for Economic Co-operation and Development, "The Arctic May Contain Almost ¼ of the World's Undiscoverd Oil & Gas Reserves," *Twitter*, April 17, 2014, https://twitter.com/OECD/status/456779972179292161.

Organization of the Petroleum Exporting Countries, "Member Countries," accessed February 18, 2015, http://www.opec.org/opec_web/en/about_us/25.htm.

Ostryzniuk, Evan, "Pasqual: Europe Doesn't Need Russia's Gazprom," *KyivPost*, March 21, 2015, http://www.kyivpost.com/.

Page, Susan, "A New Cold War? Why Crimea Should Matter to Americans," *USA Today*, March 14, 2014, http://www.usatoday.com/.

Panin, Alexander, "Nuclear Icebreakers Clear the Way for Arctic Oil," *The Moscow Times*, April 27 2014, http://www.themoscowtimes.com/.

Parker, Kathleen, "Parker: Putin Continues to Win at Global Game of Chess," *Chron*, April 19, 2014, http://www.chron.com/.

"Parsing Putin's Popularity," *Gray Falcon* (blog) June 14, 2014, http://grayfalcon.blogspot.com/.

Peritz, Ingrid, "Hillary Clinton Warns Montreal Crowd of Russia's Increased

Activity in Arctic," *The Globe and Mail*, March 18, 2014, http://www.theglobeandmail.com/.

"Petrol Giant Braced for Consumer Boycott After Buying Arctic Oil," *Click Green*, April 27, 2014,http://www.clickgreen.org.uk/.

Pettersen, Trude, "Putin Attends Nuclear Sub Ceremony," *Barents Observer*, July 31, 2012, http://barentsobserver.com/.

Pettersen, Trude, "Putin Sees Bright Future for Arctic Transport," *Barents Observer*, September 25, 2011, http://barentsobserver.com/.

Phoenix, Joaquin, "Phoenix: Household Products Harm Rainforest," *USA Today*, May 3, 2014, http://usat.ly/.

Polar Shares, "US Unprepared for Arctic Rush," *The American Interest* (blog), April 26, 2014, http://www.the-american-interest.com/blog/2014/04/26/us-unprepared-for-arctic-rush/.

"Putin Says He Wants to Boost Russia's Arctic Presence After First Oil Shipment," *South China Morning Post*, April 23, 2014, http://www.scmp.com/.

"Putin Signed a Law the Repeals the Agreements with Ukraine," *Fox 35*, April 2, 2014, http://www.kcba.com/.

Redford, Robert, "President Obama, Put the Arctic Off-Limits to Big Oil," *The Huffington Post Green*, April 17, 2014, http://www.huffingtonpost.com/.

Reed, Craig W. *Red November: Inside the U.S. – Soviet Submarine War*. New York: HarperCollins, 2010.

Rice, Doyle, "Doomsday Approaching? Clock Ticking Closer to Midnight," *USA Today*, January 23, 2015, http://www.usatoday.com//

Rice, Doyle, "May 2014 Was Earth's Warmest Day on Record," *USA Today*, June 23, 2014, http://www.usatoday.com/.

Rosen, Armin, "Norway Wants NATO to Prepare for an Arctic Showdown," *Business Insider Australia*, June 26, 2014, http://www.businessinsider.com.au/.

Rodenko, Olga, "Annexation of Crimea Not a 'Done Deal,' Obama Says," *USA Today*, March 26, 2014, http://www.usatoday.com/.

Rogers, Jillian, "Coast Guard Gears Up for Summer's Arctic Operations," *Alaska Dispatch News*, May 19, 2014, https://www.adn.com/.

Rogin, Josh, "America's Allies Are Funding ISIS," *The Daily Beast*, June 14, 2014, http://www.infowars.com/.

Rosen, Yereth, "GAO Offers Sobering Look at Shipping Prospects in US Arctic," *Alaska Dispatch News*, April 19, 2014, http://www.adn.com/.

RSIS, "Arctic LNG: The Energy on East Asia's Doorstep—Analysis," *Eurasia Review*, May 15, 2014, https://www.eurasiareview.com/.

Runnalls, David, "Next Steps in Arctic Governance," *Council of Councils*, May 14, 2014, https:// http://www.cfr.org/.

"Russia Identifies NATO as Its Biggest Threat," *Aljazeera*, December 27, 2014, http://www.aljazeera.com/.

"Russian Arctic: A New Promised Land for Oil Giants," *Daily Times*, June 23, 2014, http://www.dailytimes.com.pk/.

"Russian-Chinese Contract Likely to Be Signed in May—Chinese Diplomat," *Sputnik International*, March 25, 2014, http://voiceofrussia.com/.

"Russian Government Touts 1st Shipment of Oil from Arctic," *Latin American Herald Tribune*, accessed February 18, 2015, http://www.laht.com/.

"Russia to Submit Arctic Shelf Claim to UN in Fall—Russian Official," *Sputnik International*, April 18, 2014, http://en.ria.ru/russia/.

Save The Arctic, "Interactive Map of the First Arctic Oil on Its Way to Europe," *Twitter*, April 25, 2014, https://twitter.com/savethearctic/status/459665737687511041/photo/1/large.

"Shell's Sakhalin-2 Project Expansion Gets Putin's Support," *domain-b*, April 19, 2014, http://www.domain-b.com/.

Sreekumar, Arjun, "3 Energy Companies that Can't Wait to Drill in the Arctic," *The Motley Fool*, March 30, 2014, http://www.fool.com/.

Stoll, John D., "NATO Chief Concerned about Russia's Future Arctic Plans," *The Wall Street Journal*, accessed February 18, 2015, http://online.wsj.com/.

Strauss, Gary, "Crude Oil's Collapse Will Cost 9,000 Jobs at Schlumberger," *USA Today*, January 19, 2015, http://www.usatoday.com/.

Sukhoy, Yevgeniy, "Russia Holds Key to Arctic Explorations, Expert Conference Highlights Impacts," *The Voice of Russia*, April 18, 2014, http://voiceofrussia.com/.

Surowiecki, James, "Putin's Power Play," *The New Yorker*, March 24, 2014, http://www.newyorker.com/talk/financial/2014/03/24/140324ta_talk_surowiecki.

Swaine, Jon, "Russian Troops May Invade Ukraine, Says White House," *The Guardian*, March 23, 2014, http://www.theguardian.com/.

Tan, Michelle, "Inside the Army's Growing Arctic Circle Mission," *Army Times*, May 7, 2014, http://www.armytimes.com/.

"The Sinking of the Russian Sub *Kursk*!" last modified February 2, 2002, accessed February 16, 2015, http://whatreallyhappened.com/WRHARTICLES/KURSK/kursk.html.

"Twenty Countries with the Largest Foreign Exchange Rates," *Rediff Business*, April 25, 2013, http://www.rediff.com/.

"Ukraine Misses Gas Payment Deadline, Risks Halt on Supplies—Gazprom," *RT*,

March 7, 2014, http://rt.com/business/ukraine-gas-payment-cuts-490/.

United Nations, "Commission on Limits of Continental Shelf Concludes Thirty-Fourth Session at Headquarters, 27 Jan–13 March," March 18, 2014, http://www.un.org/News/Press/docs/2014/sea1999.doc.htm.

United Nations: Oceans & Law of the Sea, "Submissions, though the Secretary-General of the United Nations, to the Commission on the Limits of the Continental Shelf, pursuant to article 76, paragraph 8, of the United Nations Convention of the Law of the Sea of 10 December 1982," December 17, 2014, http://www.un.org/depts/los/clcs_new/commission_submissions.htm.

U.S. Navy, Office of Corporate Communication. *United States Navy Fact File: Attack Submarines*. http://www.navy.mil/navydata/fact_print.asp?cid=4100&tid=100&ct=4&page=1.

Walker, Shaun, "I Feel No Responsibility for Rouble's Collapse, Says Putin," *The Guardian*, December 18, 2014, http://www.theguardian.com/.

Viñas, Maria-José, "NASA Researchers and National Snow and Ice Data Center Reports Melting Season in Arctic Lasting Longer," *Clarksville Online*, April 1, 2014, http://www.clarksvilleonline.com/.

Walker, Shaun, Leonid Ragozin, Matthew Weaver, "Putin Likens Ukraine Forces to Nazis and Threatens Standoff in the Arctic," *The Guardian*, August 29, 2014, http://www.theguardian.com/.

Wikipedia, s.v. "Cold War," last modified February 13, 2015, http://en.wikipedia.org/wiki/Cold_War.

Wikipedia, s.v. "Gazprom," last modified February 10, 2015, http://en.wikipedia.org/wiki/Gazprom.

Wikipedia, s.v. "Gulf of Ob," last modified February, 13, 2015, http://en.wikipedia.org/wiki/Gulf_of_Ob.

Wikipedia, s.v. "Russia in the European energy sector," last modified February 5, 2015, http://en.wikipedia.org/wiki/Russia_in_the_European_energy_sector.

Wikipedia, s.v. "Siege of Sevastopol," last modified February 18, 2015, http://en.wikipedia.org/wiki/Siege_of_Sevastopol_(1941%E2%80%9342).

Wikipedia, s.v. "Ukraine-European Union Association Agreement," last modified February 7, 2015, http://en.wikipedia.org/wiki/Ukraine%E2%80%93European_Union_Assochttp://rt.com/business/crimea-gazprom-exploration-request-598/iation_Agreement.

Wikipedia, s.v. "Vladimir Putin," last modified February 18, 2015, http://en.wikipedia.org/wiki/Vladimir_Putin.

Wikipedia, s.v. "Yamal Peninsula," last modified January 25, 2015, http://en.wikipedia.org/wiki/Yamal_Peninsula.

Wilson, Scott and Will Englund, "Obama Says Military Force Will Not be Used to Dislodge Russia from Crimea," *The Washington Post*, March 25, 2014, http://www.washingtonpost.com/.

Zachs Equity Research, "Statoil to Develop Arctic Field Using FPSO," *Zachs* (blog), May 16, 2014, http:// http://www.zacks.com/stock/news/133837/statoil-to-develop-arctic-field-using-fpso.

Zigfeld, Kim, "Russia through the Peanut Hole," *American Thinker*, November 21, 2013, http://www.americanthinker.com/.

Zolotukhin, Anatoly, "Russia's Arctic Resources: Opportunities and Challenges," Russian Gubkin State University of Oil and Gas, Norweigan-Russian Arctic Offshore Workshop, Oslo June 17–18, 2009, http://www.forskningsradet.no/.

ABOUT THE AUTHOR

William Craig Reed is the author of the non-fiction book *Red November: Inside the Secret U.S. – Soviet Submarine War* (HarperCollins, 2010) and *The Eagle and the Snake: A SEAL Team Six Interactive Thriller* (DiversionBooks, 2012), and *Tarzan, My Father* with the late Johnny Weissmuller, Jr. (ECW Press, 2002).

Reed served as a U.S. Navy diver and submarine special operations photographer aboard nuclear fast attack submarines and earned commendations for completing secret missions during the Cold War, several in concert with Navy SEAL teams. Reed was the only author invited by the U.S. Navy to observe the 2011 ICEX operations in the Arctic, and is an alumnus or member of numerous military, veteran, and technology associations. Reed serves on the board of directors for the US4Warriors (us4warriors.org) nonprofit veteran's assistance foundation.

When not writing, Reed is a partner in Aventi Group—a technology marketing consulting firm. Reed holds an MBA in marketing and was a former vice president and board director for the Silicon Valley American Marketing Association. He founded two software companies and developed an innovative mobile device app called PIERbook™ that automatically customizes e-book content based on a reader's personal preferences and selections. This technology was used to create a mobile app and customizable e-book titled *Bad Boss: How to Use Neuroscience to Transform Your Professional Life from Miserable to Miraculous.*